Copyright ©1991 by John J. Murphy
Published by John Wiley & Sons, Inc.

Library of Congress Cataloging-in-Publication Data

Murphy, John J.
    Intermarket technical analysis: trading strategies
for the global stock, bond, commodity, and currency markets /
John J. Murphy.
        p.   cm. — (Wiley finance editions)
    Includes index.
    ISBN 0-471-52433-6 (cloth)
    1. Investment analysis.   2. Portfolio management.   I. Title.
II. Series.
HG4529.M86 1991
332.6—dc20   90-48567

Printed in the United States of America

20   19   18   17   16   15   14   13   12

INTERMARKET TECHNICAL ANALYSIS
TRADING STRATEGIES FOR THE GLOBAL STOCK, BOND, COMMODITY AND CURRENCY MARKETS

John J. Murphy

Wiley Finance Editions
JOHN WILEY & SONS, INC.

New York • Chichester • Brisbane • Toronto • Singapore

Contents

To Patty, my friend

and

to Clare and Brian

Preface

Like that of most technical analysts, my analytical work for many years relied on traditional chart analysis supported by a host of internal technical indicators. About five years ago, however, my technical work took a different direction. As consulting editor for the Commodity Research Bureau (CRB), I spent a considerable amount of time analyzing the Commodity Research Bureau Futures Price Index, which measures the trend of commodity prices. I had always used the CRB Index in my analysis of commodity markets in much the same way that equity analysts used the Dow Jones Industrial Average in their analysis of common stocks. However, I began to notice some interesting correlations with markets outside the commodity field, most notably the bond market, that piqued my interest.

The simple observation that commodity prices and bond yields trend in the same direction provided the initial insight that there was a lot more information to be got from our price charts, and that insight opened the door to my intermarket journey. As consultant to the New York Futures Exchange during the launching of a futures contract on the CRB Futures Price Index, my work began to focus on the relationship between commodities and stocks, since that exchange also trades a stock index futures contract. I had access to correlation studies being done between the various financial sectors: commodities, Treasury bonds, and stocks. The results of that research confirmed what I was seeing on my charts—namely, that *commodities, bonds, and stocks are closely linked,* and that *a thorough analysis of one should include consideration of the other two.* At a later date, I incorporated the dollar into my work because of its direct impact on the commodity markets and its indirect impact on bonds and stocks.

The turning point for me came in 1987. The dramatic market events of that year turned what was an interesting theory into cold reality. A collapse in the bond market during the spring, coinciding with an explosion in the commodity sector, set the stage for the stock market crash in the fall of that year. The interplay between the dollar, the commodity markets, bonds, and stocks during 1987 convinced me that intermarket analysis represented a critically important dimension to technical work that could no longer be ignored.

Another by-product of 1987 was my growing awareness of the importance of international markets as global stock markets rose and fell together that year. I noticed that activity in the global bond and stock markets often gave advance warnings of what our markets were up to. Another illustration of global forces at work was given at the start of 1990, when the collapse in the American bond market during the first quarter was foreshadowed by declines in the German, British, and Japanese markets. The collapse in the Japanese stock market during the first quarter of 1990 also gave advance warning of the coming drop in other global equity markets, including our own, later that summer.

This book is the result of my continuing research into the world of intermarket analysis. I hope the charts that are included will clearly demonstrate the interrelationships that exist among the various market sectors, and why it's so important to be aware of those relationships. I believe the greatest contribution made by intermarket analysis is that it improves the technical analyst's peripheral trading vision. Trying to trade the markets without intermarket awareness is like trying to drive a car without looking out the side and rear windows—in other words, it's very dangerous.

The application of intermarket analysis extends into all markets everywhere on the globe. By turning the focus of the technical analyst outward instead of inward, intermarket analysis provides a more rational understanding of technical forces at work in the marketplace. It provides a more unified view of global market behavior. Intermarket analysis uses activity in surrounding markets in much the same way that most of us have employed traditional technical indicators, that is, for directional clues. Intermarket analysis doesn't replace other technical work, but simply adds another dimension to it. It also has some bearing on interest rate direction, inflation, Federal Reserve policy, economic analysis, and the business cycle.

The work presented in this book is a beginning rather than an end. There's still a lot that remains to be done before we can fully understand how markets relate to one another. The intermarket principles described herein, while evident in most situations, are meant to be used as guidelines in market analysis, not as rigid or mechanical rules. Although the scope of intermarket analysis is broad, forcing us to stretch our imaginations and expand our vision, the potential benefit is well worth the extra effort. I'm excited about the prospects for intermarket analysis, and I hope you'll agree after reading the following pages.

John J. Murphy
February 1991

A New Dimension in Technical Analysis

One of the most striking lessons of the 1980s is that all markets are interrelated—financial and nonfinancial, domestic and international. The U.S. stock market doesn't trade in a vacuum; it is heavily influenced by the bond market. Bond prices are very much affected by the direction of commodity markets, which in turn depend on the trend of the U.S. dollar. Overseas markets are also impacted by and in turn have an impact on the U.S. markets. Events of the past decade have made it clear that markets don't move in isolation. As a result, the concept of technical analysis is now evolving to take these intermarket relationships into consideration. *Intermarket technical analysis refers to the application of technical analysis to these intermarket linkages.*

The idea behind intermarket analysis seems so obvious that it's a mystery why we haven't paid more attention to it sooner. It's not unusual these days to open a financial newspaper to the stock market page only to read about bond prices and the dollar. The bond page often talks about such things as the price of gold and oil, or sometimes even the amount of rain in Iowa and its impact on soybean prices. Reference is frequently made to the Japanese and British markets. The financial markets haven't really changed, but our perception of them has.

Think back to 1987 when the stock market took its terrible plunge. Remember how all the other world equity markets plunged as well. Remember how those same world markets, led by the Japanese stock market, then led the United States out of those 1987 doldrums to record highs in 1989 (see Figure 1.1).

Turn on your favorite business show any morning and you'll get a recap of the overnight developments that took place overseas in the U.S. dollar, gold and oil, treasury bond prices, and the foreign stock markets. The world continued trading while we slept and, in many cases, already determined how our markets were going to open that morning.

FIGURE 1.1
A COMPARISON OF THE WORLD'S THREE LARGEST EQUITY MARKETS: THE UNITED STATES, JAPAN, AND BRITAIN. GLOBAL MARKETS COLLAPSED TOGETHER IN 1987. THE SUBSEQUENT GLOBAL STOCK MARKET RECOVERY THAT LASTED THROUGH THE END OF 1989 WAS LED BY THE JAPANESE MARKET.

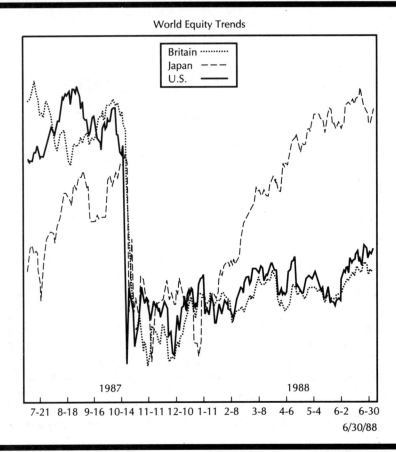

World Equity Trends

ALL MARKETS ARE RELATED

What this means for us as traders and investors is that *it is no longer possible to study any financial market in isolation*, whether it's the U.S. stock market or gold futures. Stock traders have to watch the bond market. Bond traders have to watch the commodity markets. And everyone has to watch the U.S. dollar. Then there's the Japanese stock market to consider. So who needs intermarket analysis? I guess just about everyone; since all sectors are influenced in some way, it stands to reason that anyone interested in any of the financial markets should benefit in some way from knowledge of how intermarket relationships work.

IMPLICATIONS FOR TECHNICAL ANALYSIS

Technical analysis has always had an inward focus. Emphasis was placed on a particular market to which a host of internal technical indicators were applied. There was a time when stock traders didn't watch bond prices too closely, when bond traders didn't pay too much attention to commodities. Study of the dollar was left to interbank traders and multinational corporations. Overseas markets were something we knew existed, but didn't care too much about.

It was enough for the technical analyst to study only the market in question. To consider outside influences seemed like heresy. To look at what the other markets were doing smacked of fundamental or economic analysis. All of that is now changing. Intermarket analysis is a step in another direction. *It uses information in related markets in much the same way that traditional technical indicators have been employed.* Stock technicians talk about the divergence between bonds and stocks in much the same way that they used to talk about divergence between stocks and the advance/decline line.

Markets provide us with an enormous amount of information. Bonds tell us which way interest rates are heading, a trend that influences stock prices. Commodity prices tell us which way inflation is headed, which influences bond prices and interest rates. The U.S. dollar largely determines the inflationary environment and influences which way commodities trend. Overseas equity markets often provide valuable clues to the type of environment the U.S. market is a part of. The job of the technical trader is to sniff out clues wherever they may lie. If they lie in another market, so be it. As long as price movements can be studied on price charts, and as long as it can be demonstrated that they have an impact on one another, why not take whatever useful information the markets are offering us? Technical analysis is the study of market action. No one ever said that we had to limit that study to only the market or markets we're trading.

Intermarket analysis represents an evolutionary step in technical analysis. Intermarket work builds on existing technical theory and adds another step to the analytical process. Later in this chapter, I'll discuss why technical analysis is uniquely suited to this type of investigative work and why technical analysis represents the preferred vehicle for intermarket analysis.

THE PURPOSE OF THIS BOOK

The goal of this book is to demonstrate how these intermarket relationships work in a way that can be easily recognized by technicians and nontechnicians alike. You won't have to be a technical expert to understand the argument, although some knowledge of technical analysis wouldn't hurt. For those who are new to technical work, some of the principles and tools employed throughout the book are explained in the Glossary. However, the primary focus here is to study interrelationships between markets, not to break any new ground in the use of traditional technical indicators.

We'll be looking at the four market sectors—currencies, commodities, bonds, and stocks—as well as the overseas markets. This is a book about the study of market action. Therefore, it will be a very visual book. The charts should largely speak for themselves. Once the basic relationships are described, charts will be employed to show how they have worked in real life.

Although economic forces, which are impossible to avoid, are at work here, the discussions of those economic forces will be kept to a minimum. It's not possible to do intermarket work without gaining a better understanding of the fundamental forces behind those moves. However, our intention will be to stick to market action and keep economic analysis to a minimum. We will devote one chapter to a brief discussion of the role of intermarket analysis in the business cycle, however, to provide a useful chronological framework to the interaction between commodities, bonds, and stocks.

FOUR MARKET SECTORS: CURRENCIES, COMMODITIES, BONDS, AND STOCKS

The key to intermarket work lies in dividing the financial markets into these four sectors. How these four sectors interact with each other will be shown by various visual means. The U.S. dollar, for example, usually trades in the opposite direction of the commodity markets, in particular the gold market. While individual commodities such as gold and oil are discussed, special emphasis will be placed on the Commodity Research Bureau (CRB) Index, which is a basket of 21 commodities and the most

---

FIGURE 1.2

A LOOK AT THE FOUR MARKET SECTORS—CURRENCIES, COMMODITIES, BONDS, AND STOCKS—IN 1989. FROM THE SPRING TO THE AUTUMN OF 1989, A FIRM U.S. DOLLAR HAD A BEARISH INFLUENCE ON COMMODITIES. WEAK COMMODITY PRICES COINCIDED WITH A RISING BOND MARKET, WHICH IN TURN HAD A BULLISH INFLUENCE ON THE STOCK MARKET.

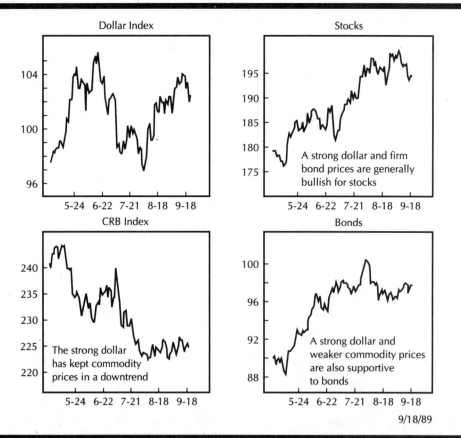

9/18/89

widely watched gauge of commodity price direction. Other commodity indexes will be discussed as well.

The strong inverse relationship between the CRB Index and bond prices will be shown. Events of 1987 and thereafter take on a whole new light when activity in the CRB Index is factored into the financial equation. Comparisons between bonds and stocks will be used to show that bond prices provide a useful confirming indicator and often lead stock prices.

I hope you'll begin to see that if you're not watching these relationships, you're missing vital market information (see Figure 1.2).

You'll also see that very often stock market moves are the end result of a ripple effect that flows through the other three sectors—a phenomenon that carries important implications in the area of *program trading*. Among the financial media and those who haven't acquired intermarket awareness, "program trading" is often unfairly blamed for stock market drops without any consideration of what caused the program trading in the first place. We'll deal with the controversial subject of program trading in Chapter 14.

BASIC PREMISES OF INTERMARKET WORK

Before we begin to study the individual relationships, I'd like to lay down some basic premises or guidelines that I'll be using throughout the book. This should provide a useful framework and, at the same time, help point out the direction we'll be going. Then I'll briefly outline the specific relationships we'll be focusing on. There are an infinite number of relationships that exist between markets, but our discussions will be limited to those that I have found most useful and that I believe carry the most significance. After completion of the overview contained in this chapter, we'll proceed in Chapter 2 to the events of 1987 and begin to approach the material in more specific fashion. These, then, are our basic guidelines:

1. All markets are interrelated; markets don't move in isolation.
2. Intermarket work provides important background data.
3. Intermarket work uses external, as opposed to internal, data.
4. Technical analysis is the preferred vehicle.
5. Heavy emphasis is placed on the futures markets.
6. Futures-oriented technical indicators are employed.

These premises form the basis for intermarket analysis. If it can be shown that all markets—financial and nonfinancial, domestic and global—are interrelated, and that all are just part of a greater whole, then it becomes clear that focusing one's attention on only one market without consideration of what is happening in the others leaves one in danger of missing vital directional clues. Market analysis, when limited to any one market, often leaves the analyst in doubt. Technical analysis can tell an important story about a common stock or a futures contract. More often than not, however, technical readings are uncertain. It is at those times that a study of a related market may provide critical information as to market direction. *When in doubt, look to related markets for clues.* Demonstrating that these intermarket relationships exist, and how they can be incorporated into our technical work, is the major task of this book.

INTERMARKET ANALYSIS AS BACKGROUND INFORMATION

The key word here is "background." Intermarket work provides *background* information, not *primary* information. Traditional technical analysis still has to be applied to the markets on an individual basis, with primary emphasis placed on the market being traded. Once that's done, however, the next step is to take intermarket relationships into consideration to see if the individual conclusions make sense from an intermarket perspective.

Suppose intermarket work suggests that two markets usually trend in opposite directions, such as Treasury bonds and the Commodity Research Bureau Index. Suppose further that a separate analysis of the top markets provides a bullish outlook for both at the same time. Since those two conclusions, arrived at by separate analysis, contradict their usual inverse relationship, the analyst might want to go back and reexamine the individual conclusions.

There will be times when the usual intermarket relationships aren't visible or, for a variety of reasons, appear to be temporarily out of line. What is the trader to do when traditional technical analysis clashes with intermarket analysis? At such times, traditional analysis still takes precedence but with increased caution. The trader who gets bullish readings in two markets that usually don't trend in the same direction knows one of the markets is probably giving false readings, but isn't sure which one. The prudent course at such times is to fall back on one's separate technical work, but to do so very cautiously until the intermarket work becomes clearer.

Another way to look at it is that intermarket analysis warns traders when they can afford to be more aggressive and when they should be more cautious. They may remain faithful to the more traditional technical work, but intermarket relationships may serve to warn them not to trust completely what the individual charts are showing. There may be other times when intermarket analysis may cause a trader to override individual market conclusions. Remember that intermarket analysis is meant to add to the trader's data, not to replace what has gone before. I'll try to resolve this seeming contradiction as we work our way through the various examples in succeeding chapters.

EXTERNAL RATHER THAN INTERNAL DATA

Traditional technical work has tended to focus its attention on an individual market, such as the stock market or the gold market. All the market data needed to analyze an individual market technically—price, volume, open interest—was provided by the market itself. As many as 40 different technical indicators—on balance volume, moving averages, oscillators, trendlines, and so on—were applied to the market along with various analytical techniques, such as Elliott Wave theory and cycles. The goal was to analyze the market separately from everything else.

Intermarket analysis has a totally different focus. It suggests that important directional clues can be found in related markets. Intermarket work has a more outward focus and represents a different emphasis and direction in technical work.

One of the great advantages of technical analysis is that it is very transferable. A technician doesn't have to be an expert in a given market to be able to analyze it technically. If a market is reasonably liquid, and can be plotted on a chart, a technical analyst can do a pretty adequate job of analyzing it. Since intermarket analysis requires the analyst to look at so many different markets, it should be obvious why the technical analyst is at such an advantage.

Technicians don't have to be experts in the stock market, bond market, currency market, commodity market, or the Japanese stock market to study their trends and their technical condition. They can arrive at technical conclusions and make intermarket comparisons without understanding the fundamentals of each individual market. Fundamental analysts, by comparison, would have to become familiar with all the economic forces that drive each of these markets individually—a formidable task that is probably impossible. It is mainly for this reason that technical analysis is the preferred vehicle for intermarket work.

EMPHASIS ON THE FUTURES MARKETS

Intermarket awareness parallels the development of the futures industry. The main reason that we are now aware of intermarket relationships is that price data is now readily available through the various futures markets that wasn't available just 15 years ago. The price discovery mechanism of the futures markets has provided the catalyst that has sparked the growing interest in and awareness of the interrelationships among the various financial sectors.

In the 1970s the New York commodity exchanges expanded their list of traditional commodity contracts to include inflation-sensitive markets such as gold and energy futures. In 1972 the Chicago Mercantile Exchange pioneered the development of the first financial futures contracts on foreign currencies. Starting in 1976 the Chicago exchanges introduced a new breed of financial futures contracts covering Treasury bonds and Treasury bills. Later on, other interest rate futures, such as Eurodollars and Treasury notes, were added. In 1982 stock index futures were introduced. In the mid-1980s in New York, the Commodity Research Bureau Futures Price Index and the U.S. Dollar Index were listed.

Prior to 1972 stock traders followed only stocks, bond traders only bonds, currency traders only currencies, and commodity traders only commodities. After 1986, however, traders could pick up a chart book to include graphs on virtually every market and sector. They could see right before their eyes the daily movements in the various futures markets, including agricultural commodities, copper, gold, oil, the CRB Index, the U.S. dollar, foreign currencies, bond, and stock index futures. Traders in brokerage firms and banks could now follow on their video screens the minute-by-minute quotes and chart action in the four major sectors: commodities, currencies, bonds, and stock index futures. It didn't take long for them to notice that these four sectors, which used to be looked at separately, actually fed off one another. A whole new way to look at the markets began to evolve.

On an international level, stock index futures were introduced on various overseas equities, in particular the British and Japanese stock markets. As various financial futures contracts began to proliferate around the globe, the world suddenly seemed to grow smaller. In no small way, then, our ability to monitor such a broad range of markets and our increased awareness of how they interact derive from the development of the various futures markets over the past 15 years.

It should come as no surprise, then, that the main emphasis in this book will be on the futures markets. Since the futures markets cover every financial sector, they provide a useful framework for our intermarket work. Of course, when we talk about stock index futures and bond futures, we're also talking about the stock market and the Treasury bond market as well. We're simply using the futures markets as proxies for all of the sectors under study.

Since most of our attention will be focused on the futures markets, I'll be employing technical indicators that are used primarily in the futures markets. There is an enormous amount of overlap between technical analysis of stocks and futures, but there are certain types of indicators that are more heavily used in each area.

For one thing, I'll be using mostly price-based indicators. Readers familiar with traditional technical analysis such as price pattern analysis, trendlines, support and resistance, moving averages, and oscillators should have no trouble at all.

Those readers who have studied my previous book, *Technical Analysis of the Futures Markets* (New York Institute of Finance/Prentice-Hall, 1986) are already well prepared. For those newer to technical analysis, the Glossary gives a brief introduction to some of the work we will be employing. However, I'd like to stress that while some technical work will be employed, it will be on a very basic level and is not the primary focus. Most of the charts employed will be overlay, or comparison, charts that simply compare the price activity between two or three markets. You should be able to see these relationships even with little or no knowledge of technical analysis.

Finally, one other advantage of the price-based type of indicators widely used in the futures markets is that they make comparison with related markets, particularly overseas markets, much easier. Stock market work, as it is practiced in the United States, is very heavily oriented to the use of sentiment indicators, such as the degree of bullishness among trading advisors, mutual fund cash levels, and put/call ratios. Since many of the markets we will be looking at do not provide the type of data needed to determine sentiment readings, the price-oriented indicators I will be employing lend themselves more readily to intermarket and overseas comparisons.

THE IMPORTANT ROLE
OF THE COMMODITY MARKETS

Although our primary goal is to examine intermarket relationships between financial sectors, a lot of emphasis will be placed on the commodity markets. This is done for two reasons. First, we'll be using the commodity markets to demonstrate how relationships within one sector can be used as trading information. This should prove especially helpful to those who actually trade the commodity markets. The second, and more important, reason is based on my belief that commodity markets represent the least understood of the market sectors that make up the intermarket chain. For reasons that we'll explain later, the introduction of a futures contract on the CRB Index in mid-1986 put the final piece of the intermarket structure in place and helped launch the movement toward intermarket awareness.

The key to understanding the intermarket scenario lies in recognizing the often overlooked role that the commodity markets play. Those readers who are more involved with the financial markets, and who have not paid much attention to the commodity markets, need to learn more about that area. I'll spend some time, therefore, talking about relationships within the commodity markets themselves, and then place the commodity group as a whole into the intermarket structure. To perform the latter task, I'll be employing various commodity indexes, such as the CRB Index. However, an adequate understanding of the workings of the CRB Index involves monitoring the workings of certain key commodity sectors, such as the precious metals, energy, and grain markets.

KEY MARKET RELATIONSHIPS

These then are the primary intermarket relationships we'll be working on. We'll begin in the commodity sector and work our way outward into the three other financial sectors. We'll then extend our horizon to include international markets. The key relationships are:

1. Action *within* commodity groups, such as the relationship of gold to platinum or crude to heating oil.
2. Action *between* related commodity groups, such as that between the precious metals and energy markets.
3. The relationship between the CRB Index and the various commodity groups and markets.
4. The *inverse* relationship between commodities and bonds.
5. The *positive* relationship between bonds and the stock market.
6. The *inverse* relationship between the U.S. dollar and the various commodity markets, in particular the gold market.
7. The relationship between various futures markets and related stock market groups, for example, gold versus gold mining shares.
8. U.S. bonds and stocks versus overseas bond and stock markets.

THE STRUCTURE OF THIS BOOK

This chapter introduces the concept of intermarket technical analysis and provides a general foundation for the more specific work to follow. In Chapter 2, the events leading up to the *1987 stock market crash* are used as the vehicle for providing an intermarket *overview* of the relationships between the four market sectors. I'll show how the activity in the commodity and bond markets gave ample warning that the strength in the stock market going into the fall of that year was on very shaky ground. In Chapter 3 the crucial link between *the CRB Index and the bond market*, which is the most important relationship in the intermarket picture, will be examined in more depth. The real breakthrough in intermarket work comes with the recognition of how commodity markets and bond prices are linked (see Figure 1.3).

Chapter 4 presents the positive relationship between *bonds and stocks*. More and more, stock market analysts are beginning to use bond price activity as an important indication of stock market strength. The link between *commodities and the U.S. dollar* will be treated in Chapter 5. Understanding how movements in the U.S. dollar affect the general commodity price level is helpful in understanding why a rising dollar is considered bearish for commodity markets and generally positive for bonds and stocks. In Chapter 6 the activity in the *U.S. dollar* will then be compared *to interest rate* futures.

Chapter 7 will delve into the world of *commodities.* Various commodity indexes will be compared for their predictive value and for their respective roles in influencing the direction of inflation and interest rates. The CRB Index will be examined closely, as will various commodity subindexes. Other popular commodity gauges, such as the Journal of Commerce and the Raw Industrial Indexes, will be studied. The relationship of commodity markets to the Producer Price Index and the Consumer Price Index will be treated along with an explanation of how the Federal Reserve Board uses commodity markets in its policy making.

FIGURE 1.3
BONDS AND COMMODITIES USUALLY TREND IN OPPOSITE DIRECTIONS. THAT INVERSE RELATIONSHIP CAN BE SEEN DURING 1989 BETWEEN TREASURY BOND FUTURES AND THE CRB FUTURES PRICE INDEX.

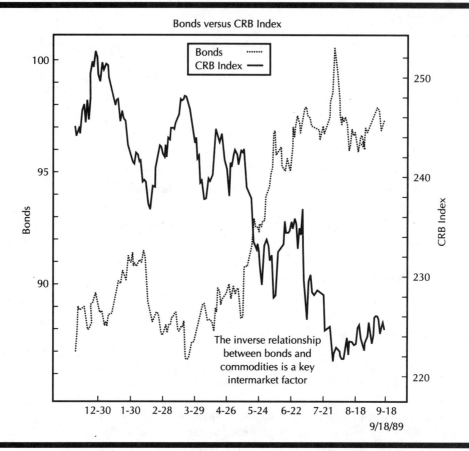

Bonds versus CRB Index

The inverse relationship between bonds and commodities is a key intermarket factor

9/18/89

International markets will be discussed in Chapter 8, where comparisons will be made between the U.S. markets and those of the other two world leaders, Britain and Japan. You'll see why knowing what's happening overseas may prove beneficial to your investing results. Chapter 9 will look at intermarket relationships from a different perspective. We'll look at how various inflation and interest-sensitive *stock market groups* and individual stocks are affected by activity in the various futures sectors.

The *Dow Jones Utility Average* is recognized as a leading indicator of the stock market. The Utilities are very sensitive to interest rate direction and hence the action in the bond market. Chapter 10 is devoted to consideration of how the relationship between bonds and commodities influence the Utility Average and the impact of that average on the stock market as a whole. I'll show in Chapter 11 how *relative strength*, or *ratio analysis*, can be used as an additional method of comparison between markets and sectors.

Chapter 12 discusses how ratio analysis can be employed in the *asset allocation* process and also makes the case for treating commodity markets as an asset class in the asset allocation formula. The business cycle provides the economic backdrop that determines whether the economy is in a period of expansion or contraction. The financial markets appear to go through a predictable, chronological sequence of peaks and troughs depending on the stage of the business cycle. The business cycle provides some economic rationale as to why the financial and commodity markets interact the way they do at certain times. We'll look at the *business cycle* in Chapter 13.

Chapter 14 will consider whether *program trading* is really a *cause* of stock market moves—or, as the evidence seems to indicate, whether program trading is itself an *effect* of events in other markets. Finally, I'll try to pull all of these relationships together in Chapter 15 to provide you with a *comprehensive picture* of how all of these intermarket relationships work. It's one thing to look at one or two key relationships; it's quite another to put the whole thing together in a way that it all makes sense.

I should warn you before we begin that intermarket work doesn't make the work of an analyst any easier. In many ways, it makes our market analysis more difficult by forcing us to take much more information into consideration. As in any other market approach or technique, the messages being sent by the markets aren't always clear, and sometimes they appear to be in conflict. The most intimidating feature of intermarket analysis is that it forces us to take in so much more information and to move into areas that many of us, who have tended to specialize, have never ventured into before.

The way the world looks at the financial markets is rapidly changing. Instant communications and the trend toward globalization have tied all of the world markets together into one big jigsaw puzzle. Every market plays some role in that big puzzle. The information is there for the taking. The question is no longer whether or not we should take intermarket comparisons into consideration, but rather how soon we should begin.

2

The 1987 Crash Revisited— an Intermarket Perspective

The year 1987 is one that most stock market participants would probably rather forget. The stock market drop in the fall of that year shook the financial markets around the world and led to a lot of finger pointing as to what actually caused the global equity collapse. Many took the narrow view that various futures-related strategies, such as program trading and portfolio insurance, actually caused the selling panic. They reasoned that there didn't seem to be any economic or technical justification for the stock collapse. The fact that the equity collapse was global in scope, and not limited to the U.S. markets, would seem to argue against such a narrow view, however, since most overseas markets at the time weren't affected by program trading or portfolio insurance.

In Chapter 14 it will be argued that what is often blamed on program trading is in reality usually some manifestation of intermarket linkages at work. The more specific purpose in this chapter is to reexamine the market events leading up to the October 1987 collapse and to demonstrate that, while the stock market itself may have been taken by surprise, those observers who were monitoring activity in the commodity and bond markets were aware that the stock market advance during 1987 was on very shaky ground. In fact, the events of 1987 provide a textbook example of how the intermarket scenario works and make a compelling argument as to why stock market participants need to monitor the other three market sectors—the dollar, bonds, and commodities.

THE LOW-INFLATION ENVIRONMENT AND THE BULL MARKET IN STOCKS

I'll start the examination of the 1987 events by looking at the situation in the commodity markets and the bond market. Two of the main supporting factors behind the bull market in stocks that began in 1982 were falling commodity prices (lower inflation) and falling interest rates (rising bond prices). Commodity prices (represented by the Commodity Research Bureau Index) had been dropping since 1980. Long-term interest rates topped out in 1981. Going into the 1980s, therefore, falling commodity prices signaled that the inflationary spiral of the 1970s had ended. The subsequent drop in commodity prices and interest rate yields provided a low inflation environment, which fueled strong bull markets in bonds and stocks.

In later chapters many of these relationships will be examined in more depth. For now, I'll simply state the basic premise that generally the CRB Index moves in the *same* direction as interest rate yields and in the *opposite* direction of bond prices. Falling commodity prices are generally bullish for bonds. In turn, rising bond prices are generally bullish for stocks.

Figure 2.1 shows the inverse relationship between the CRB Index and Treasury bonds from 1985 through the end of 1987. Going into 1986 bond prices were rising and commodity prices were falling. In the spring of 1986 the commodity price level began to level off and formed what later came to be seen as a "left shoulder" in a major inverse "head and shoulders" bottom that was resolved by a bullish breakout in the spring of 1987. Two specific events help explain that recovery in the CRB Index

---

FIGURE 2.1
THE INVERSE RELATIONSHIP BETWEEN BOND PRICES AND COMMODITIES CAN BE SEEN FROM 1985 THROUGH 1987. THE BOND MARKET COLLAPSE IN THE SPRING OF 1987 COINCIDED WITH A BULLISH BREAKOUT IN COMMODITIES. THE BULLISH "HEAD AND SHOULDERS" BOTTOM IN THE CRB INDEX WARNED THAT THE BULLISH "SYMMETRICAL TRIANGLE" IN BONDS WAS SUSPECT.

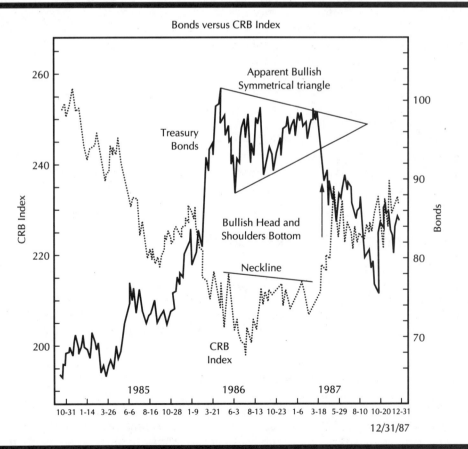

in 1986. One was the Chernobyl nuclear accident in Russia in April 1986 which caused strong reflex rallies in many commodity markets. The other factor was that crude oil prices, which had been in a freefall from $32.00 to $10.00, hit bottom the same month and began to rally.

Figure 2.1 shows that the actual top in bond prices in the spring of 1986 coincided with the formation of the "left shoulder" in the CRB Index. (The bond market is particularly sensitive to trends in the oil market.) The following year saw sideways movement in both the bond market and the CRB Index, which eventually led to major trend reversals in both markets in 1987. What happened during the ensuing 12 months is a dramatic example not only of the strong inverse relationship between commodities and bonds but also of why it's so important to take intermarket comparisons into consideration.

The price pattern that the bond market formed throughout the second half of 1986 and early 1987 was viewed at the time as a bullish "symmetrical triangle." The pattern is clearly visible in Figure 2.1. Normally, this type of pattern with two converging trendlines is a continuation pattern, which means that the prior trend (in this case, the bullish trend) would probably resume. The consensus of technical opinion at that time was for a bullish resolution of the bond triangle.

On its own merits that bullish interpretation seemed fully justified if the technical trader had been looking only at the bond market. However, the trader who was also monitoring the CRB Index should have detected the formation of the potentially bullish "head and shoulders" bottoming pattern. Since the CRB Index and bond prices usually trend in opposite directions, something was clearly wrong. If the CRB Index actually broke its 12-month "neckline" and started to rally sharply, it would be hard to justify a simultaneous bullish breakout in bonds.

This, then, is an excellent example of two independent technical readings giving simultaneous bullish interpretations to two markets that seldom move in the same direction. At the very least the bond bull should have been warned that his bullish interpretation might be faulty.

Figure 2.1 shows that the bullish breakout by the CRB Index in April 1987 coincided with the bearish breakdown in bond prices. It became clear at that point that two major props under the bull market in stocks (rising bond prices and falling commodity prices) had been removed. Let's look at what happened between bonds and stocks.

THE BOND COLLAPSE—A WARNING FOR STOCKS

Figure 2.2 compares the action between bonds and stocks in the three-year period prior to October 1987. Since 1982 bonds and stocks had been rallying together. Both markets had undergone a one-year consolidation throughout most of 1986. Early in 1987 stocks began another advance but for the first time in four years, the stock rally was not confirmed by a similar rally in bonds. What made matters worse was the bond market collapse in April 1987 (coinciding with the commodity price rally). At the very least stock traders who were following the course of events in commodities and bonds were warned that something important had changed and that it was time to start worrying about stocks.

What about the long lead time between bonds and stocks? It's true that the stock market peak in August 1987 came four months after the bond market collapse that took place in April. It's also true that there was a lot of money to be made in stocks during those four months (provided the trader exited the stock market on time). However, the action in bonds and commodities warned that it was time to be cautious.

FIGURE 2.2
BONDS USUALLY PEAK BEFORE STOCKS. BONDS PEAKED IN 1986 BUT DIDN'T START TO DROP UNTIL THE SPRING OF 1987. THE COLLAPSE IN BOND PRICES IN APRIL OF 1987 (WHICH COINCIDED WITH AN UPTURN IN COMMODITIES) WARNED THAT THE STOCK MARKET RALLY (WHICH PEAKED IN AUGUST) WAS ON SHAKY GROUND.

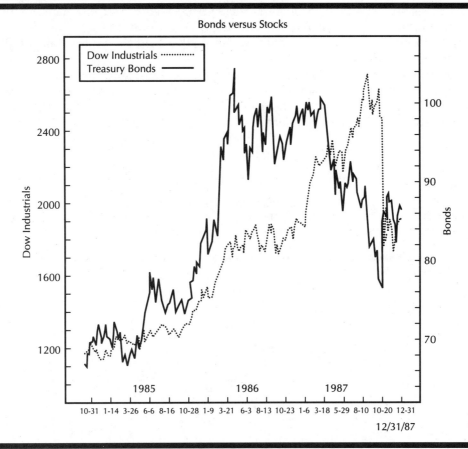

Many traditional stock market indicators gave "sell" signals in advance of the October collapse. Negative divergences were evident in many popular oscillators; several mechanical systems flashed "sell" signals; a Dow Theory sell signal was given the week prior to the October crash. The problem was that many technically oriented traders paid little attention to the bearish signals because many of those signals had often proven unreliable during the previous five years. The action in the commodity and bond markets might have suggested giving more credence to the bearish technical warnings in stocks this time around.

Although the rally in the CRB Index and the collapse in the bond market didn't provide a specific timing signal as to when to take long profits in stocks, there's no question that they provided plenty of time for the stock trader to implement a more defensive strategy. By using intermarket analysis to provide a background that suggested this stock rally was not on solid footing, the technical trader could have monitored various stock market technical indicators with the intention of exiting long positions or taking some appropriate defensive action to protect long profits on the first sign of breakdowns or divergences in those technical indicators.

Figure 2.3 shows bond, commodities, and stocks on one chart for the same three-year period. This type of chart from 1985 through the end of 1987 clearly shows the interplay between the three markets. It shows the bullish breakout in the CRB Index, the simultaneous bearish breakdown in bonds in April 1987, and the subsequent stock market peak in August of the same year. The rally in the commodity markets and bond decline had pushed interest rates sharply higher. Probably more than any other factor, the surge in interest rates during September and October of 1987 (as a direct result of the action in the other two sectors) caused the eventual downfall of the stock market.

Figure 2.4 compares Treasury bond yields to the Dow Jones Industrial Average. Notice on the left scale that bond yields rose to double-digit levels (over 10 percent) in October. This sharp jump in bond yields coincided with a virtual collapse in the bond market. Market commentators since the crash have cited the interest rate

---

FIGURE 2.3

A COMPARISON OF BONDS, STOCKS, AND COMMODITIES FROM 1985 THROUGH 1987. THE STOCK MARKET PEAK IN THE SECOND HALF OF 1987 WAS FORESHADOWED BY THE RALLY IN COMMODITIES AND THE DROP IN BOND PRICES DURING THE FIRST HALF OF THAT YEAR.

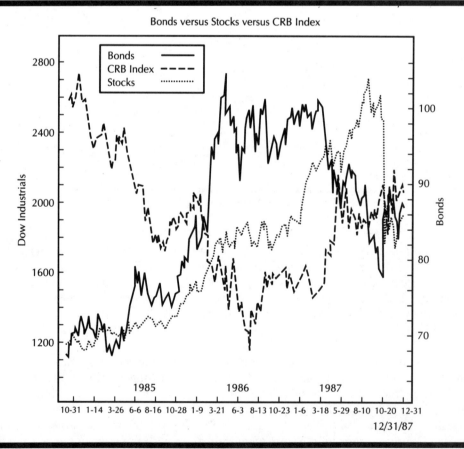

FIGURE 2.4
THE SURGE IN BOND YIELDS IN THE SUMMER AND FALL OF 1987 HAD A BEARISH INFLUENCE ON STOCKS. FROM JULY TO OCTOBER OF THAT YEAR, TREASURY BOND YIELDS SURGED FROM 8.50 PERCENT TO OVER 10.00 PERCENT. THE SURGE IN BOND YIELDS WAS TIED TO THE COLLAPSING BOND MARKET AND RISING COMMODITIES.

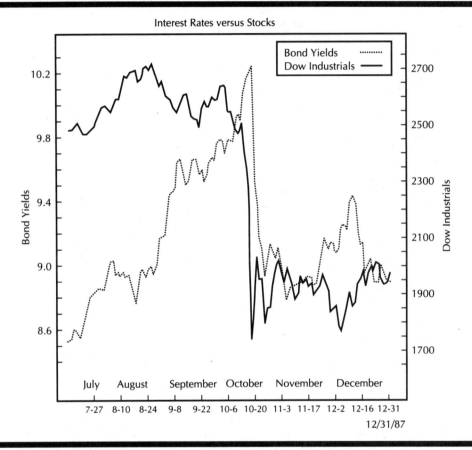

surge as the primary factor in the stock market selloff. If that's the case, the whole scenario had begun to play itself out several months earlier in the commodity and bond markets.

THE ROLE OF THE DOLLAR

Attention during this discussion of the events of 1987 has primarily focused on the commodity, bond, and stock markets. The U.S. dollar played a role as well in the autumn of 1987. Figure 2.5 compares the U.S. stock market with the action in the dollar. It can be seen that a sharp drop in the U.S. currency coincided almost exactly with the stock market decline. The U.S. dollar had actually been in a bear market since early 1985. However, for several months prior, the dollar had staged an impressive rally. There was considerable speculation at the time as to whether or not the dollar had actually bottomed. As the chart in Figure 2.5 shows, however, the dollar rally

FIGURE 2.5

THE FALLING U.S. DOLLAR DURING THE SECOND HALF OF 1987 ALSO WEIGHED ON STOCK PRICES. THE TWIN PEAKS IN THE U.S. CURRENCY IN AUGUST AND OCTOBER OF THAT YEAR COINCIDED WITH SIMILAR PEAKS IN THE STOCK MARKET. THE COLLAPSE IN THE U.S. DOLLAR IN OCTOBER ALSO PARALLELED THE DROP IN EQUITIES.

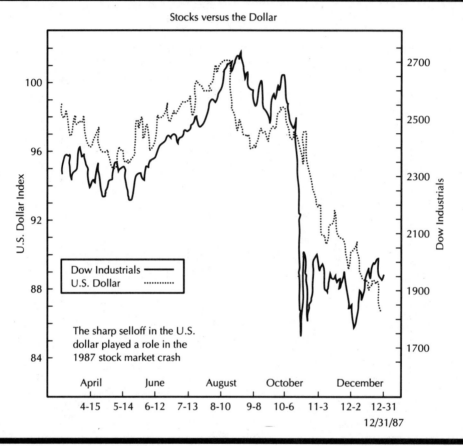

Stocks versus the Dollar

peaked in August along with the stock market. A second rally failure by the dollar in October and its subsequent plunge coincided almost exactly with the stock market selloff. It seems clear that the plunge in the dollar contributed to the weakness in equities.

Consider the sequence of events going into the fall of 1987. Commodity prices had turned sharply higher, fueling fears of renewed inflation. At the same time interest rates began to soar to double digits. The U.S. dollar, which was attempting to end its two-year bear market, suddenly went into a freefall of its own (fueling even more inflation fears). Is it any wonder, then, that the stock market finally ran into trouble? Given all of the bearish activity in the surrounding markets, it's amazing the stock market held up as well as it did for so long. There were plenty of reasons why stocks should have sold off in late 1987. Most of those reasons, however, were visible in the action of the surrounding markets and not necessarily in the stock market itself.

RECAP OF KEY RELATIONSHIPS

I'll briefly restate the key relationships here as they were demonstrated in 1987. In subsequent chapters, I'll break down the relationships more finely and examine each of them in isolation and in more depth. After examining each of them separately, I'll then put them all back together again.

- Bond prices and commodities usually trend in opposite directions.
- Bonds usually trend in the same direction as stocks. Any serious divergence between bonds and stocks usually warns of a possible trend reversal in stocks.
- A falling dollar will eventually cause commodity prices to rally which in turn will have a bearish impact on bonds and stocks. Conversely, a rising dollar will eventually cause commodity prices to weaken which is bullish for bonds and stocks.

LEADS AND LAGS IN THE DOLLAR

The role of the dollar in 1987 isn't as convincing as that of bonds and stocks. Despite its plunge in October 1987, which contributed to stock market weakness, the dollar had already been falling for over two years. It's important to recognize that although the dollar plays an important role in the intermarket picture, long lead times must at times be taken into consideration. For example, the dollar topped in the spring of 1985. That peak in the dollar started a chain of events in motion and led to the eventual bottom in the CRB Index and tops in bonds and stocks. However, the bottom in the commodity index didn't take place until a year after the dollar peak. A falling dollar becomes bearish for bonds and stocks when its inflationary impact begins to push commodity prices higher.

Although my analysis begins with the dollar, it's important to recognize that there's really no starting point in intermarket work. The dollar affects commodity prices, which affect interest rates, which in turn affect the dollar. A period of falling interest rates (1981–1986) will eventually cause the dollar to weaken (1985); the weaker dollar will eventually cause commodities to rally (1986–1987) along with higher interest rates, which is bearish for bonds and stocks (1987). Eventually the higher interest rates will pull the dollar higher, commodities and interest rates will peak, exerting a bullish influence on bonds and stocks, and the whole cycle starts over again.

Therefore, it is possible to have a falling dollar along with falling commodity prices and rising financial assets for a period of time. The trouble starts when commodities turn higher. Of the four sectors that we will be examining, the role of the U.S. dollar is probably the least precise and the one most difficult to pin down.

SUMMARY

The events of 1987 provided a textbook example of how the financial markets interrelate with each other and also an excellent vehicle for an overview of the four market sectors. I'll return to this time period in Chapters 8, 10, and 13, which discuss various other intermarket features, such as the business cycle, the international markets, and the leading action of the Dow Jones Utility Average. Let's now take a closer look at the most important relationship in the intermarket picture: the linkage between commodities and bonds.

3

Commodity Prices and Bonds

Of all the intermarket relationships explored in this book, the link between commodity markets and the Treasury bond market is the most important. The commodity-bond link is the fulcrum on which the other relationships are built. It is this inverse relationship between the commodity markets (represented by the Commodity Research Bureau Futures Price Index) and Treasury bond prices that provides the breakthrough linking commodity markets and the financial sector.

Why is this so important? If a strong link can be established between the commodity sector and the bond sector, then a link can also be established between the commodity markets and the stock market because the latter is influenced to a large extent by bond prices. Bond and stock prices are both influenced by the dollar. However, the dollar's impact on bonds and stocks comes through the commodity sector. Movements in the dollar influence commodity prices. Commodity prices influence bonds, which then influence stocks. *The key relationship that binds all four sectors together is the link between bonds and commodities.* To understand why this is the case brings us to the critical question of inflation.

THE KEY IS INFLATION

The reason commodity prices are so important is because of their role as a leading indicator of inflation. In Chapter 7, I'll show how commodity markets lead other popular inflation gauges such as the Consumer Price Index (CPI) and the Producer Price Index (PPI) by several months. We'll content ourselves here with the general statement that *rising commodity prices are inflationary*, while *falling commodity prices are non-inflationary*. Periods of inflation are also characterized by rising interest rates, while noninflationary periods experience falling interest rates. During the 1970s soaring commodity markets led to double-digit inflation and interest rate yields in excess of 20 percent. The commodity markets peaked out in 1980 and declined for six years, ushering in a period of disinflation and falling interest rates.

The major premise of this chapter is that *commodity markets trend in the same direction as Treasury bond yields and in the opposite direction of bond prices.* Since the early 1970s every major turning point in long-term interest rates has been accompanied by or preceded by a major turn in the commodity markets in the same direction. Figure 3.1 shows that the CRB Index and interest rates rose simultaneously

FIGURE 3.1

A DEMONSTRATION OF THE POSITIVE CORRELATION BETWEEN THE CRB INDEX AND 10-YEAR TREASURY YIELDS FROM 1973 THROUGH 1987. (*SOURCE: CRB INDEX WHITE PAPER: AN INVESTIGATION INTO NON-TRADITIONAL TRADING APPLICATIONS FOR CRB INDEX FUTURES*, PREPARED BY POWERS RESEARCH, INC., 30 MONTGOMERY STREET, JERSEY CITY, NJ 07302, MARCH 1988.)

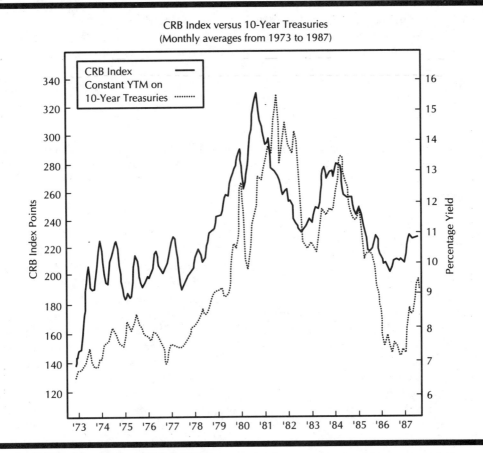

CRB Index versus 10-Year Treasuries
(Monthly averages from 1973 to 1987)

during the early 1970s, trended sideways together from 1974 to 1977, and then rose dramatically into 1980. In late 1980 commodity prices began to drop sharply. Bond yields topped out a year later in 1981. Commodities and bond yields dropped together to mid-1986 when both measures troughed out together.

For those readers who are unfamiliar with Treasury bond pricing, it's important to recognize that bond *prices* and bond *yields* move in opposite directions. When Treasury bond *yields* are rising (during a period of rising inflation like the 1970s), bond *prices* fall. When bond *yields* are falling (during a period of disinflation like the early 1980s), bond *prices* are rising. This is how the inverse relationship between bond *prices* and commodity *prices* is established. If it can be shown that interest rate *yields* and commodity prices trend in the same direction, and if it is understood that bond *yields* and bond *prices* move in opposite directions, then it follows that bond *prices* and commodity prices trend in opposite directions.

ECONOMIC BACKGROUND

It isn't necessary to understand why these economic relationships exist. All that is necessary is the demonstration that they do exist and the application of that knowledge in trading decisions. The purpose in this and succeeding chapters is to demonstrate that these relationships do exist and can be used to advantage in market analysis. However, it is comforting to know that there are economic explanations as to why commodities and interest rates move in the same direction.

During a period of economic expansion, demand for raw materials increases along with the demand for money to fuel the economic expansion. As a result prices of commodities rise along with the price of money (interest rates). A period of rising commodity prices arouses fears of inflation which prompts monetary authorities to raise interest rates to combat that inflation. Eventually, the rise in interest rates chokes off the economic expansion which leads to the inevitable economic slowdown and recession. During the recession demand for raw materials and money decreases, resulting in lower commodity prices and interest rates. Although it's not the main concern in this chapter, it should also be obvious that activity in the bond and commodity markets can tell a lot about which way the economy is heading.

MARKET HISTORY IN THE 1980s

Comparison of the bond and commodity markets begins with the events leading up to and following the major turning points of the 1980–1981 period which ended the inflationary spiral of the 1970s and began the disinflationary period of the 1980s. This provides a useful background for closer scrutiny of the market action of the past five years. The major purpose in this chapter is simply to demonstrate that *a strong inverse relationship exists between the CRB Index and the Treasury bond market* and to suggest ways that the trader or analyst could have used this information to advantage. Since the focus is on the Commodity Research Bureau Futures Price Index, a brief explanation is necessary.

The CRB Index, which was created by the Commodity Research Bureau in 1956, represents a basket of 21 actively-traded commodity markets. It is the most widely-watched barometer of general commodity price trends and is regarded as the commodity markets' equivalent of the Dow Jones Industrial Average. It includes grains, livestock, tropical, metals, and energy markets. It uses 1967 as its base year. While other commodity indexes provide useful trending information, the wide acceptance of the CRB Index as the main barometer of the commodity markets, the fact that all of its components are traded on futures markets, and the fact that it is the only commodity index that is also a futures contract itself make it the logical choice for intermarket comparisons. In Chapter 7, I'll explain the CRB Index in more depth and compare it to some other commodity indexes.

The 1970s witnessed virtual explosions in the commodity markets, which led to spiraling inflation and rising interest rates. From 1971 to 1980 the CRB Index appreciated in value by approximately 250 percent. During that same period of time, bond yields appreciated by about 150 percent. In November of 1980, however, a collapse in the CRB Index signaled the end of the inflationary spiral and began the disinflationary period of the 1980s. (An even earlier warning of an impending top in the commodity markets was sounded by the precious metals markets which began to fall during the first quarter of 1980.) Long-term bond rates continued to rise into the middle of 1981 before finally peaking in September of that year.

The 1970s had been characterized by rising commodity prices and a weak bond market. In the six years after the 1980 peak, the CRB Index lost 40 percent of its value while bond yields dropped by about half. The inflation rate descended from the 12–13 percent range at the beginning of the 1980s to its lowpoint of 2 percent in 1986. The 1980 peak in the CRB Index set the stage for the major bottom in bonds the following year (1981). A decade later the 1980 top in the CRB Index and the 1981 bottom in the bond market have still not been challenged.

The disinflationary period starting in 1980 saw falling commodity markets along with falling interest rates (see Figure 3.1). One major interruption of those trends took place from the end of 1982 through early 1984, when the CRB Index recovered about half of its earlier losses. Not surprisingly during that same time period interest rates rose. In mid-1984, however, the CRB index resumed its major downtrend. At the same time that the CRB Index was resuming its decline, bond yields started the second leg of their decline that lasted for another two years. Figure 3.2 compares the CRB Index and bond yields on a *rate of change* basis.

FIGURE 3.2

THE LINKAGE BETWEEN THE CRB INDEX AND TREASURY BOND YIELDS CAN BE SEEN ON A 12-MONTH RATE OF CHANGE BASIS FROM 1964 TO 1986. (*SOURCE:* COMMODITY RESEARCH BUREAU, 75 WALL STREET, NEW YORK, N.Y. 10005.)

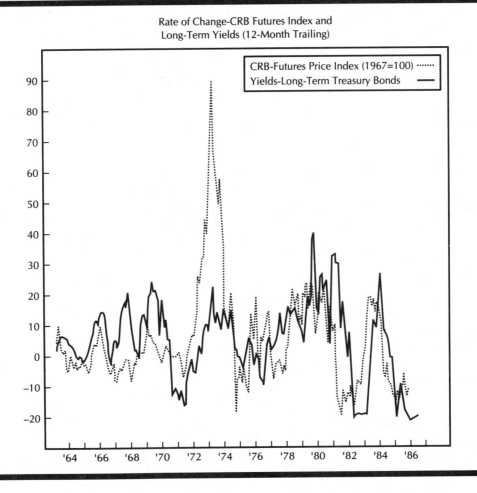

Rate of Change-CRB Futures Index and
Long-Term Yields (12-Month Trailing)

CRB-Futures Price Index (1967=100) ⋯⋯
Yields-Long-Term Treasury Bonds ——

Although the focus of this chapter is on the relationship of commodities and bonds, it should be mentioned at this point that the 1980 peak in the commodity markets was accompanied by a major bottom in the U.S. dollar, a subject that is explained in Chapter 5. The bottom in the bond market during 1981 and the subsequent upside breakout in 1982 helped launch the major bull market in stocks that began the same year. It's instructive to point out here that the action in the dollar played an important role in the reversals in commodity and bonds in 1980 and 1981 and that the stock market was the eventual beneficiary of the events in those other three markets.

The rising bond market and falling CRB Index reflected disinflation during the early 1980s and provided a supportive environment for financial assets at the expense of hard assets. That all began to change, however, in 1986. In another example of the linkage between the CRB Index and bonds, both began to change direction in 1986. The commodity price level began to level off after a six-year decline. Interest rates bottomed at the same time and the bond market peaked. I discussed in Chapter 2 the beginning of the "head and shoulders" bottom that began to form in the CRB Index during 1986 and the warning that bullish pattern gave of the impending top in the bond market. Although the collapse in the bond market in early 1987, accompanied by a sharp rally in the CRB Index, provided a dramatic example of their inverse relationship, there's no need to repeat that analysis here. Instead, attention will be focused on the events following the 1987 peak in bonds and the bottom in the CRB Index to see if the intermarket linkage holds up.

BONDS AND THE CRB INDEX FROM THE 1987 TURNING POINTS

Figures 3.3 through 3.8 provide different views of the price action of bonds versus the CRB Index since 1987. Figure 3.3 provides a four-year view of the interaction between bond *yields* and the CRB Index from the end of 1985 into the second half of 1989. Although not a perfect match it can be seen that both lines generally rose and fell together. Figure 3.4 uses bond *prices* in place of *yields* for the same time span. The three major points of interest on this four-year chart are the major peak in bonds and the bottom in the CRB Index in the spring of 1987, the major spike in the CRB Index in mid-1988 (caused by rising grain prices resulting from the midwestern drought in the United States) during which time the bond market remained on the defensive, and finally the rally in the bond market and the accompanying decline in the CRB Index going into the second half of 1989. This chart shows that the inverse relationship between the CRB Index and bonds held up pretty well during that time period.

Figure 3.5 provides a closer view of the 1987 price trends and demonstrates the inverse relationship between the CRB Index and bond prices during that year. The first half of 1987 saw strong commodity markets and a falling bond market. Going into October the bond market was falling sharply while commodity prices were firming. The strong rebound in bond prices in late-October (reflecting a flight to safety during that month's stock market crash) witnessed a sharp pullback in commodities. Commodities then rallied during November while bonds weakened. In an unusual development both markets then rallied together into early 1988. That situation didn't last long, however.

Figure 3.6 shows that early in January of 1988 bonds rallied sharply into March while the CRB Index sold off sharply. In March, bonds peaked and continued to drop into August. The March peak in bonds coincided with a major lowpoint in the CRB

FIGURE 3.3

A COMPARISON OF THE CRB INDEX AND TREASURY BOND YIELDS FROM 1986 TO 1989. INTEREST RATES AND COMMODITY PRICES USUALLY TREND IN THE SAME DIRECTION.

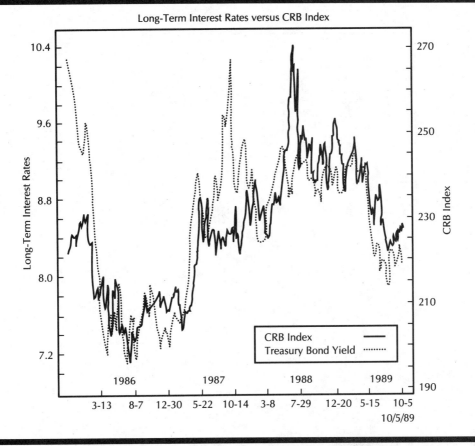

Long-Term Interest Rates versus CRB Index

Index which then rallied sharply into July. Whereas the first quarter of 1988 had seen a firm bond market and falling commodity markets, the spring and early summer saw surging commodity markets and a weak bond market. This surge in the CRB Index was caused mainly by strong grain and soybean markets, which rallied on a severe drought in the midwestern United States, culminating in a major peak in the CRB Index in July. The bond market didn't hit bottom until August, over a month after the CRB Index had peaked out.

Figure 3.7 shows the events from October 1988 to October 1989 and provides a closer look at the way bonds and commodities trended in opposite directions during those 12 months. The period from the fall of 1988 to May of 1989 was a period of indecision in both markets. Both went through a period of consolidation with no clear trend direction. Figure 3.7 shows that even during this period of relative trendlessness, peaks in one market tended to coincide with troughs in the other. The final bottom in the bond market took place during March which coincides with an important peak in the CRB Index.

The most dramatic manifestation of the negative linkage between the two markets during 1989 was the breakdown in the CRB Index during May, which coincided with

FIGURE 3.4
THE INVERSE RELATIONSHIP BETWEEN THE CRB INDEX AND TREASURY BOND PRICES CAN BE SEEN FROM 1986 TO 1989.

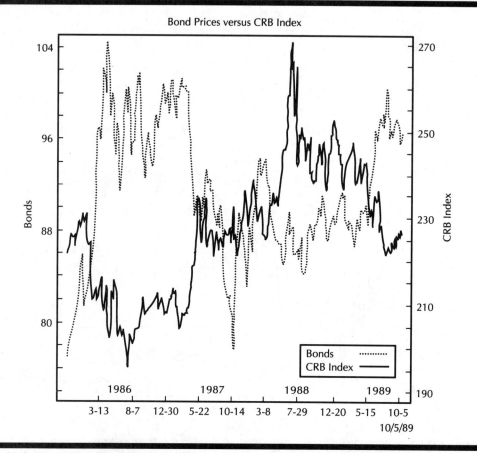

Bond Prices versus CRB Index

FIGURE 3.5
EVEN DURING THE HECTIC TRADING OF 1987, THE TENDENCY FOR COMMODITY PRICES AND TREASURY BOND PRICES TO TREND IN THE OPPOSITE DIRECTION CAN BE SEEN.

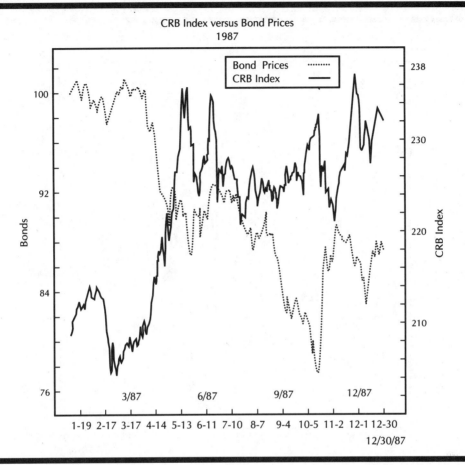

CRB Index versus Bond Prices
1987

FIGURE 3.6
**BOND PRICES AND COMMODITIES TRENDED IN OPPOSITE DIRECTIONS DURING 1988. THE
BOND PEAK DURING THE FIRST QUARTER COINCIDED WITH A SURGE IN COMMODITIES.
THE COMMODITY PEAK IN JULY PRECEDED A BOTTOM IN BONDS A MONTH LATER.**

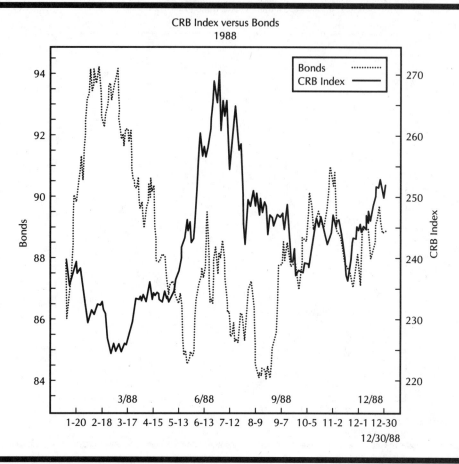

CRB Index versus Bonds
1988

FIGURE 3.7
THE INVERSE RELATIONSHIP BETWEEN THE CRB INDEX AND BOND PRICES CAN BE SEEN FROM THE THIRD QUARTER OF 1988 THROUGH THE THIRD QUARTER OF 1989. THE CORRESPONDING PEAKS AND TROUGHS ARE MARKED BY VERTICAL LINES. THE BREAKDOWN IN COMMODITIES DURING MAY OF 1989 COINCIDED WITH A MAJOR BULLISH BREAKOUT IN BONDS. IN AUGUST OF 1989, A BOTTOM IN THE CRB INDEX COINCIDED WITH A PEAK IN BONDS.

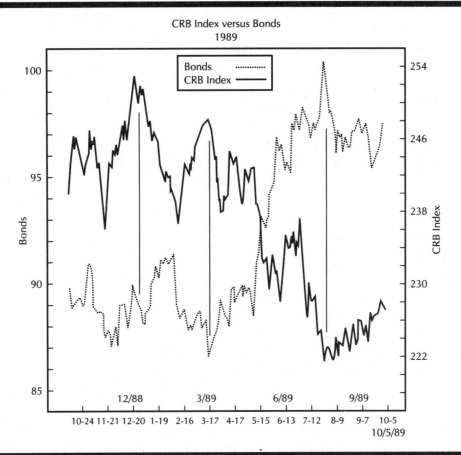

FIGURE 3.8
THE POSITIVE LINK BETWEEN THE CRB INDEX AND BOND YIELDS CAN BE SEEN FROM THE THIRD QUARTER OF 1988 TO THE THIRD QUARTER OF 1989. BOTH MEASURES DROPPED SHARPLY DURING MAY OF 1989 AND BOTTOMED TOGETHER IN AUGUST.

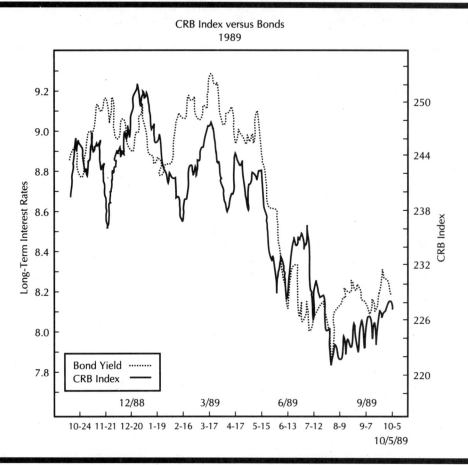

CRB Index versus Bonds
1989

an upside breakout in bonds during that same month. Notice that to the far right of the chart in Figure 3.7 a rally beginning in the CRB Index during the first week in August 1989 coincided exactly with a pullback in the bond market.

Figure 3.8 turns the picture around and compares the CRB Index to bond *yields* during that same 12-month period from late 1988 to late 1989. Notice how closely the CRB Index and Treasury bond yields tracked each other during that period of time. The breakdown in the CRB Index in May correctly signaled a new downleg in interest rates.

HOW THE TECHNICIAN CAN USE THIS INFORMATION

So far, the inverse relationship between bonds and the CRB Index has been demonstrated. Now some practical ways that a technical analyst can use this inverse relationship to some advantage will be shown. Figures 3.9 and 3.10 are monthly charts of the CRB Index and nearby Treasury bond futures. The indicator along the bottom

FIGURE 3.9

A MONTHLY CHART OF THE CRB INDEX FROM 1975 THROUGH AUGUST, 1989. THE INDICATOR ALONG THE BOTTOM IS A 14 BAR SLOW STOCHASTIC OSCILLATOR. MAJOR TURNING POINTS CAN BE SEEN IN 1980, 1982, 1984, 1986, AND 1988. MAJOR TREND SIGNALS IN THE CRB INDEX SHOULD BE CONFIRMED BY OPPOSITE SIGNALS IN THE BOND MARKET. (*SOURCE:* COMMODITY TREND SERVICE, P. O. BOX 32309, PALM BEACH GARDENS, FLORIDA 33420.)

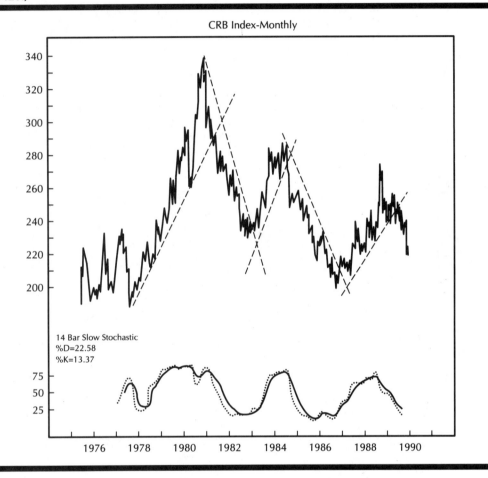

of both charts is a 14-month *stochastics* oscillator. For those not familiar with this indicator, when the dotted line crosses below the solid line and the lines are above 75, a *sell* signal is given. When the dotted line crosses over the solid line and both lines are below 25, a *buy* signal is given.

Notice that buy signals in one market are generally accompanied (or followed) by a sell signal in the other. Therefore, the concept of confirmation is carried a step further. A buy signal in the CRB Index should be confirmed by a sell signal in bonds. Conversely, a buy signal in bonds should be confirmed by a sell signal in the CRB Index. *We're now using signals in a related market as a confirming indicator of signals in another market.* Sometimes a signal in one market will act as a leading indicator for the other. When two markets that usually trend in opposite

FIGURE 3.10
**MONTHLY CHART OF TREASURY BOND FUTURES FROM 1978 THROUGH AUGUST, 1989. THE
INDICATOR ALONG THE BOTTOM IS A 14 BAR SLOW STOCHASTIC OSCILLATOR. MAJOR
TURNING POINTS CAN BE SEEN IN 1981, 1983, 1984, 1986, AND 1987. BUY AND SELL SIGNALS
ON THE TREASURY BOND CHART SHOULD BE CONFIRMED BY OPPOSITE SIGNALS IN THE
CRB INDEX. (*SOURCE:* COMMODITY TREND SERVICE, P.O. BOX 32309, PALM BEACH GARDENS,
FLORIDA 33420.)**

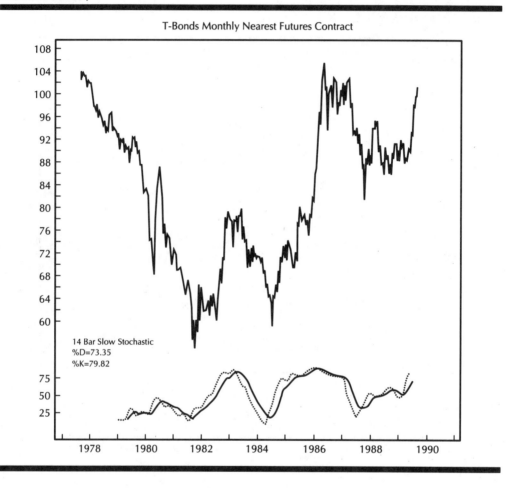

directions give simultaneous buy signals or simultaneous sell signals, the trader
knows something is wrong and should be cautious of the signals.

The analysis of the stochastics signals will be supplemented with simple
trendline and breakout analysis. Notice that at the 1980 top in Figure 3.9, the monthly
stochastics oscillator gave a major sell signal for commodity prices. The sell signal
was preceded by a major *negative divergence* in the stochastics oscillator which then
turned down in late 1980. The actual breaking of the major uptrend line in the CRB
Index didn't occur until June of 1981. From November of 1980 until September of
1981, bond and commodities dropped together. However, the CRB collapse warned
that that situation wouldn't last for long. Bonds actually bottomed in September
of 1981 when the stochastics oscillator also started to turn up and the inverse
relationship reestablished itself.

The next major turn in the CRB Index took place in late 1982, when a major down trendline was broken, and commodities turned higher. The bond market started to drop sharply within a couple of months. In June 1984 the CRB Index broke its up trendline and gave a stochastics sell signal. A month later the bond market began a major advance supported by a stochastics buy signal.

Moving ahead to 1986, a stochastics sell signal in bonds was followed by a buy signal in the CRB Index. This buy signal in the CRB Index lasted until mid-1988, when commodity prices peaked. A CRB sell signal was followed by a trendline breakdown in the spring of 1989. Bonds had given an original buy signal in late 1987 and gave a repeat buy signal in early 1989. The late 1987 buy signal in bonds preceded the mid-1988 CRB sell signal. However, it wasn't until mid-1988, when the CRB Index gave its stochastics sell signal, that bonds actually began a serious rally.

Figure 3.11 shows that the May 1989 breakdown in the CRB Index coincided exactly with a bullish breakout in bonds. That bearish "descending triangle" in the CRB Index provided a hint that commodity prices were headed lower and bonds higher. Going into late 1989 the bond market had reached a major resistance area

FIGURE 3.11
THE "DESCENDING TRIANGLE" IN THE CRB INDEX FORMED DURING THE FIRST HALF OF 1989 GAVE ADVANCE WARNING OF FALLING COMMODITIES AND RISING BOND PRICES. THE BEARISH BREAKDOWN IN COMMODITIES IN MAY OF THAT YEAR COINCIDED WITH A BULLISH BREAKOUT IN BONDS. AS THE FOURTH QUARTER OF 1989 BEGAN, COMMODITIES WERE RALLYING AND BONDS WERE WEAKENING.

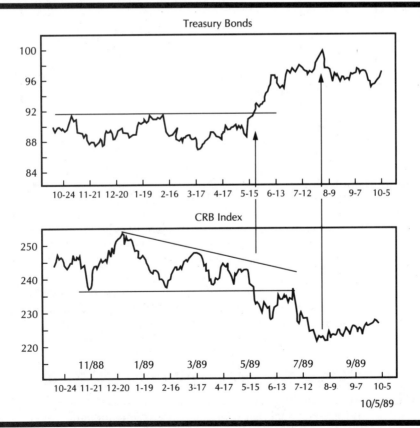

FIGURE 3.12
A COMPARISON OF WEEKLY CHARTS OF TREASURY BONDS AND THE CRB INDEX FROM 1986 TO OCTOBER OF 1989. IN EARLY 1987 RISING COMMODITIES WERE BEARISH FOR BONDS. IN MID-1988 A COMMODITY PEAK PROVED TO BE BULLISH FOR BONDS. ENTERING THE FOURTH QUARTER OF 1989, RISING BONDS WERE BACKING OFF FROM MAJOR RESISTANCE NEAR 100 WHILE THE FALLING CRB INDEX WAS BOUNCING OFF SUPPORT NEAR 220.

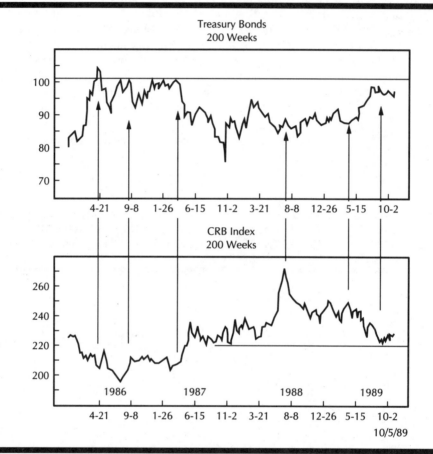

Treasury Bonds
200 Weeks

CRB Index
200 Weeks

10/5/89

near 100. At the same time the CRB Index had reached a major support level near 220. Those two events, occurring at the same time, suggested at the time that bonds were overbought and due for some weakness while the commodity markets were oversold and due for a bounce.

To the far right of Figure 3.11, the simultaneous pullback in bonds and the bounce in the CRB Index can be seen. Figure 3.12, a weekly chart of bonds and the CRB Index from 1986 to 1989, shows bonds testing overhead resistance near 100 in the summer of 1989 at the same time that the CRB Index is testing support near 220.

LINKING TECHNICAL ANALYSIS OF COMMODITIES AND BONDS

The purpose of the preceding exercise was simply to demonstrate the practical application of intermarket analysis. Those readers who are more experienced in technical analysis will no doubt see many more applications that are possible. The message itself is relatively simple. If it can be shown that two markets generally trend in opposite directions, such as the CRB Index and Treasury bonds, that information is extremely valuable to participants in both markets. It isn't my intention to claim that one market always leads the other, but simply to show that knowing what is happening in the commodity sector provides valuable information for the bond market. Conversely, knowing which way the bond market is most likely to trend tells the commodity trader a lot about which way the commodity markets are likely to trend. This type of combined analysis can be performed on monthly, weekly, daily, and even intraday charts.

THE USE OF RELATIVE–STRENGTH ANALYSIS

There is another technical tool which is especially helpful in comparing bond prices to commodity prices: relative strength, or ratio, analysis. Ratio analysis, where one market is divided by the other, enables us to compare the relative strength between two markets and provides another useful visual method for comparing bonds and the CRB Index. Ratio analysis will be briefly introduced in this section but will be covered more extensively in Chapters 11 and 12.

Figure 3.13 is divided into two parts. The upper portion is an overlay chart of the CRB Index and bonds for the three-year period from late 1986 to late 1989. The bottom chart is a ratio of the CRB Index divided by the bond market. When the line is rising, such as during the periods from March to October of 1987 and from March to July of 1988, commodity prices are outperforming bonds, and inflation pressures are intensifying. In this environment financial markets like bonds and stocks are generally under pressure. A major peak in the ratio line in the summer of 1988 marked the top of a two-year rise in the ratio and signaled the peak in inflation pressures. Financial markets strengthened from that point. (Popular inflation gauges such as the Consumer Price Index—CPI—and the Producer Price Index—PPI— didn't peak until early 1989, almost half a year later.)

In mid-1989 the ratio line broke down again from a major sideways pattern and signaled another significant shift in the commodity-bond relationship. The falling ratio line signaled that inflation pressures were waning even more, which was bearish for commodities, and that the pendulum was swinging toward the financial markets. Both bonds and stocks rallied strongly from that point.

THE ROLE OF SHORT-TERM RATES

All interest rates move in the same direction. It would seem, then, that the positive relationship between the CRB Index and long-term bond yields should also apply to shorter-term rates, such as 90-day Treasury bill and Eurodollar rates. Short-term interest rates are more volatile than long-term rates and are more responsive to changes in monetary policy. Attempts by the Federal Reserve Board to fine-tune monetary policy, by increasing or decreasing liquidity in the banking system, are reflected more in short-term rates, such as the overnight Federal funds rate or the 90-day Treasury Bill rate, than in 10-year Treasury note and 30-year bond rates which are more influenced by longer range inflationary expectations. It should come as no surprise then that the CRB Index correlates better with Treasury notes and bonds, with longer maturities, than with Treasury bills, which have much shorter maturities.

Even with this caveat, it's a good idea to keep an eye on what Treasury bill and Eurodollar futures prices are doing. Although movements in these short-term rate markets are much more volatile than those of bonds, turning points in T-bill and

FIGURE 3.13
THE BOTTOM CHART IS A RATIO OF THE CRB INDEX DIVIDED BY TREASURY BOND PRICES FROM 1987 THROUGH OCTOBER 1989. A RISING RATIO SHOWS THAT COMMODITIES ARE OUTPERFORMING BONDS AND IS INFLATIONARY. A FALLING RATIO FAVORS BONDS OVER COMMODITIES AND IS NONINFLATIONARY.

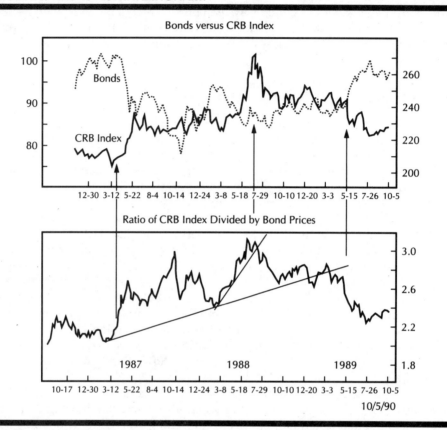

Eurodollar futures usually coincide with turning points in bonds and often pinpoint important trend reversals in the latter. When tracking the movement in the Treasury bond market for a good entry point, very often the actual signal can be found in the shorter-term T-bill and Eurodollar markets.

As a rule of thumb, all three markets should be trending in the same direction. It's not a good idea to buy bonds while T-bill and Eurodollar prices are falling. Wait for the T-bill and Eurodollar markets to turn first in the same direction of bonds before initiating a new long position in the bond market. To carry the analysis a step further, if turns in short-term rate futures provide useful clues to turns in bond prices, then short-term rate markets also provide clues to turns in commodity prices, which usually go in the opposite direction.

THE IMPORTANCE OF T-BILL ACTION

One example of how T-bills, T-bonds, and the CRB Index are interrelated can be seen in Figure 3.14. This chart compares the prices of T-bill futures and T-bond futures in the upper chart with the CRB Index in the lower chart from the end of 1987 to late

FIGURE 3.14
**THE UPPER CHART COMPARES PRICES OF TREASURY BILLS AND TREASURY BONDS. THE
BOTTOM CHART COMPARES THE CRB INDEX TO PRICES IN THE UPPER CHART. MAJOR
TURNING POINTS IN TREASURY BILLS CAN BE HELPFUL IN PINPOINTING TURNS IN BONDS
AND THE CRB INDEX. DURING MARCH OF 1988, BILLS AND BONDS TURNED DOWN
TOGETHER (WHILE COMMODITIES BOTTOMED). IN THE SPRING OF 1989, A MAJOR UPTURN
IN T-BILLS MARKED A BOTTOM IN BONDS AND WARNED OF AN IMPENDING BREAKDOWN
IN COMMODITIES.**

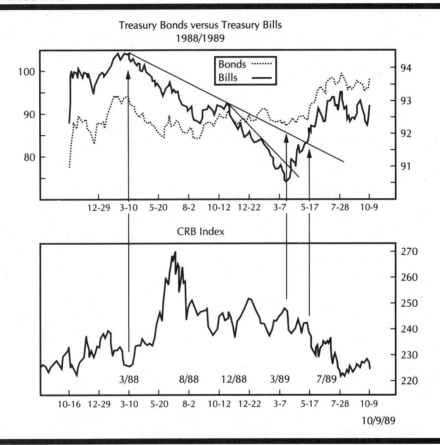

1989. It can be seen that bonds and bills trend in the same direction and turn at the
same time but that T-bill prices swing much more widely than bonds. To the upper
left of Figure 3.14, both turned down in March of 1988. This downturn in T-bills
and T-bonds coincided with a major upturn in the CRB Index, which rose over 20
percent in the next four months to its final peak in mid-1988.

The bond market hit bottom in August of the same year but was unable to gain
much ground. This sideways period in the bond market over the ensuing six months
coincided with similar sideways activity in the CRB Index. Treasury bill prices continued to drop sharply into March of 1989. It wasn't until T-bill futures put in a
bottom in March of 1989 and broke a tight down trendline that the bond market
began to rally seriously. The upward break of a one-year down trendline by T-bill
futures two months later in May of 1989 coincided exactly with a major bullish

breakout in bond futures. At the same time the CRB was resolving its trading range on the downside by dropping to the lowest level since the spring of the previous year.

In this case, the bullish turnaround in the T-bill market in March of 1989 did two things. It gave the green light to bond bulls to begin buying bonds more aggressively, and it set in motion the eventual bullish breakout in bonds and the bearish breakdown in the CRB Index.

"WATCH EVERYTHING"

The preceding discussion illustrates that important information in the bond market can be found by monitoring the trend action in the T-Bill market. It's another example of looking to a related market for directional clues. To carry this analysis another step, T-Bills and Eurodollars also trend in the same direction. Therefore, when monitoring the short-term rate markets, it's advisable to track both T-Bill and Eurodollar markets to ensure that both of them are confirming each other's actions. Treasury notes, which cover maturities from 2 to 10 years and lie between the maturities of the 90-day T-bills and 30-year bonds on the interest rate yield curve, should also be followed closely for trend indications. In other words, watch everything. You never know where the next clue will come from.

The focus of the previous paragraphs was on the necessity of monitoring all of the interest rate markets from the shorter to the longer range maturities to find clues to interest rate direction. Then that analysis is put into the intermarket picture to see how it fits with our commodity analysis. A bullish forecast in interest rate futures should be accompanied by a bearish forecast on the commodity markets. Otherwise, something is out of line. This chapter has concentrated on the CRB Index as a proxy for the commodity markets. However, the CRB Index represents a basket of 21 active commodity markets. Some of those markets are important in their own right as inflation indicators and often play a dominant role in the intermarket picture.

Gold and oil are two markets that are inflation-sensitive and that, at times, can play a decisive role in the intermarket picture. Sometimes the bond market will respond in the opposite direction to any strong trending action by either or both of those two markets. At other times, such as in the spring of 1988, during the worst drought in half a century, the grain markets in Chicago can dominate. It's necessary to monitor activity in each of the commodity markets as well as the CRB Index. The respective roles of the individual commodities will be discussed in Chapter 7.

SOME CORRELATION NUMBERS

This work so far has been based on visual comparisons. Statistical analysis appears to confirm what the charts are showing, namely that there is a strong negative correlation between the CRB Index and bond prices. A study prepared by Powers Research, Inc. (Jersey City, NJ 07302), entitled *The CRB Index White Paper: An Investigation into Non-Traditional Trading Applications for CRB Index Futures* (March, 1988), reported the results of correlation analysis over several time periods between the CRB Index and the other financial sectors. The results showed that over the 10 years from 1978 to 1987, the CRB Index had an 82 percent positive correlation with 10-year Treasury yields with a lead time of four months.

In the five years from 1982 to 1987, the correlation was an even more impressive +92 percent. Besides providing statistical evidence supporting the linkage between the CRB Index and bond yields, the study also suggests that, at least during the time span under study, the CRB Index led turns in bond yields by an average of four months.

In a more recent work, the *CRB Index Futures Reference Guide* (New York Futures Exchange, 1989), correlation comparisons are presented between prices of the CRB Index futures contract and bond futures prices. In this case, since the comparison was made with bond *prices* instead of bond *yields*, a negative correlation should have been present. In the period from June 1988 to June 1989, a negative correlation of −91 percent existed between CRB Index futures and bond futures, showing that the negative linkage held up very well during those 12 months.

The 1989 study provided another interesting statistic which takes us to our next step in the intermarket linkage and the subject of the next chapter—*the relationship between bonds and stocks*. During that same 12-month period, from June 1988 to June 1989, the statistical correlation between bond futures prices and futures prices of the New York Stock Exchange Composite Index was +94 percent. During that 12-month span, bond prices showed a negative 91 percent correlation to commodities and a positive 94 percent correlation to stocks, which demonstrates the fulcrum effect of the bond market alluded to earlier in the chapter.

The numbers also demonstrate why so much importance is placed on the inverse relationship between bonds and the commodity markets. If the commodity markets are linked to bonds and bonds are linked to stocks, then the commodity markets become indirectly linked to stocks through their influence on the bond market. It follows that if stock market traders want to analyze the bond market (and they should), it also becomes necessary to monitor the commodity markets.

SUMMARY

This chapter presented graphic and statistical evidence that commodity prices, represented by the CRB Index, trend in the same direction as Treasury bond yields and in the opposite direction of bond prices. Technical analysis of bonds or commodities is incomplete without a corresponding technical analysis of the other. The relative strength between bonds and the CRB Index, arrived at by ratio analysis, also provides useful information as to which way inflation is trending and whether or not the investment climate favors financial or hard assets.

4

Bonds Versus Stocks

In the previous chapter, the inverse relationship between bonds and commodities was studied. In this chapter, another vital link will be added to the intermarket chain in order to study the positive relationship between bonds and common stocks. The stock market is influenced by many factors. Two of the most important are the direction of inflation and interest rates. As a general rule of thumb, rising interest rates are bearish for stocks; falling interest rates are bullish. Put another way, *a rising bond market is generally bullish for stocks*. Conversely, *a falling bond market is generally bearish for stocks.* It can also be shown that bonds often act as a leading indicator of stocks. The purpose of this chapter is to demonstrate the strong positive linkage between bonds and stocks and to suggest that a technical analysis of stocks is incomplete without a corresponding analysis of the bond market.

Treasury bond futures, which have become the most actively traded futures contract in the world, were launched at the Chicago Board of Trade in 1977. In keeping with the primary focus on the futures markets, our attention in this chapter will be concentrated on the period since then, with special emphasis on the events of the 1980s. Toward the end of the book, a glance backward a bit further will reveal a larger historical perspective.

FINANCIAL MARKETS ON THE DEFENSIVE

As Chapter 3 suggested, the 1970s were a period of rising inflation and rising interest rates. It was the decade for tangible assets. Bond prices had been dropping sharply since 1977 and continued to do so until 1981. The weight of rising commodity prices kept downward pressure on bond prices as the 1970s ended. During that decade, bond market troughs in 1970 and 1974 preceded trading bottoms in the equity markets. A bond market top in 1977, however, pushed stock prices lower that year and kept the stock market relatively dormant through the end of the decade. In 1980 a major top in the commodity prices set the stage for a significant bullish turnaround in bond prices in 1981. This bullish turnaround in bonds set the stage for the major bull market in stocks that started in 1982.

To put things in proper perspective, the period from 1977 to 1980 was also characterized by a falling U.S. dollar, which boosted inflation pressures and kept downward pressure on the bond market. The U.S. dollar bottomed out in 1980, which was mainly responsible for the bearish top in the commodity sector. The rising dollar in the early 1980s provided a supportive influence for financial assets like bonds and stocks and was mainly responsible for the swing away from tangible assets.

THE BOND MARKET BOTTOM OF 1981 AND THE STOCK BOTTOM OF 1982

The comparison of bonds and stocks will begin with the events surrounding the 1981 bottom in bonds and the 1982 bottom in stocks. Then a gradual analysis through the simultaneous bull markets in both sectors culminating in the events of 1987 and 1989 will be given. Figures 4.1 and 4.2 are monthly charts of Treasury bonds and the Dow

---

FIGURE 4.1
MONTHLY CHART OF TREASURY BOND FUTURES FROM 1978 THROUGH SEPTEMBER 1989. THE INDICATOR ALONG THE BOTTOM IS A 14 BAR SLOW STOCHASTIC OSCILLATOR. A MONTHLY CHART IS HELPFUL IN IDENTIFYING MAJOR TURNING POINTS. TURNS IN THE BOND MARKET USUALLY PRECEDE SIMILAR TURNS IN THE STOCK MARKET. THE BOTTOM IN BONDS IN 1981 GAVE AN EARLY WARNING OF THE MAJOR BULL MARKET THAT BEGAN IN STOCKS THE FOLLOWING YEAR. (SOURCE : COMMODITY TREND SERVICE, P.O. BOX 32309, PALM BEACH GARDENS, FLORIDA 33420.)

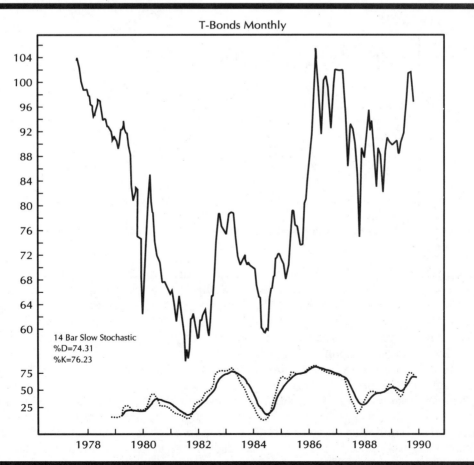

T-Bonds Monthly

14 Bar Slow Stochastic
%D=74.31
%K=76.23

FIGURE 4.2
MONTHLY CHART OF THE DOW JONES INDUSTRIAL AVERAGE FROM 1971 THROUGH SEPTEM-BER 1989. THE INDICATOR ALONG THE BOTTOM IS A 14 BAR SLOW STOCHASTIC OSCILLA-TOR. MAJOR TRENDS IN THE STOCK MARKET USUALLY FOLLOW SIMILAR TURNS IN BONDS. THE STOCK MARKET BOTTOM IN 1982 AND THE PEAK IN 1987 WERE PRECEDED BY SIMILAR TURNS IN BONDS BY ELEVEN AND FOUR MONTHS, RESPECTIVELY. (*SOURCE* : COMMODITY TREND SERVICE, P.O. BOX 32309, PALM BEACH GARDENS, FLORIDA 33420.)

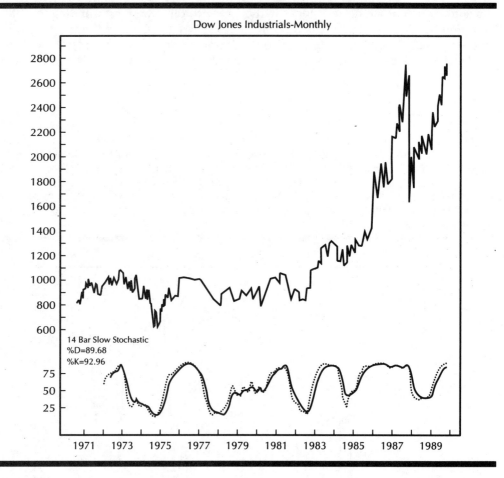

Dow Jones Industrials-Monthly

Industrials with a monthly *stochastics* oscillator along the bottom of each. These are the same types of charts that were used in Chapter 3 in comparing bond activity to the CRB Index, except in this case the comparison is of bonds to stocks. Instead of looking for signals in the *opposite* direction as was done with bonds and the CRB Index, the analyst will be looking for buy and sell signals in both bonds and stocks to be in the *same* direction.

As the charts show, the period from 1977 to 1981 saw a falling bond market and a relatively flat stock market. From 1977 to early 1980 the downward pull of the bond market kept stocks in a relatively narrow trading range. In early 1980 a sharp bond rally began in March which helped launch a stock market rally the following month. The bond rally proved short-lived as prices began to drop again into 1981. After testing the upper end of its 14-year trading range, the Dow Industrials sold off again into 1982.

The bullish turnaround began in 1981. In September of that year, bonds hit their lowpoint and began a basing process that culminated in an important bullish breakout in August 1982. From September of 1981 to August of 1982, the bonds formed a pattern of three rising bottoms. Those three rising bottoms in bonds coincide with three declining bottoms in stocks. *A major positive divergence was in place.* As stocks continued to drop, the lack of downside confirmation by the bond market provided an early warning that a significant turn might be in progress.

August 1982 stands out as a milestone in stock market history. During that month, while many stock market traders were relaxing at the seashore, the great bull market of the 1980s began. During that month, the Dow Industrials dropped to a two-year low before recovering enough to register a bullish *monthly reversal*. At the same time bonds were breaking out from the basing pattern that had been forming for a year. After diverging from stocks for a year, the bullish breakout in bonds confirmed that something important was happening on the upside.

In Figures 4.1 and 4.2, notice the action of the stochastics oscillator during the bottoming process. The dotted line in the stochastics oscillator on the bond chart crossed above the solid line in the fall of 1981 from a level below 25, providing a buy signal in bonds. *A similar buy signal in stocks didn't occur until the summer of 1982.* The technical action in bonds preceded the bottom in stocks by almost a year. It should seem clear that stock market traders would have benefited from a technical analysis of bonds during that historic turnaround.

BONDS AS A LEADING INDICATOR OF STOCKS

The purpose of this chapter is twofold. One is to demonstrate a strong positive relationship between bonds and stocks. In other words, the price action and technical readings in the two markets should confirm each other. As long as they are moving in the same direction, analysts can say that the two markets are confirming each other and their trends are likely to continue. *It's when the two markets begin to trend in opposite directions that analysts should begin to worry.*

The second point is *that the bond market usually turns first.* Near market tops, the bond market will usually turn down first. At market bottoms, the bond market will usually turn up first. Therefore, the technical action of the bond market becomes a leading technical indicator for the stock market.

The young bull market in bonds and stocks continued into early 1983. In May of 1983, however, the bond market suffered a bearish monthly reversal, setting up a potential *double top* on the bond chart (see Figure 4.1). At the same time, the stochastics oscillator gave a sell signal. As Figure 4.2 shows, stocks began to roll over toward the end of 1983 and flashed a stochastics sell signal as the year ended. The setback in stocks wasn't nearly as severe as that in bonds. However, the weakness in bonds warned that it was time to take some profits prior to the 15 percent stock market decline.

In mid-1984 both markets flashed new stochastics buy signals at about the same time. (Bonds actually began to rally a month before stocks.) The beginning of the second bull leg in the bond market had a lot to do with resumption of the bull market in stocks. Both markets rallied together for another two years. It wasn't until early 1987, when the two markets began to move in opposite directions, that another negative divergence was given.

In April 1987 bonds began to drop (flashing a stochastics sell signal), which set the stage for the 1987 stock market crash in October of that year. Once again the bond market had proven its worth as a leading indicator of stocks. The bullish monthly reversal in bonds in October 1987 also set the stage for the stock market recovery from the 1987 bottom. A stochastics buy signal in bonds at the end of 1987 preceded a similar buy signal in stocks by almost a year. During the entire decade of the 1980s, *every significant turn in the stock market was either accompanied by or preceded by a similar turn in the bond market.*

Overlay charts will show comparison of the relative action of bonds and stocks over shorter time periods. On the monthly charts used in preceding paragraphs, price breakouts and stochastics buy and sell signals were emphasized. In the overlay charts, attention will shift to relative price action. Price divergences are easier to spot on overlay charts, and the leads and lags between the two markets are more obvious.

Figure 4.3 compares the two markets from 1982 through the third quarter of 1989. The similar trend characteristics of the two markets are more easily seen. The most prominent points of interest on this chart are the simultaneous rallies in 1982; the breakdown in bonds in 1983 leading to a stock market correction; the simultaneous

FIGURE 4.3
A COMPARISON OF TREASURY BONDS AND STOCKS FROM 1982 TO 1989. ALTHOUGH BOTH MARKETS GENERALLY TREND IN THE SAME DIRECTION, BONDS HAVE A TENDENCY TO TURN AHEAD OF STOCKS. BONDS SHOULD BE VIEWED AS A LEADING INDICATOR FOR STOCKS.

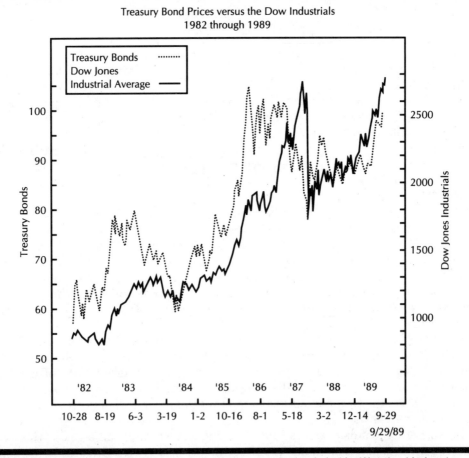

Treasury Bond Prices versus the Dow Industrials
1982 through 1989

Reproduced with permission by Knight Ridder's Tradecenter. Tradecenter is a registered trademark of Knight Ridder's Financial Information.

upturn in both markets in 1984; the top in bonds in early 1987, preceding the stock market crash of 1987; and both markets rallying together into 1989. To the upper right it can be seen that the breakout by stocks above their 1987 pre-crash highs has not been confirmed by a similar bullish breakout in bonds.

Figures 4.4 through 4.9 break the period from 1982 to 1989 into shorter time intervals to provide closer visual comparisons. I'll take a closer look at the events immediately preceding and following the October 1987 stock market crash and will also examine the market events of 1989 in more detail. Figure 4.4 shows the relative action of bonds and stocks at the 1982 major bottom. Notice that as the Dow Industrials hit succeeding lows in March, June, and August of 1982, the bond market was forming rising troughs in the same three months. In August, although both markets rallied together, bonds were the clear leader on the upside.

In May of 1983, bonds formed a prominent *double top* and began to drop. That bearish divergence led to an intermediate stock market peak at the end of the year, which led to a 15 percent downward correction in the equity market. The downward correction in both markets continued into the summer of 1984 (see Figure 4.5). A

FIGURE 4.4

A COMPARISON OF BONDS AND STOCKS DURING 1982 AND 1983. BONDS TURNED UP PRIOR TO STOCKS IN 1982 AND CORRECTED DOWNWARD FIRST DURING 1983.

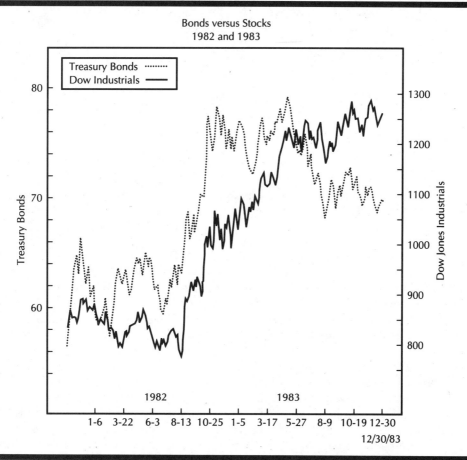

Bonds versus Stocks
1982 and 1983

FIGURE 4.5
**BONDS VERSUS STOCKS DURING 1984 AND 1985. BONDS TURNED UP A MONTH BEFORE
STOCKS IN 1984. DURING 1985 TWO DOWNWARD CORRECTIONS IN TREASURY BONDS
WARNED OF SIMILAR CORRECTIONS IN EQUITIES.**

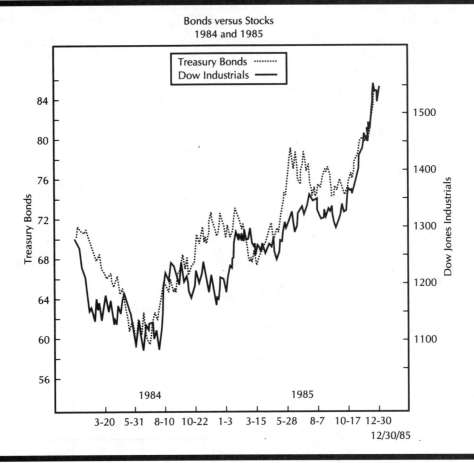

Bonds versus Stocks
1984 and 1985

close inspection of Figure 4.5 will show that the mid-1984 upturn in bonds preceded
stocks by almost a month. Both entities then rallied together through the end of 1985.
Notice, however, that short-term tops in bonds in the first quarter and summer of 1985
preceded downward corrections in the stock market.

Figure 4.6 compares the two markets during 1986 and 1987. After rising for
almost four years, both markets spent 1986 in a consolidation phase. However, at the
beginning of 1987, stocks resumed their bull trend. As the chart shows, bonds did
not confirm the bullish breakout in stocks. What was even more alarming was the
bearish breakdown in bonds in April of 1987 (influenced by a sharp drop in the U.S.
dollar and a bullish breakout in the commodity markets). Stocks dipped briefly during
the bond selloff. During June the bond market bounced a bit, and stocks resumed the
uptrend. However, bonds broke down again in July and August as stocks rallied. You'll
notice that bonds broke support at the May lows in August, thereby flashing another
bear signal. *This bear signal in bonds during August 1987 coincided with the 1987
peak in stocks the same month.*

FIGURE 4.6

BONDS VERSUS STOCKS DURING 1986 AND 1987. BONDS COLLAPSED IN APRIL OF 1987 AND PRECEDED THE AUGUST PEAK IN STOCKS BY FOUR MONTHS.

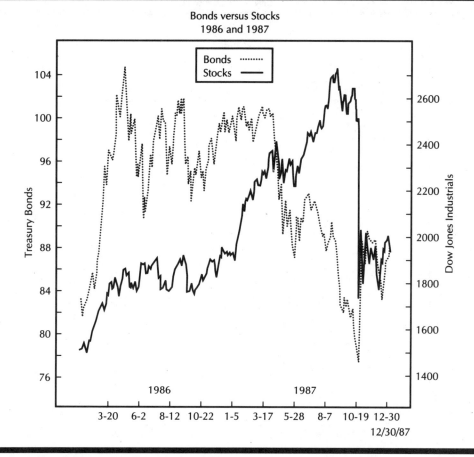

Bonds versus Stocks
1986 and 1987

Bonds not only led stocks on the downside in the fall of 1987, they also led stocks on the upside. Figure 4.7 shows the precipitous slide in bond prices which preceded the stock market crash in October 1987. The bearish breakdown in bonds was too serious to be ignored by stock market technicians. However, as the actual stock market crash began, the bond market soared in a flight to quality. Funds pulled out of the stock market in panic were quickly funneled into the relative safety of Treasury bills and Treasury bonds. There was another important factor that helps explain the sharp rally in interest rate futures in October 1987.

In the ensuing panic during the stock market crash, the Federal Reserve flooded the financial system with liquidity in an attempt to calm the markets and cushion the stock market fall. At the time the consensus view was that a serious recession was at hand. As a result the sudden monetary easing pushed interest rates sharply lower. The lowering of interest rate yields pushed up the prices of interest rate futures.

At such times the normal positive relationship of bonds and stocks is temporarily disturbed. Until the markets stabilized, an inverse relationship between the two

FIGURE 4.7
BONDS VERSUS STOCKS DURING THE LATTER HALF OF 1987 THROUGH THE SUMMER OF 1988. THE STRONG REBOUND IN BONDS THAT BEGAN IN OCTOBER OF 1987 HELPED STABILIZE THE STOCK MARKET FOLLOWING THE 1987 CRASH.

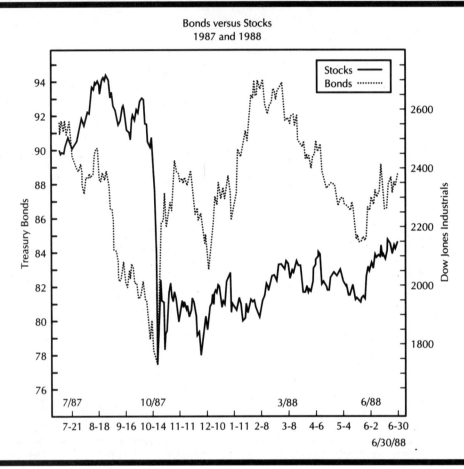

Bonds versus Stocks
1987 and 1988

sectors was evident. However, as Figure 4.7 shows, that inverse relationship was short-lived. In fact, it's remarkable how quickly the positive relationship was resumed. Within a matter of days, the peaks and troughs in bonds and stocks begin to move in the same direction. However, the sharp rally in bonds into the first quarter of 1988 reflected continued concerns about an impending recession (or depression) and the desire on the part of the Federal Reserve Board to lower interest rates to prevent such an eventuality.

By the middle of 1988, things seemed pretty much back to normal. However, through it all, on the downside first and then on the upside, *important directional clues about stock market direction during the summer and fall of 1987 could be discovered by monitoring the bond market.*

Figure 4.8 gives us a view of 1988 and the first three quarters of 1989. It can be seen that from the spring of 1988 to the fall of 1989, the peaks and troughs in both sectors were closely correlated and that both markets rallied together. However, in

FIGURE 4.8
BONDS AND STOCKS ARE SHOWN RALLYING TOGETHER FROM 1988 THROUGH THE FOURTH QUARTER OF 1989. THE BULLISH BREAKOUT BY BONDS IN THE SPRING OF 1989 GAVE THE STOCK RALLY A BOOST.

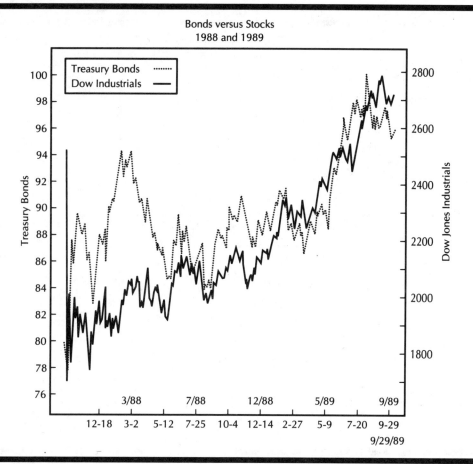

Bonds versus Stocks
1988 and 1989

Reproduced with permission by Knight Ridder's Tradecenter. Tradecenter is a registered trademark of Knight Ridder's Financial Information.

FIGURE 4.9

A COMPARISON OF BONDS AND STOCKS FROM OCTOBER 1988 TO SEPTEMBER 1989. THE VERTICAL LINES SHOW THE SIMILARITIES BETWEEN THE CORRESPONDING PEAKS AND TROUGHS. DURING SEPTEMBER OF 1989, THE RALLY TO NEW HIGHS BY STOCKS HAS NOT BEEN CONFIRMED BY THE BOND MARKET, WHICH IS BEGINNING TO WEAKEN.

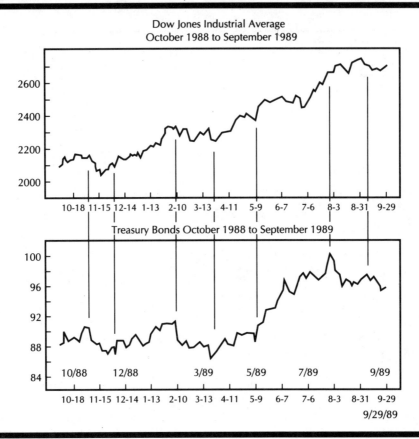

Dow Jones Industrial Average
October 1988 to September 1989

Treasury Bonds October 1988 to September 1989

this instance the stock market proved to be the stronger of the two. Although both markets moved in the same direction, it wasn't until May of 1989 that bonds finally broke out to the upside to confirm the stock market advance.

Figure 4.9 gives a closer look at 1989. This chart shows the close visual correlation of both markets. The timing of the peaks and troughs is extremely close together. To the upper right, however, the bond market is beginning to show some signs of weakness in what could be the beginning of a negative divergence between the two markets.

BONDS AND STOCKS SHOULD BE ANALYZED TOGETHER

The moral of this chapter is that since bonds and stocks are historically linked together, technical analysis of one without a corresponding analysis of the other is incomplete. At the very least a stock market trader or investor should be monitoring the bond market for confirmation. A bullish technical forecast for bonds is also a bullish technical forecast for stocks. Conversely, a bearish analysis for bonds is a bearish forecast for stocks. As demonstrated in Figures 4.1 and 4.2, the technical signals in bonds (such as stochastics buy and sell signals) usually lead similar signals in stocks. At the worst the signals are usually coincident. Analysts can use moving averages or any other tools at their disposal. The important thing is that bond activity be factored into the stock market analysis.

WHAT ABOUT LONG LEAD TIMES?

Although the charts of recent market history show a remarkable day-to-day correlation between bonds and stocks, turns in the bond market often lead those of stocks by long periods of time. The September 1981 bottom in bonds, for example, preceded the stock market bottom in August 1982 by 11 months. The April 1987 breakdown in bonds preceded the August stock market top by four months. How, then, does the stock market analyst take these long lead times into consideration?

The bond market is an important background factor in stock market analysis. Buy and sell signals for stocks are given by the stock market itself. If the bond market starts to diverge from the stock market, a warning is being given—the more serious the divergence, the more important the warning. In the summer of 1987, as an example, the collapse in the bond market simply warned the stock market trader that something was wrong. The stock market trader, while not necessarily abandoning long positions in stocks during the summer of 1987, might have paid greater attention to initial signs of impending weakness on his stock charts.

In 1981 and 1982 the bottoming action in the bond market gave the stock market traders plenty of warning that the tide might be turning. Even if the stock trader ignored the bottoming activity in bonds up to the summer of 1982, the bullish breakout in bonds in August of 1982 might have caused a stock market trader to become more aggressive in buying into the stock market rally. The long lead times in both instances, while less helpful to the short-term trader, were probably most useful to portfolio managers or those investors with a longer time horizon.

Having acknowledged the existence of occasional long lead times between the two markets, it should also be pointed out that on a day-to-day basis there is often a remarkable correlation between the two markets. This correlation can even be seen on an hour-to-hour basis on many days. Even for short-term timing, it's a good idea to monitor the activity in the bond market.

SHORT-TERM INTEREST RATE MARKETS AND THE BOND MARKET

Our main concern has been with the bond market. However, for reasons that were touched on in Chapter 3, it's also important to monitor the trend action in the Treasury bill and Eurodollar markets because of their impact on the bond market. Action in these short-term money markets often provides important clues to bond market direction.

During periods of monetary tightness, short-term interest rates will rise faster than long-term rates. If the situation persists long enough, short-term rates may eventually exceed long-term rates. This condition, known as an *inverted yield curve*, is considered bearish for stocks. (The normal situation is a *positive yield curve*, where long-term bond yields exceed short-term market rates.) An inverted yield curve occurs when the Federal Reserve raises short-term rates in an attempt to control inflation and keep the economy from overheating. This type of situation usually takes place near the end of an economic expansion and helps pave the way for a downturn in the financial markets, which generally precedes an economic slowdown or a recession.

The action of short-term rate futures relative to bond futures tells whether or not the Federal Reserve Board is pursuing a policy of monetary tightness. In general, when T-bill futures are rising faster than bond futures, a period of monetary ease is in place, which is considered supportive to stocks. When T-bill futures are dropping faster than bond prices, a period of tightness is being pursued, which is potentially bearish for stocks. Another weapon used by the Federal Reserve Board to tighten monetary policy is to raise the discount rate.

THE "THREE-STEPS-AND-A-STUMBLE" RULE

Another manifestation of the relationship between interest rates and stocks is the so-called "three-steps-and-a-stumble rule." This rule states that when the Federal Reserve Board raises the discount rate three times in succession, a bear market in stocks usually follows. In the 12 times that the Fed pursued this policy in the past 70 years, a bear market in stocks followed each time. In the two-year period from 1987 to 1989, the Fed raised the discount rate three times in succession, activating the "three-steps-and-a-stumble rule" and, in doing so, placed the seven-year bull market in equities in jeopardy (see Figure 4.10).

Changing the discount rate is usually the last weapon the Fed uses and usually lags behind market forces. Such Fed action often occurs after the markets have begun to move in a similar direction. In other words the raising of the discount rate generally occurs after a rise in short-term money rates, which is signalled by a decline in the T-bill futures market. Lowering of the discount rate is usually preceded by a rise in T-bill futures. So, for a variety of reasons, short-term futures should be watched closely.

It's not always necessary that the bond and stock markets trend in the same direction. What's most important is that they don't trend in *opposite* directions. In other words if a bond market decline begins to level off, that stability might be enough to push stock prices higher. A severe bond market selloff might not actually push stock prices lower but might stall the stock market advance. It's important to realize that the two markets may not always move in lockstep. However, it's rare when the impact of the bond market on the stock market is nonexistent. In the end it's up to the judgment of the technical analyst to determine whether an important trend change is taking place in the bond market and what impact that trend change might have on the stock market.

FIGURE 4.10
**AN EXAMPLE OF THE "THREE STEPS AND A STUMBLE" RULE. SINCE 1987, THE FEDERAL RE-
SERVE BOARD HAS RAISED THE DISCOUNT RATE THREE TIMES IN SUCCESSION. HISTORICAL-
LY, SUCH ACTION BY THE FED HAS PROVEN TO BE BEARISH FOR STOCKS.**

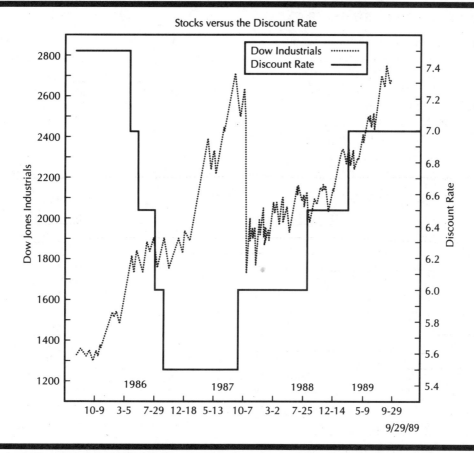

HISTORICAL PERSPECTIVE

Most of the focus of this study has been on the market events of the past 15 years. It would be natural to ask at this point if these intermarket comparisons hold up over a longer span of time. This brings us to a critical question. How far back in history can or should the markets be researched for intermarket comparisons? Prior to 1970 we had fixed exchange rates. Movements in the U.S. dollar and foreign currencies simply didn't exist. Gold was set at a fixed price and couldn't be owned by Americans. The price of oil was regulated. All of these markets are critical ingredients in the intermarket picture.

There were no futures markets in currencies, gold, oil, or Treasury bonds. Stock index futures and program trading hadn't been invented. The instant communication between markets that is so common today was still in the future. Globalization was an idea whose time hadn't yet come, and most market analysts were unaware of the overseas markets. Computers didn't exist to permit study of interrelationships. Technical analysis, which is the basis for intermarket work, was still practiced behind closed doors. In other words, a lot has changed in the last two decades.

What needs to be determined is whether or not these developments have changed the way the markets interact with each other. If so, then comparisons prior to 1970 may not be helpful.

THE ROLE OF THE BUSINESS CYCLE

Understanding the economic rationale that binds commodities, bonds, and the stock market requires some discussion of the business cycle and what happens during periods of expansion and recession. For example, the bond market is considered an excellent leading indicator of the U.S. economy. A rising bond market presages economic strength. A weak bond market usually provides a leading indication of an economic downturn (although the lead times can be quite long). The stock market benefits from economic expansion and weakens during times of economic recession.

Both bonds and stocks are considered leading indicators of the economy. They usually turn down prior to a recession and bottom out after the economy is well into a recession. However, turns in the bond market usually occur first. Going back through the last 80 years, *every major downturn in the stock market has either come after or at the same time as a major downturn in the bond market.* During the last six recessions *bonds have bottomed out an average of almost four months prior to bottoms in the stock market.* During the postwar era stocks have begun to turn down an average of six months prior to the onset of a recession and have begun to turn up about six months prior to the end of a recession.

Tops in the bond market, which usually give earlier warnings of an impending recession, are generally associated with rising commodity markets. Conversely, during a recession falling commodity markets are usually associated with a bottom in the bond market. Therefore, movements in the commodity markets also play an important role in the analysis of bonds and stocks. The economic background of these intermarket relationships will be discussed in more depth in Chapter 13.

WHAT ABOUT THE DOLLAR?

Discussions so far have turned on the how the commodity markets affect the bond market and how the bond market affects stocks. The activity in the U.S. dollar plays an important role in the intermarket picture as well. Most market participants would agree with the general statement that a rising dollar is bullish for bonds and stocks and that a falling dollar is bearish for bonds and stocks. However, it's not as simple as that. The U.S. dollar hit a major top in 1985 and dropped all the way to January 1988. For a large part of that time, bonds and stocks rose as the dollar weakened. Clearly, there must be something missing in this analysis.

The impact of the dollar on the bond and the stock markets is not a direct one but an indirect one. The impact of the dollar on bonds and stocks must be understood from the standpoint of the dollar's impact on inflation, which brings us back to the commodity markets. To fully understand how a falling dollar can be bullish for bonds and stocks, one must look to the commodity markets for answers. This will be the subject of Chapter 5.

SUMMARY

This chapter discussed the strong link between Treasury bonds and equities. A rising bond market is considered bullish for stocks; a falling bond market is considered bearish. However, there are some qualifiers. Although a falling bond market is almost always bearish for equities, *a rising bond market does not ensure a strong equity market*. Deteriorating corporate earnings during an economic slowdown may overshadow the positive effect of a rising bond market (and falling interest rates). While a rising bond market doesn't *guarantee* a bull market in stocks, a bull market in stocks is *unlikely* without a rising bond market.

5

Commodities and the U.S. Dollar

The *inverse* relationship between bonds and commodity prices and the *positive* relationship between bonds and equities have been examined. Now the important role the dollar plays in the intermarket picture will be considered. As mentioned in the previous chapter, it is often said that a rising dollar is considered bullish for bonds and stocks and that a falling dollar is considered bearish for both financial markets. However, that statement doesn't always hold up when examined against the historical relationship of the dollar to both markets. The statement also demonstrates the danger of taking shortcuts in intermarket analysis.

The relationship of the dollar to bonds and stocks makes more sense, and holds up much better, when factored through the commodity markets. In other words, there is a path through the four sectors. Let's start with the stock market and work backwards. The stock market is sensitive to interest rates and hence movements in the bond market. The bond market is influenced by inflation expectations, which are demonstrated by the trend of the commodity markets. The inflationary impact of the commodity markets is largely determined by the trend of the U.S. dollar. Therefore, *we begin our intermarket analysis with the dollar.* The path to take is from the dollar to the commodity markets, then from the commodity markets to the bond market, and finally from the bond market to the stock market.

THE DOLLAR MOVES INVERSELY TO COMMODITY PRICES

A rising dollar is noninflationary. As a result a rising dollar eventually produces lower commodity prices. Lower commodity prices, in turn, lead to lower interest rates and higher bond prices. Higher bond prices are bullish for stocks. A falling dollar has the exact opposite effect; it is bullish for commodities and bearish for bonds and equities. Why, then, can't we say that a rising dollar is bullish for bonds and stocks and just forget about commodities? The reason lies with long lead times in these relationships and with the troublesome question of inflation.

It is possible to have a falling dollar along with strong bond and equity markets. Figure 5.1 shows that after topping out in the spring of 1985, the U.S. dollar dropped for almost three years. During most of that time, the bond market (and the stock market) remained strong while the dollar was falling. More recently, the dollar hit an intermediate bottom at the end of 1988 and began to rally. The bond market, although steady, didn't really explode until May of 1989.

FIGURE 5.1

THE U.S. DOLLAR VERSUS TREASURY BOND PRICES FROM 1985 THROUGH 1989. ALTHOUGH A RISING DOLLAR IS EVENTUALLY BULLISH FOR BONDS AND A FALLING DOLLAR IS EVENTUALLY BEARISH FOR BONDS, LONG LEAD TIMES DIMINISH THE VALUE OF DIRECT COMPARISON BETWEEN THE TWO MARKETS. DURING ALL OF 1985 AND MOST OF 1986, BONDS WERE STRONG WHILE THE DOLLAR WAS WEAK.

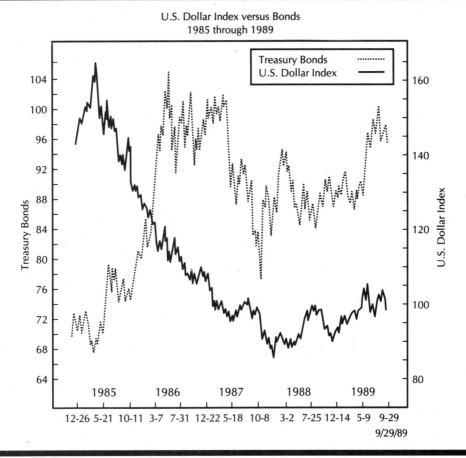

U.S. Dollar Index versus Bonds
1985 through 1989

COMMODITY PRICE TRENDS—THE KEY TO INFLATION

Turns in the dollar eventually have an impact on bonds (and an even more delayed impact on stocks) but only after long lead times. The picture becomes much clearer, however, if the impact of the dollar on bonds and stocks is viewed through the commodity markets. A falling dollar is bearish for bonds and stocks because it is inflationary. However, it takes time for the inflationary effects of a falling dollar to filter through the system. How does the bond trader know when the inflationary effects of the falling dollar are taking hold? The answer is *when the commodity markets start to move higher.* Therefore, we can qualify the statement regarding the relationship between the dollar and bonds and stocks. A falling dollar becomes bearish for bonds and stocks *when commodity prices start to rise.* Conversely, a rising dollar becomes bullish for bonds and stocks *when commodity prices start to drop.*

The upper part of Figure 5.2 compares bonds and the U.S. dollar from 1985 through the third quarter of 1989. The upper chart shows that the falling dollar, which started to drop in early 1985, eventually had a bearish effect on bonds which started to drop in the spring of 1987 (two years later). The bottom part of the chart shows the CRB Index during the same period of time. The arrows on the chart show how the peaks in the bond market correspond with troughs in the CRB Index. It wasn't until the commodity price level started to rally sharply in April 1987 that the bond market started to tumble. The stock market peaked that year in August, leading to the October crash. The inflationary impact of the falling dollar eventually pushed commodity prices higher, which began the topping process in bonds and stocks.

The dollar bottomed as 1988 began. A year later, in December of 1988, the dollar formed an intermediate bottom and started to rally. Bonds were stable but locked in a trading range. Figure 5.3 shows that the eventual upside breakout in bonds was delayed for another six months until May of 1989, which coincided with the bearish breakdown in the CRB Index. The strong dollar by itself wasn't enough to push the

FIGURE 5.2

A COMPARISON OF BONDS AND THE DOLLAR (UPPER CHART) AND COMMODITY PRICES (LOWER CHART) FROM 1985 THROUGH 1989. A FALLING DOLLAR IS BEARISH FOR BONDS WHEN COMMODITY PRICES ARE RALLYING. A RISING DOLLAR IS BULLISH FOR BONDS WHEN COMMODITY PRICES ARE FALLING. THE INFLATIONARY OR NONINFLATIONARY IMPACT OF THE DOLLAR ON BONDS SHOULD BE FACTORED THROUGH THE COMMODITY MARKETS.

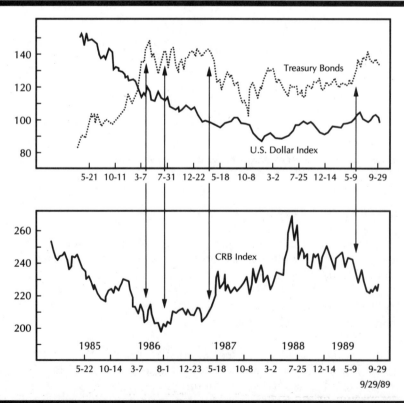

FIGURE 5.3
A COMPARISON OF THE BONDS AND THE DOLLAR (UPPER CHART) AND COMMODITY PRICES (LOWER CHART) FROM LATE 1988 TO LATE 1989. THE BULLISH IMPACT OF THE FIRMING DOLLAR ON THE BOND MARKET WASN'T FULLY FELT UNTIL MAY OF 1989 WHEN COMMODITY PRICES CRASHED THROUGH CHART SUPPORT. TOWARD THE END OF 1989, THE WEAKENING DOLLAR IS BEGINNING TO PUSH COMMODITY PRICES HIGHER, WHICH ARE BEGINNING TO PULL BONDS LOWER.

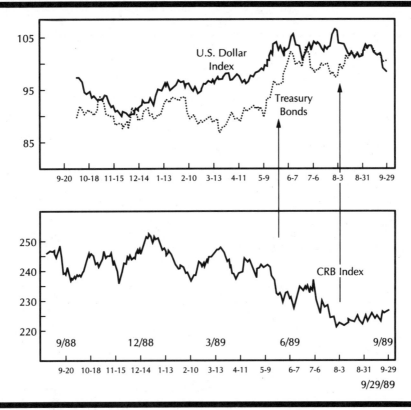

bond (and stock) market higher. *The bullish impact of the rising dollar on bonds was realized only when the commodity markets began to topple.*

The sequence of events in May of 1989 involved all three markets. The dollar scored a bullish breakout from a major basing pattern. That bullish breakout in the dollar pushed the commodity prices through important chart support, resuming their bearish trend. The bearish breakdown in the commodity markets corresponded with the bullish breakout in bonds. It seems clear, then, that taking shortcuts is dangerous work. The impact of the dollar on bonds and stocks is an indirect one and usually takes effect after some time has passed. The impact of the dollar on bonds and stocks becomes more pertinent when its more direct impact on the commodity markets is taken into consideration.

THE DOLLAR VERSUS THE CRB INDEX

Further discussion of the indirect impact of the dollar on bonds and equities will be deferred until Chapter 6. In this chapter, the inverse relationship between the

FIGURE 5.4
THE U.S. DOLLAR VERSUS THE CRB INDEX FROM 1985 THROUGH THE FOURTH QUARTER OF 1989. A FALLING DOLLAR WILL EVENTUALLY PUSH THE CRB INDEX HIGHER. CONVERSELY, A RISING DOLLAR WILL EVENTUALLY PUSH THE CRB INDEX LOWER. THE 1986 BOTTOM IN THE CRB INDEX OCCURRED A YEAR AFTER THE 1985 PEAK IN THE DOLLAR. THE 1988 PEAK IN THE CRB INDEX TOOK PLACE A HALF YEAR AFTER THE 1988 BOTTOM IN THE DOLLAR.

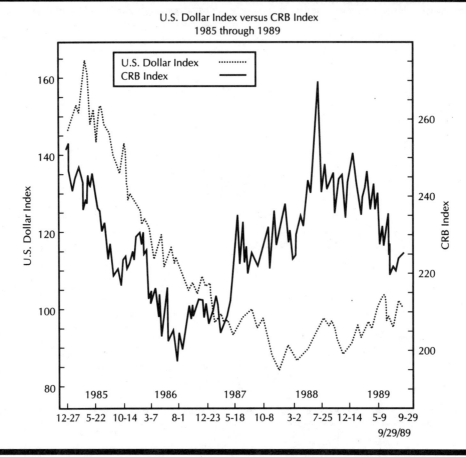

U.S. Dollar Index versus CRB Index
1985 through 1989

U.S. dollar and the commodity markets will be examined. I'll show how movements in the dollar can be used to predict changes in trend in the CRB Index. Commodity prices are a leading indicator of inflation. Since commodity markets represent raw material prices, this is usually where the inflationary impact of the dollar will be seen first. The important role the gold market plays in this process as well as the action in the foreign currency markets will also be considered. I'll show how monitoring the price of gold and the foreign currency markets often provides excellent leading indications of inflationary trends and how that information can be used in commodity price forecasting. But first a brief historical rundown of the relationship between the CRB Index and the U.S. dollar will be given.

The decade of the 1970s witnessed explosive commodity prices. One of the driving forces behind that commodity price explosion was a falling U.S. dollar. The entire decade saw the U.S. currency on the defensive.

FIGURE 5.5
THE U.S. DOLLAR VERSUS THE CRB INDEX DURING 1988 AND 1989. THE DOLLAR BOTTOM AT THE START OF 1988 WAS FOLLOWED BY A CRB PEAK ABOUT SIX MONTHS LATER. THE BULLISH BREAKOUT IN THE DOLLAR DURING MAY OF 1989 COINCIDED WITH A MAJOR BREAKDOWN IN THE COMMODITY MARKETS.

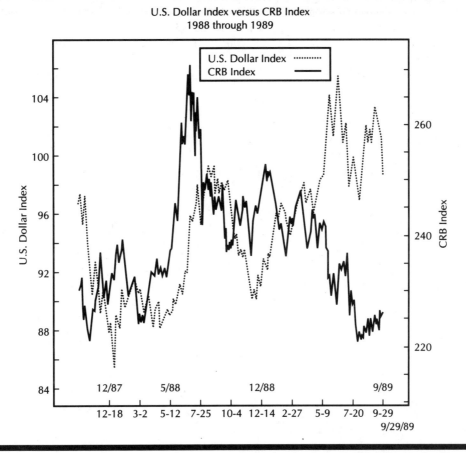

U.S. Dollar Index versus CRB Index
1988 through 1989

The fall in the dollar accelerated in 1972, which was the year the commodity explosion started. Another sharp selloff in the U.S. unit began in 1978, which helped launch the final surge in commodity markets and led to double-digit inflation by 1980. In 1980 the U.S. dollar bottomed out and started to rally in a powerful ascent that lasted until the spring of 1985. This bullish turnaround in the dollar in 1980 contributed to the major top in the commodity markets that took place the same year and helped provide the low inflation environment of the early 1980s, which launched spectacular bull markets in bonds and stocks.

The 1985 peak in the dollar led to a bottom in the CRB Index one year later in the summer of 1986. I'll begin analysis of the dollar and the CRB Index with the descent in the dollar that began in 1985. However, bear in mind that *in the 20 years from 1970 through the end of 1989, every important turn in the CRB Index has been preceded by a turn in the U.S. dollar.* In the past decade, the dollar has made three

FIGURE 5.6
THE DOLLAR VERSUS COMMODITIES DURING 1989. A RISING DOLLAR DURING MOST OF 1989 EXERTED BEARISH PRESSURE ON COMMODITIES. A "DOUBLE TOP" IN THE DOLLAR IN JUNE AND SEPTEMBER OF THAT YEAR, HOWEVER, IS BEGINNING TO HAVE A BULLISH IMPACT ON COMMODITIES. COMMODITIES USUALLY TREND IN THE OPPOSITE DIRECTION OF THE DOLLAR BUT WITH A TIME LAG.

U.S. Dollar Index versus CRB Index
Dec. 1988 through Sept. 1989

significant trend changes which correspond with trend changes in the CRB Index. The 1980 bottom in the dollar corresponded with a major peak in the CRB Index the same year. The 1985 peak in the dollar corresponded with a bottom in the CRB Index the following year. The bottom in the dollar in December 1987 paved the way for a peak in the CRB Index a half-year later in July of 1988.

Figures 5.4 through 5.6 demonstrate the inverse relationship between the commodity markets, represented by the CRB Index, and the U.S. Dollar Index from 1985 to 1989. Figure 5.4 shows the entire five years from 1985 through the third quarter of 1989. Figures 5.5 and 5.6 zero in on more recent time periods. The charts demonstrate two important points. First, *a rising dollar is bearish for the CRB Index*, and *a falling dollar is bullish for the CRB Index*. The second important point is that turns in the dollar occur before turns in the CRB Index.

THE PROBLEM OF LEAD TIME

Although the inverse relationship between both markets is clearly visible, there's still the problem of lead and lag times. It can be seen that turns in the dollar lead turns in the CRB Index. The 1985 top in the dollar preceded the 1986 bottom in the CRB Index by 17 months. The 1988 bottom in the dollar preceded the final peak in the CRB Index by six months. How, then, does the chartist deal with these lead times? Is there a faster or a more direct way to measure the impact of the dollar on the commodity markets? Fortunately, the answer to that question is yes. This brings us to an additional step in the intermarket process, which forms a bridge between the dollar and the CRB Index. This bridge is the gold market.

THE KEY ROLE OF GOLD

In order to better understand the relationship between the dollar and the CRB Index, it is necessary to appreciate the important role the gold market plays. This is true for

---

FIGURE 5.7
THE STRONG INVERSE RELATIONSHIP BETWEEN THE GOLD MARKET AND THE U.S. DOLLAR CAN BE SEEN OVER THE PAST FIVE YEARS. GOLD AND THE DOLLAR USUALLY TREND IN OPPOSITE DIRECTIONS.

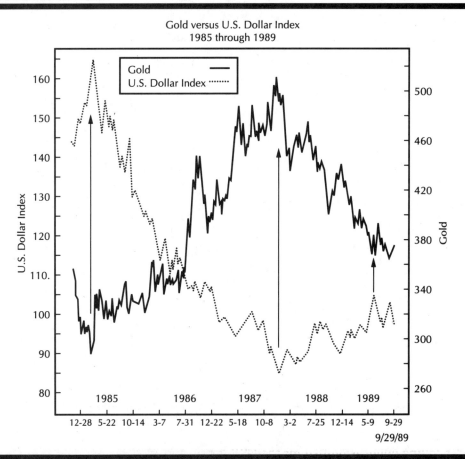

Gold versus U.S. Dollar Index
1985 through 1989

two reasons. First, of the 21 commodity markets in the CRB Index, gold is the most sensitive to dollar trends. Second, *the gold market leads turns in the CRB Index.* A trend change in the dollar will produce a trend change in gold, in the opposite direction, almost immediately. This trend change in the gold market will eventually begin to spill over into the general commodity price level. Close monitoring of the gold market becomes a crucial step in the process. To understand why, an examination of the strong inverse relationship between the gold market and the U.S. dollar is necessary.

Figure 5.7 compares price action in gold and the dollar from 1985 through 1989. The chart is striking for two reasons. First, both markets clearly trend in opposite directions. Second, turns in both markets occur at the same time. Figure 5.7 shows three important turns in both markets (see arrows). The 1985 bottom in the gold market coincided exactly with the peak in the dollar the same year. The major top

FIGURE 5.8
THE DOLLAR VERSUS GOLD DURING 1988 AND 1989. PEAKS AND TROUGHS IN THE DOLLAR USUALLY ACCOMPANY OPPOSITE REACTIONS IN THE GOLD MARKET. THE DOLLAR RALLY THROUGH ALL OF 1988 AND HALF OF 1989 SAW FALLING GOLD PRICES. THESE TWO MARKETS SHOULD ALWAYS BE ANALYZED TOGETHER.

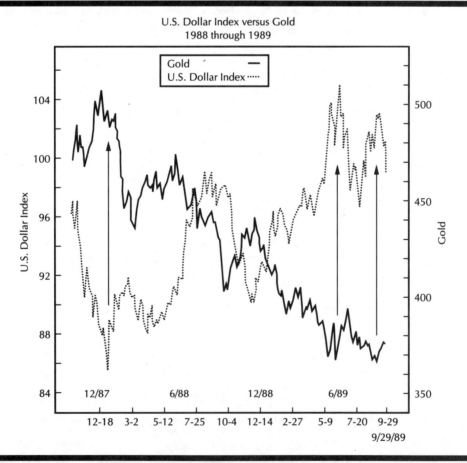

U.S. Dollar Index versus Gold
1988 through 1989

in gold in December 1987 took place as the dollar bottomed at the same time. The leveling off process in the gold market in June of 1989 coincided with a top in the dollar.

Figure 5.8 provides a closer view of the turns in late 1987 and mid-1989 and demonstrates the strong inverse link between the two markets. Figure 5.9 compares turns at the end of 1988 and the summer and fall of 1989. Notice in Figure 5.9 how the two peaks in the dollar in June and September of 1989 coincided perfectly with a possible "double bottom" developing in the gold market. Given the strong inverse link between gold and the dollar, it should be clear that analysis of one market is incomplete without analysis of the other. A gold bull, for example, should probably think twice about buying gold while the dollar is still strong. A sell signal in the dollar usually implies a buy signal for gold. A buy signal in the dollar is usually a sell signal for gold.

FIGURE 5.9
THE DECEMBER 1988 BOTTOM IN THE DOLLAR OCCURRED SIMULTANEOUSLY WITH A PEAK IN GOLD. THE JUNE AND SEPTEMBER 1989 PEAKS IN THE DOLLAR ARE CORRESPONDING WITH TROUGHS IN THE GOLD MARKET.

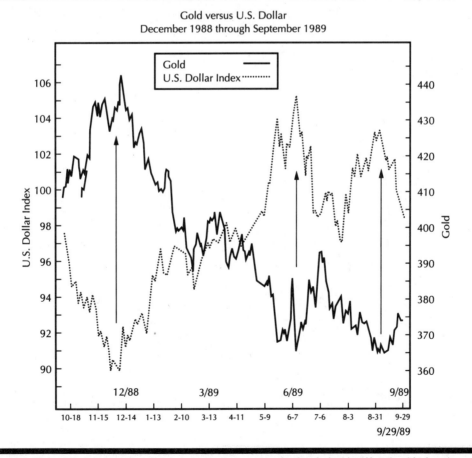

Gold versus U.S. Dollar
December 1988 through September 1989

FOREIGN CURRENCIES AND GOLD

Now another dimension will be added to this comparison. Gold trends in the opposite direction of the dollar. So do the foreign currency markets. As the dollar rises, foreign currencies fall. As the dollar falls, foreign currencies rise. Therefore, *foreign currencies and gold should trend in the same direction.* Given that tendency the deutsche mark will be used as a vehicle to take a longer historical look at the comparison of the gold market and the currencies. It's easier to compare the gold's relationship with the dollar by using a foreign currency chart, since foreign currencies trend in the same direction as gold.

Figure 5.10 shows the strong positive relationship between gold and the deutsche mark in the ten years from 1980 through 1989. (Although the mark is used in these examples, comparisons can also be made with most of the overseas currency markets—especially the British pound, the Swiss franc, and the Japanese yen—or

FIGURE 5.10
GOLD AND THE DEUTSCHE MARK (OVERSEAS CURRENCIES) USUALLY TREND IN THE SAME DIRECTION (OPPOSITE TO THE DOLLAR). GOLD AND THE MARK PEAKED SIMULTANEOUSLY IN 1980 AND 1987 AND TROUGHED TOGETHER IN 1985.

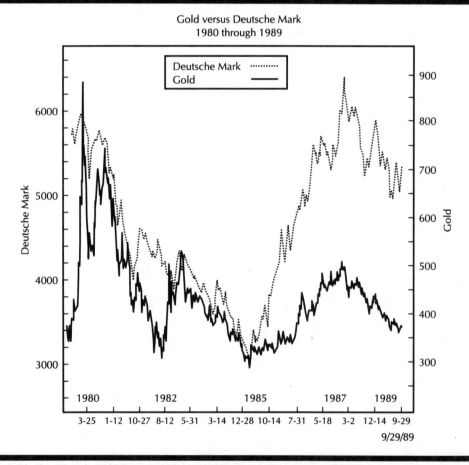

some index of overseas currencies.) Notice how closely the turns occur in both markets in the same direction. Three major turns took place in both markets during that 10-year span. Both markets peaked out together in the first half of 1980 (leading the downturn in the CRB Index by half a year). They bottomed together in the first half of 1985, and topped out together in December of 1987. Going into the summer of 1989, the mark (along with other overseas currencies) was dropping (meaning the dollar was rising) and gold was also dropping (Figure 5.11). The mark and gold both hit a bottom in June of 1989 (coinciding with a pullback in the dollar).

In September of 1989, the mark formed a second bottom which was much higher than the first. The gold market hit a second bottom at the exact same time, forming a "double bottom." The pattern of "rising bottoms" in the mark entering the fall of 1989 formed a "positive divergence" with the gold market and warned of a possible bottom in gold. Needless to say, the rebound in the mark and the gold market corresponded

FIGURE 5.11
GOLD VERSUS THE DEUTSCHE MARK FROM 1987 THROUGH MOST OF 1989. BOTH PEAKED TOGETHER AT THE END OF 1987 AND FELL UNTIL THE SUMMER OF 1989. THE PATTERN OF "RISING BOTTOMS" IN THE MARK DURING SEPTEMBER OF 1989 IS HINTING AT UPWARD PRESSURE IN THE OVERSEAS CURRENCIES AND THE GOLD MARKET.

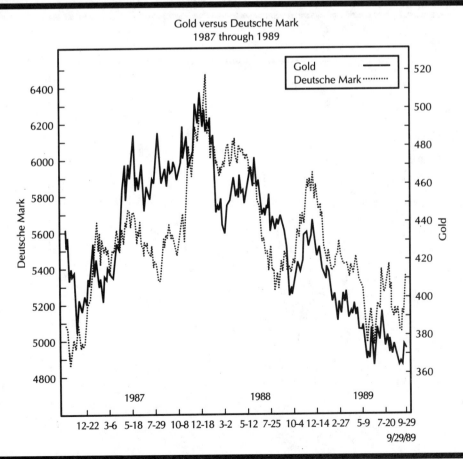

Gold versus Deutsche Mark
1987 through 1989

with a setback in the dollar. Given the close relationship between the gold market and the deutsche mark (and most major overseas currencies), it can be seen that analysis of the overseas markets plays a vital role in an analysis of the gold market and of the general commodity price level. Since it has already been stated that the gold market is a leading indicator of the CRB Index, and given gold's close relationship to the overseas currencies, it follows that *the overseas currencies are also leading indicators of the commodity markets priced in U.S. dollars.* Figure 5.12 shows why this is so.

GOLD AS A LEADING INDICATOR OF THE CRB INDEX

Gold's role as a leading indicator of the CRB Index can be seen in Figures 5.12 and 5.13. Figure 5.12 shows gold leading major turns in the CRB Index at the 1985 bottom and the 1987 top. (Gold also led the downturn in the CRB Index in 1980.) The 1985 bottom in gold was more than a year ahead of the 1986 bottom in the CRB Index. The December 1987 peak in the gold market preceded the CRB Index top, which occurred in the summer of 1988, by over half a year.

FIGURE 5.12
GOLD USUALLY LEADS TURNS IN THE CRB INDEX. GOLD BOTTOMED A YEAR AHEAD OF THE CRB INDEX IN 1985 AND PEAKED ABOUT A HALF YEAR AHEAD OF THE CRB INDEX IN 1988.

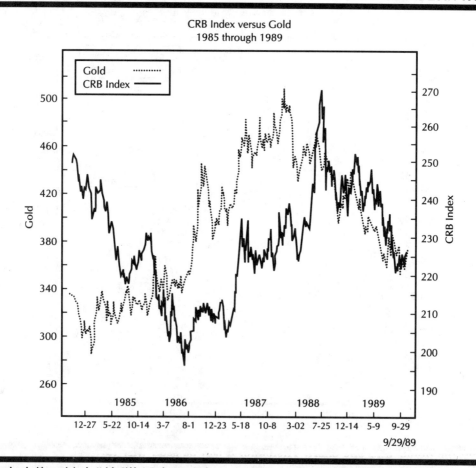

CRB Index versus Gold
1985 through 1989

FIGURE 5.13
DURING THE SPRING OF 1989, GOLD LED THE CRB INDEX LOWER AND ANTICIPATED THE CRB BREAKDOWN THAT OCCURRED DURING MAY BY TWO MONTHS. FROM JUNE THROUGH SEPTEMBER OF 1989, A POTENTIAL "DOUBLE BOTTOM" IN GOLD IS HINTING AT A BOTTOM IN THE CRB INDEX.

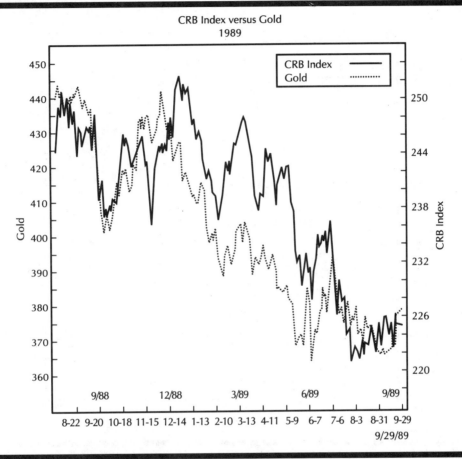

CRB Index versus Gold
1989

Figure 5.13 gives a closer view of the events entering the fall of 1989. While the CRB Index has continued to drop into August/September of that year, the gold market is holding above its June bottom near $360. The ability of the gold market in September of 1989 to hold above its June low appears to be providing a "positive divergence" with the CRB Index and may be warning of stability in the general price level. Bear in mind also that the "double bottom" in the gold market was itself being foreshadowed by a pattern of "rising bottoms" in the deutsche mark. The sequence of events entering the fourth quarter of 1989, therefore, is this: Strength in the deutsche mark provided a warning of a possible bottom in gold, which in turn provided a warning of a possible bottom in the CRB Index.

The relationship between the dollar and the gold market is very important in forecasting the trend of the general commodity price level, and using a foreign currency market, such as the deutsche mark, provides a shortcut. The deutsche mark example in Figures 5.10 and 5.11 combines the inverse relationship of the gold market and the dollar into one chart. Therefore, it can be seen why turns in the mark usually lead turns in the CRB Index. Figure 5.14 shows the mark leading the CRB Index in

FIGURE 5.14

THE DEUTSCHE MARK (OR OTHER OVERSEAS CURRENCIES) CAN BE USED AS A LEADING INDICATOR OF THE CRB INDEX. IN 1985 THE MARK TURNED UP A YEAR AHEAD OF THE CRB INDEX. IN LATE 1987 THE MARK TURNED DOWN SEVEN MONTHS PRIOR TO THE CRB INDEX.

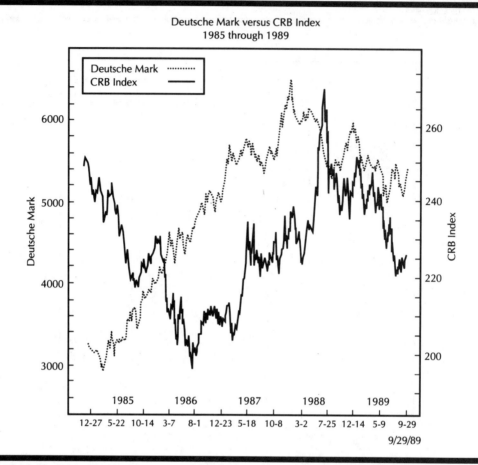

Deutsche Mark versus CRB Index
1985 through 1989

the period from 1985 through the third quarter of 1989. Figure 5.15 shows the mark leading the CRB Index lower in May of 1989 (coinciding with bullish breakout in the dollar and bonds) and hinting at a bottom in the CRB Index in September of the same year. Going further back in history, Figure 5.10 shows the major peak in the deutsche mark and gold in the first quarter of 1980, which foreshadowed the major downturn in the CRB Index that occurred in the fourth quarter of that same year.

COMBINING THE DOLLAR, GOLD, AND THE CRB INDEX

It's not enough to simply compare the dollar to the CRB Index. A rising dollar will eventually cause the CRB Index to turn lower, while a falling dollar will eventually push the CRB Index higher. The lead time between turns in the dollar and the CRB Index is better understood if the gold market is used as a bridge between the other two markets. At major turning points the lead time between turns in gold and the CRB Index can be as long as a year. At the more frequent turning points that occur

major

FIGURE 5.15
THE DEUTSCHE MARK VERSUS THE CRB INDEX FROM SEPTEMBER 1988 TO SEPTEMBER 1989. FROM DECEMBER TO JUNE, THE MARK LED THE CRB INDEX LOWER. THE "DOUBLE BOTTOM" IN THE MARK IN THE FALL OF 1989 IS HINTING AT UPWARD PRESSURE IN THE CRB INDEX. SINCE OVERSEAS CURRENCIES TREND IN THE OPPOSITE DIRECTION OF THE DOLLAR, THEY TREND IN THE SAME DIRECTION AS U.S. COMMODITIES WITH A CERTAIN AMOUNT OF LEAD TIME.

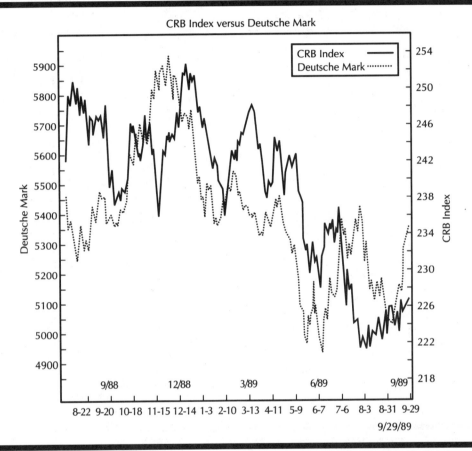

CRB Index versus Deutsche Mark

at short-term and intermediate changes in trend, *gold will usually lead turns in the CRB Index by about four months on average.* This being the case, the same can be said for the lead time between turns in the U.S. dollar and the CRB Index.

Figure 5.16 compares all three markets from September 1988 through September 1989. The upper chart shows movement in the U.S. Dollar Index. It shows a bottom in December 1988, a bullish breakout in May 1989, and two peaks in June and September of the same year. The bottom chart compares gold and the CRB Index during the same time span. The December 1988 peak in gold (coinciding with the dollar bottom) preceded a peak in the CRB Index by a month. The setting of new lows by gold in March of 1989 provided an early warning of the impending breakdown in the CRB Index two months later. The actual breakdown in the CRB Index in May was caused primarily by the bullish breakout in the dollar that occurred during the same month.

FIGURE 5.16
A COMPARISON OF THE DOLLAR (UPPER CHART), GOLD, AND THE CRB INDEX (BOTTOM CHART). THE LATE 1988 BOTTOM IN THE DOLLAR PUSHED GOLD LOWER, WHICH LED THE CRB DOWNTURN. ALTHOUGH THE BULLISH BREAKOUT IN THE DOLLAR DURING MAY OF 1989 PUSHED THE CRB INDEX THROUGH SUPPORT, GOLD HAD ALREADY BROKEN DOWN. IN THE FALL OF 1989, A FALLING DOLLAR IS PULLING UP GOLD, WHICH IS BEGINNING TO PULL THE CRB INDEX HIGHER.

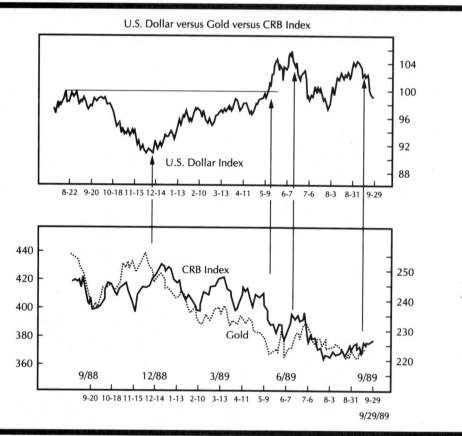

U.S. Dollar versus Gold versus CRB Index

Dollar peaks in June and September of 1989 (upper chart of Figure 5.16) coincided with "double bottoms" in gold, which may in turn be signaling a bottom in the CRB Index. In all three cases, the dollar remains the dominant market. However, the dollar's impact on the gold market is the conduit through which the dollar impacts on the CRB Index. Therefore, it is necessary to use all three markets in one's analysis.

SUMMARY

The relationship between the U.S. dollar and bonds and stocks is an indirect one. The more direct relationship exists between the U.S. dollar and the CRB Index, which in turn impacts on bonds and stocks. The dollar moves in the opposite direction of the CRB Index. A falling dollar, being inflationary, will eventually push the CRB Index higher. A rising dollar, being noninflationary, will eventually push the CRB Index lower. The bullish impact of a rising dollar on bonds and stocks is felt when the commodity markets start to decline. The bearish impact of a falling dollar on bonds and stocks is felt when commodities start to rise.

Gold is the commodity market most sensitive to dollar movements and usually trends in the opposite direction of the U.S. currency. The gold market leads turns in the CRB Index by about four months (at major turning points, the lead time has averaged about a year) and provides a bridge between the dollar and the commodity index. Foreign currency markets correspond closely with movements in gold and can often be used as a leading indicator for the CRB Index.

In the next chapter, a more direct examination of the relationship between the dollar, interest rates, and the stock market will be given. A comparison of the CRB Index to the stock market will also be made to see if any convincing link exists between the two. Having already considered the important impact the dollar has on the gold market, the interplay between the gold market and the stock market will be viewed.

6

The Dollar Versus
Interest Rates and Stocks

Up to now I've stressed the importance of following a path through the four market sectors, starting with the dollar and working our way through commodities, bonds, and stocks in that order. The necessity of placing the commodity markets in between the dollar and the bond market has also been stressed. In this chapter, however, movements in the dollar will be directly compared to the bond and stock markets. I'll also take a look at the direct link, if any, between the CRB Index and the stock market. Since gold is often viewed as an alternative investment in times of adversity in stocks, gold movements will also be compared to the stock market during the 1980s.

Intermarket analysis usually begins with the dollar and works its way through the other three sectors. In reality there is no starting point. Consider the sequence of events that unfolds during a bull and bear stock market cycle. The dollar starts to rally (1980). The rising dollar, being noninflationary, pushes commodity prices lower (1980–1981). Interest rates follow commodity prices lower, pushing up bond prices (1981). The rising bond market pulls stock prices higher (1982). For awhile we have a rising dollar, falling commodity process, falling interest rates, and rising bond and stock prices (1982–1985).

Then, falling interest rates begin to exert a downward pull on the dollar (falling interest rates diminish the attractiveness of a domestic currency by lowering yields on interest-bearing investments denominated in that currency), and the dollar starts to weaken (1985–1987). We then have a falling dollar, falling commodities, falling interest rates, and rising bonds and stocks. Eventually, the falling dollar pushes commodity prices higher (1987). Rising commodity prices pull interest rates higher and bond prices lower. The lower bond market eventually pulls stock prices lower (1987). Rising interest rates start to pull the dollar higher (1988), and the bullish cycle starts all over again.

The ripple effect that flows through the four market sectors is never-ending and really has no beginning point. The dollar trend, which was used as the starting point, is really a reaction to the trend in interest rates, which was initially set in motion by the trend of the dollar. If this sounds very complicated, it isn't. Let's just consider the dollar and interest rates for now. A falling dollar, being inflationary, eventually pushes interest rates higher. Rising interest rates make the U.S. dollar more attractive relative to other currencies and eventually pull the dollar higher. The rising dollar, being noninflationary, eventually pushes interest rates lower. Lower interest rates, making the U.S. currency less attractive vis-à-vis other currencies, eventually pulls the dollar lower. And so on and so on.

Given the preceding scenario, it can be seen how closely the dollar and bonds are linked. It is also easier to see why a rising dollar is considered bullish for bonds. A rising dollar will eventually push interest rates lower, which pushes bond prices higher. A falling dollar will push interest rates higher and bond prices lower. Bond prices will then impact on the stock market, the subject of Chapter 4. The main focus of this chapter is on the more direct link between the dollar and interest rates. Although the dollar will be compared to the stock market, the impact there is more delayed and is more correctly filtered through the bond market.

DO COMMODITIES LEAD OR FOLLOW?

Although commodities aren't the main focus of this chapter, it's not possible to exclude them completely. In the relationship between the dollar and commodities, the dollar is normally placed first and used as the cause. Commodity trends are treated as the result of dollar trends. However, it could also be argued that inflationary trends caused by the commodity markets (which determine the trend of interest rates) eventually determine the direction of the dollar. Rising commodity prices and rising interest rates will in time pull the dollar higher. The rise in the dollar at the beginning of 1988 followed the rise in the CRB Index and interest rates that began in the spring of 1987. Are commodity trends the cause or the effect, then, of dollar trends? In a never-ending circle, the correct answer is both. Commodity trends (which match interest rate trends) are the result of dollar trends and in time contribute to future dollar trends.

The problem with comparing the dollar to bonds and stocks directly, without using commodities, is that it is a shortcut. While doing so may be helpful in furthering understanding of the process, it leaves analysts with the problem of irritating lead times. While analysts may understand the sequence of events, they don't know when trend changes are imminent. As pointed out in Chapter 5, usually the catalyst in the process is a rally or breakdown in the general commodity price level, which is itself often foreshadowed by the trend in the gold market. With these caveats, consider recent market history vis-à-vis the dollar and interest rates.

THE DOLLAR AND SHORT-TERM RATES

Short-term interest rates are more volatile than long-term rates and usually react quicker to changes in monetary policy. The dollar is more sensitive to movements in short-term rates than to long-term rates. Long term-rates are more sensitive to longer range inflationary expectations. The interplay between short- and long-term rates also holds important implications for the dollar and helps us determine whether the Federal Reserve is pursuing a policy of monetary ease or tightness.

Figure 6.1 compares six-month Treasury Bill rates with the dollar from 1985 through the third quarter of 1989. Interest rates had been dropping since 1981 (as a result of the rising dollar from its 1980 bottom). In 1985 falling interest rates began to pull the dollar lower. From early 1985 through 1986, both the dollar and interest rates were dropping. By late 1986, however, the inflationary impact of the lower

FIGURE 6.1
SHORT-TERM RATES VERSUS THE DOLLAR FROM 1985 THROUGH 1989. THE DOLLAR WILL FOLLOW THE DIRECTION OF INTEREST RATES BUT ONLY AFTER A PERIOD OF TIME. THE DOLLAR TOP IN 1985 WAS THE RESULT OF FALLING RATES SINCE 1981. THE LATE 1987 BOTTOM IN THE DOLLAR FOLLOWED A BOTTOM IN RATES OVER A YEAR BEFORE.

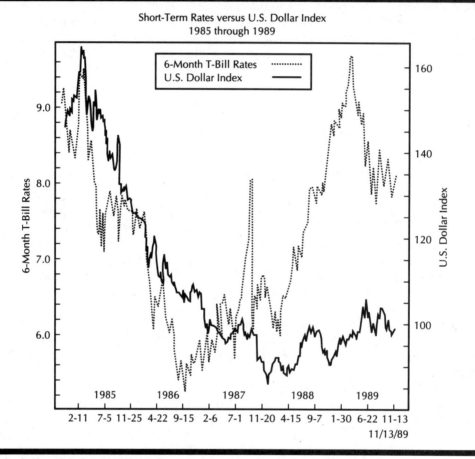

Short-Term Rates versus U.S. Dollar Index
1985 through 1989

dollar began to push interest rates (and commodity prices) higher. Although the rise in interest rates was itself the direct result of the falling dollar as inflation pressures started to build, the 1986 interest rate bottom set the stage for the bottom in the dollar a year later in December of 1987.

Heading into the fall of 1987, the year-long rise in short-term interest rates began to have a mild upward impact on the dollar. However, the October 1987 stock market crash caused rates to plunge as the Federal Reserve Board flooded the monetary system with liquidity in a dramatic easing move to stem the stock market panic. In addition, funds pulled out of the stock market poured into Treasury bills and bonds in a dramatic "flight to safety". Prices of T-bills and bonds soared, and interest rates plunged. The sharp drop in interest rates contributed to the plunge in the dollar, which immediately dropped to new lows. In the fall of 1987, the dollar collapse was caused by the sharp drop in interest rates, which in turn was caused by the stock market plunge. At such times the interplay between the stock market, interest rates, and the dollar is immediate and dramatic.

Rising interest rates eventually began to pull the dollar higher in 1988 (after the stock market had stabilized). Soaring short-term rates provided a bullish backdrop for the dollar rally. By April of 1989, short-term rates had peaked (see Figure 6.2). Within two months the dollar started to weaken as a result.

Figure 6.3 compares dollar trends to 30-year Treasury bond yields. While bond swings aren't as dramatic as the T-bill market, the relationship to the dollar is basically the same. The bond market, being a long-term investment, is more sensitive to inflationary expectations as lenders demand a higher return to protect their investment from the ravages of inflation. Bond yields turned higher in 1987 as the inflationary implications of the falling dollar (and higher commodity prices) began to take hold. The collapse in the dollar during the fourth quarter of 1987 was the direct result of the plunge in interest rates resulting from the October stock market crash. The dol-

FIGURE 6.2
THE DOLLAR FOLLOWED SHORT-TERM RATES HIGHER UNTIL MID-1989. THE PEAK IN T-BILL RATES IN MARCH OF 1989 CONTRIBUTED TO A PEAK IN THE DOLLAR THREE MONTHS LATER.

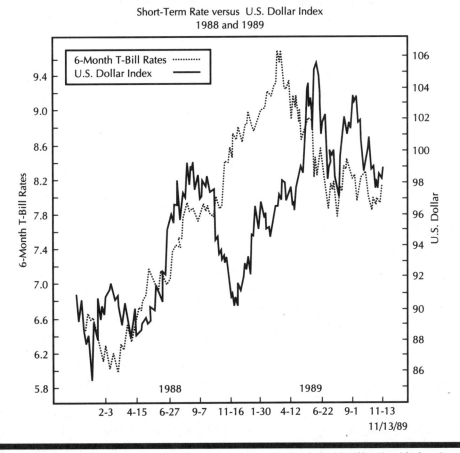

Short-Term Rate versus U.S. Dollar Index
1988 and 1989

FIGURE 6.3
**TREASURY BOND YIELDS VERSUS THE DOLLAR FROM 1985 TO 1989. A CIRCULAR RELATION-
SHIP EXISTS BETWEEN THE DOLLAR AND RATES. A FALLING DOLLAR WILL EVENTUALLY PUSH
RATES HIGHER (1986), WHICH IN TURN WILL PULL THE DOLLAR HIGHER (1988). A RISING
DOLLAR WILL EVENTUALLY PUSH RATES LOWER (1989), WHICH IN TURN WILL WEAKEN THE
DOLLAR.**

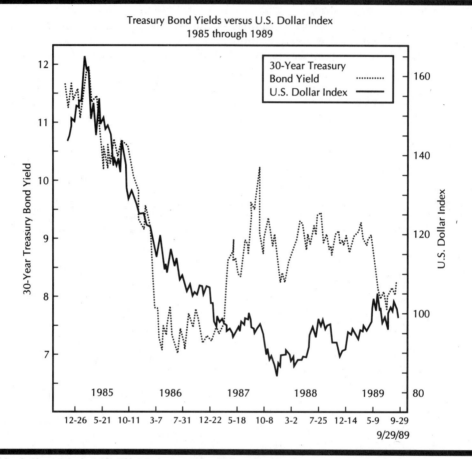

Treasury Bond Yields versus U.S. Dollar Index
1985 through 1989

lar rally from early 1988 into 1989 (resulting from higher interest rates) eventually
lowered inflation expectations (pushing commodity prices lower), and bond yields
began to drop in May of 1989 as a result. The fall in bond yields, in turn, helped
weaken the dollar during the summer of 1989.

Figure 6.4 provides a closer view of the dollar rally from its December 1987
bottom to its June 1989 peak. In May of 1989, the dollar scored a major bullish
breakout above its 1988 peak. This bullish breakout in the dollar (which pushed
commodity prices lower and bond prices higher) also had the result of dramatically
lowering interest rate yields, which contributed to its own demise just a couple of
months later. What these charts demonstrate is the close interplay between the dollar
and interest rates and why it's really not possible to determine which one leads the
other. Although it's not necessary to determine which leads and which follows, it is
necessary to understand how they interact with each other.

FIGURE 6.4
RISING BOND RATES KEPT THE DOLLAR FIRM INTO MID-1989. THE SHARP DROP IN BOND YIELDS DURING THE SPRING OF 1989 CONTRIBUTED TO A FALLING DOLLAR DURING THAT SUMMER.

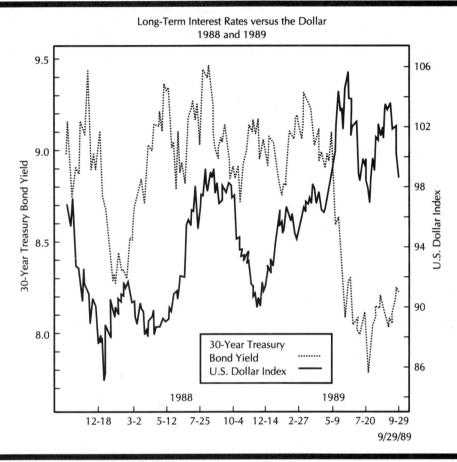

Long-Term Interest Rates versus the Dollar
1988 and 1989

SHORT-TERM RATES VERSUS LONG-TERM RATES

Figure 6.5 compares short- and long-term rates from 1985 to 1989. The chart shows that long-term yields are generally higher than short-term rates. In 1982, short-term rates were dropping much faster than long-term rates, reflecting a period of monetary ease. Not surprisingly, 1982 also marked the beginning of bull markets in bonds and stocks. The dramatic rise in short-term yields in 1988 and early 1989 reflected monetary tightness on the part of the Federal Reserve as concerns about inflation intensified, and resulted in the so-called *negative yield curve* (when short-term rates actually exceed long-term rates), as shown in Figure 6.6.

That monetary tightness, lasting from 1988 to early 1989 was bullish for the dollar. As a rule of thumb, periods of monetary tightness are supportive to the dollar. Periods of monetary ease are bearish for the dollar. (A negative, or inverted, yield curve, which existed in early 1989, has historically been bearish for stocks.) The drop in both long- and short-term rates that began in April of 1989 preceded a top

FIGURE 6.5

LONG-TERM VERSUS SHORT-TERM INTEREST RATES FROM 1982 TO 1989. LONG-TERM RATES ARE USUALLY HIGHER THAN SHORT-TERM RATES. WHEN SHORT-TERM RATES ARE DROPPING FASTER THAN LONG-TERM RATES (1982), MONETARY POLICY IS EASY, WHICH IS BULLISH FOR FINANCIAL ASSETS. WHEN SHORT-TERM RATES RISE FASTER THAN LONG-TERM RATES (1988 AND EARLY 1989), MONETARY POLICY IS TIGHT, WHICH IS BEARISH FOR FINANCIAL ASSETS.

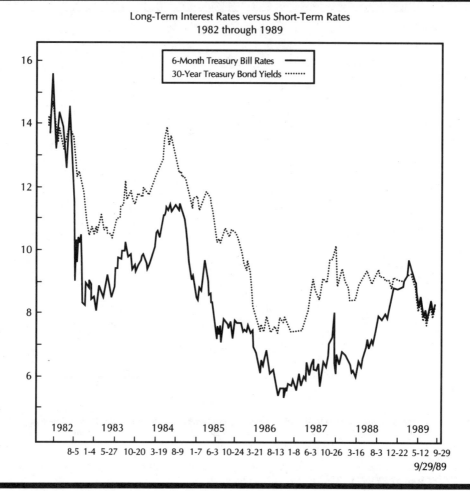

Long-Term Interest Rates versus Short-Term Rates
1982 through 1989

FIGURE 6.6
DURING THE PERIOD FROM THE SPRING OF 1988 TO THE SPRING OF 1989, SHORT-TERM RATES ROSE FASTER THAN LONG-TERM RATES, REFLECTING MONETARY TIGHTNESS. DURING THE SPRING OF 1989, SHORT-TERM RATES EXCEEDED LONG-TERM RATES (AN INVERTED YIELD CURVE), WHICH IS USUALLY BEARISH FOR FINANCIAL ASSETS. MONETARY TIGHTNESS IS BULLISH FOR THE DOLLAR, WHILE MONETARY EASE IS BEARISH FOR THE DOLLAR.

Long-Term Rates versus Short-Term Rates

in the dollar by two months. While the direction of interest rates is important to the dollar, it's also useful to monitor the relationship between short- and long-term rates (the yield curve). Having considered interest rate yields, let's turn the picture around now and compare the dollar trend to interest rate futures, which use *prices* instead of *yields*.

THE DOLLAR VERSUS BOND FUTURES

A falling dollar is bearish for bonds. Or is it? Well, yes, but only after awhile. Figure 6.7 shows why it can be dangerous to rely on generalizations. From 1985 to well into 1986, we had a rising bond market along with a collapsing dollar. Bond bulls were well-advised during that time to ignore the falling dollar. Those bond traders who looked solely at the falling dollar (and ignored the fact that commodities were also dropping) probably left the bull side prematurely. From 1988 to mid-1989, however,

FIGURE 6.7
THE DOLLAR VERSUS BOND PRICES FROM 1985 TO 1989. FROM 1985 TO 1986, THE BOND MARKET RALLIED DESPITE A FALLING DOLLAR. BOTH RALLIED TOGETHER FROM THE BEGINNING OF 1988 THROUGH THE MIDDLE OF 1989. A FALLING DOLLAR IS BEARISH FOR BONDS, AND A RISING DOLLAR BULLISH FOR BONDS BUT ONLY AFTER AWHILE.

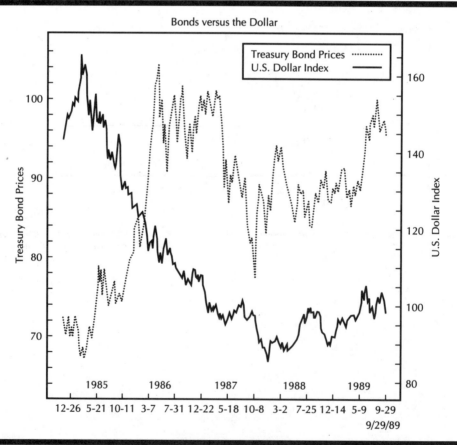

FIGURE 6.8
BOND PRICES VERSUS THE DOLLAR FROM 1987 TO 1989. BOTH MARKETS RALLIED TOGETHER FROM EARLY 1988 TO 1989. THE BULLISH BREAKOUT IN THE DOLLAR IN MAY OF 1989 CO-INCIDED WITH A BULLISH BREAKOUT IN BONDS.

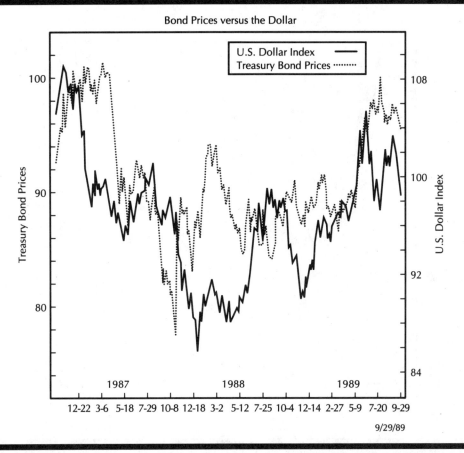

Bond Prices versus the Dollar

we had a firm bond market and a rising dollar. Figure 6.8 shows a fairly close correlation between bond futures and the dollar in the period from 1987 through 1989. The bullish breakout in the dollar in the spring of 1989 helped fuel a similar bullish breakout in the bond market.

THE DOLLAR VERSUS TREASURY BILL FUTURES

Figures 6.9 and 6.10 compare the dollar to Treasury bill futures. It can be seen that the period from early 1988 to early 1989 saw a sharp drop in T-bill futures, reflecting a sharp rise in short-term rates. A strong inverse relationship between T-bill futures and the dollar existed for that 12-month span. This also shows how the dollar reacts more to changes in short-term interest rates than to long-term rates. It explains why T-bill and the dollar often trend in opposite directions. During periods of monetary tightness, as short-term rates rise, bill prices sell off. However, the dollar rallies. During periods of monetary ease, T-bill prices will rise, short-term rates will fall, as

FIGURE 6.9
**THE U.S. DOLLAR VERSUS TREASURY BILL FUTURES PRICES FROM 1985 TO 1989. THE DOLLAR
AND TREASURY BILLS OFTEN DISPLAY AN INVERSE RELATIONSHIP. THE PEAK IN T-BILL PRICES
IN EARLY 1988 HELPED STABILIZE THE DOLLAR (BY SIGNALING HIGHER SHORT-TERM RATES).**

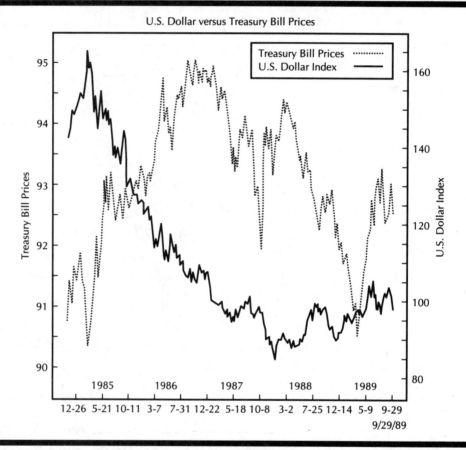

Reproduced with permission by Knight Ridder's Tradecenter. Tradecenter is a registered trademark of Knight Ridder's Financial Information.

FIGURE 6.10
THE U.S. DOLLAR VERSUS TREASURY BILL FUTURES PRICES IN 1988 AND 1989. FALLING T-BILL PRICES ARE USUALLY SUPPORTIVE FOR THE DOLLAR SINCE THEY SIGNAL HIGHER SHORT-TERM RATES (MOST OF 1988). RISING T-BILL PRICES (1989) ARE USUALLY BEARISH FOR THE DOLLAR (SIGNALING LOWER SHORT-TERM RATES).

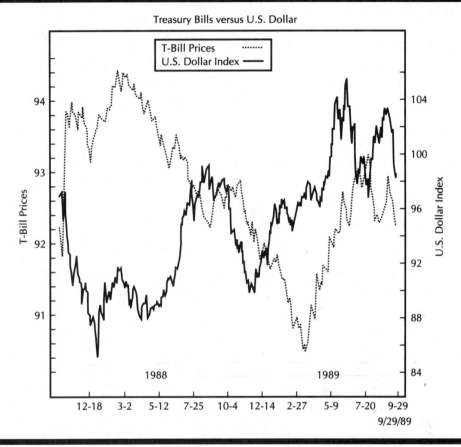

Treasury Bills versus U.S. Dollar

will the dollar. To the left of the chart in Figure 6.9, in the period from 1985 through 1986, another strong inverse relationship existed between the dollar and Treasury bill futures. Figure 6.10 shows the sharp rally in T-bill prices that began in the spring of 1989, which was the beginning of the end for the bull run in the dollar.

THE DOLLAR VERSUS THE STOCK MARKET

It stands to reason since both the dollar and the stock market are influenced by interest rate trends (as well as inflation) that there should be a direct link between the dollar and stocks. The relationship between the dollar and the stock market exists but is often subject to long lead times. A rising dollar will eventually push inflation and interest rates lower, which is bullish for stocks. A falling dollar will eventually push stock prices lower because of the rise in inflation and interest rates. However, it is an oversimplification to say that a rising dollar is always bullish for stocks, and a falling dollar is always bearish for equities.

Figure 6.11 compares the dollar to the Dow Industrials from 1985 through the third quarter of 1989. For the first two years stocks rose sharply as the dollar dropped. From 1988 through the middle of 1989, stocks and the dollar rose together. So what does the chart demonstrate? It shows that sometimes the dollar and stocks move in the opposite direction and sometimes in the same direction. The trick is in understanding the lead and lag times that usually occur and also the sequence of events that affect the two markets.

Figure 6.11 shows the dollar dropping from 1985 through 1987, during which time stocks continued to advance. Stocks didn't actually sell off sharply until the second half of 1987, more than two years after the dollar peaked. Going back to the beginning of the decade, the dollar bottomed in 1980, two years before the 1982 bottom in stocks. In 1988 and 1989 the dollar and stocks rose pretty much in tandem. The peak in the dollar in the summer of 1989, however, gave warnings that a potentially bearish scenario might be developing for the stock market.

It's not possible to discuss the relationship between the dollar and stocks without mentioning inflation (represented by commodity prices) and interest rates (represented by bonds). The dollar has an impact on the stock market, but only after a ripple effect that flows through the other two sectors. In other words, a falling dollar becomes bearish for stocks only after commodity prices and interest rates start to rise. Until that happens, it is possible to have a falling dollar along with a rising stock market (such as the period from 1985 to 1987). A rising dollar becomes bullish for stocks when commodity prices and interest rates start to decline (such as happened during 1980 and 1981). In the meantime, it is possible to have a strong dollar and a weak or flat stock market.

The peak in the dollar in the middle of 1989 led to a situation in which a weaker dollar and a strong stock market coexisted for the next several months. The potentially bearish impact of the weaker dollar would only take effect on stocks if and when commodity prices and interest rates would start to show signs of trending upward. The events of 1987 and early 1988 provide an example of how closely the dollar and stocks track each other during times of severe weakness in the equity sector.

Figure 6.12 compares the stock market to the dollar in the fall of 1987. Notice how closely the two markets tracked each other during the period from August to October of that year. As discussed earlier, interest rates had been rising for several months, pulling the dollar higher. Over the summer both the dollar and stocks began to weaken

FIGURE 6.11
THE U.S. DOLLAR VERSUS THE DOW JONES INDUSTRIAL AVERAGE FROM 1985 TO 1989. WHILE IT'S TRUE THAT A FALLING DOLLAR WILL EVENTUALLY PROVE BEARISH FOR STOCKS, A RISING STOCK MARKET CAN COEXIST WITH A FALLING DOLLAR FOR LONG PERIODS OF TIME (1985 TO 1987). BOTH ROSE DURING 1988 AND 1989.

U.S. Stocks versus the Dollar

together. Both rallied briefly in October before collapsing in tandem. The sharp selloff in the dollar during the October collapse is explained by the relationship between stocks, interest rates, and the dollar. While the stock selloff gathered momentum, interest rates began to drop sharply as the Federal Reserve Board added reserves to the system to check the equity decline. A "flight to safety" into T-bills and bonds pushed prices sharply higher in those two markets, which pushed yields lower.

As stock prices fall in such a scenario, the dollar drops primarily as a result of Federal Reserve easing. The dollar is dropping along with stocks but is really following short-term interest rates lower. Not surprisingly, after the financial markets stabilized in the fourth quarter of 1987, and short-term interest rates were allowed to trend higher once again, the dollar also stabilized and began to rally. Figure 6.13 shows the dollar and stocks rallying together through 1988 and most of 1989.

FIGURE 6.12
DURING THE 1987 STOCK MARKET CRASH, STOCKS AND THE DOLLAR BECAME CLOSELY LINKED. AFTER DROPPING TOGETHER DURING AUGUST AND OCTOBER, THEY BOTTOMED TOGETHER DURING THE FOURTH QUARTER OF THAT YEAR.

Stocks versus the Dollar
1987

FIGURE 6.13
THE DOLLAR AND EQUITIES ROSE TOGETHER DURING 1988 AND THE FIRST HALF OF 1989. THE "DOUBLE TOP" IN THE DOLLAR DURING THE THIRD QUARTER OF 1989, HOWEVER, WAS A POTENTIALLY BEARISH WARNING FOR EQUITIES.

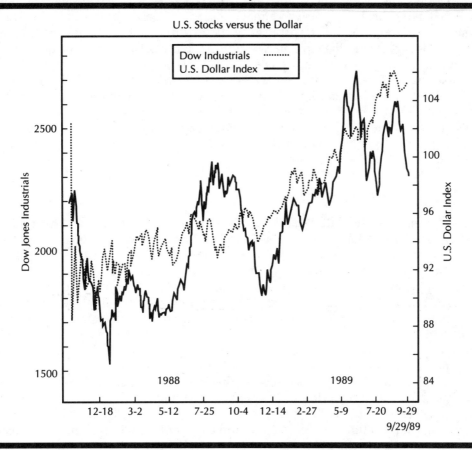

U.S. Stocks versus the Dollar

THE SEQUENCE OF THE DOLLAR, INTEREST RATES, AND STOCKS

The general sequence of events at market turns favors reversals in the dollar, bonds, and stocks in that order. The dollar will turn up first (as the result of rising interest rates). In time the rising dollar will push interest rates downward, and the bond market will rally. Stocks will turn up after bonds. After a period of falling interest rates (rising bond prices), the dollar will peak. After a while, the falling dollar will push interest rates higher, and the bond market will peak. Stocks usually peak after bonds.

This scenario generally takes place over several years. The lead times between the peaks and troughs in the three markets can often span several months to as long as two years. An understanding of this sequence explains why a falling dollar can coexist with a rising bond and stock market for a period of time. However, a falling dollar indicates that the clock has begun ticking on the bull markets in the other two sectors. Correspondingly, a bullish dollar is telling traders that it's only a matter of time before bonds and stocks follow along.

COMMODITIES VERSUS STOCKS

Figure 6.14 compares the CRB Index to the Dow Industrial Average from 1985 through the third quarter of 1989. The chart shows that stocks and commodities sometimes move in opposite directions and sometimes move in tandem. Still, some general conclusions can be drawn from this chart (and from longer-range studies), which reveals a rotational rhythm that flows through both markets. A rising CRB Index is *eventually* bearish for stocks. A falling CRB Index is *eventually* bullish for stocks. The inflationary impact of rising commodity prices (and rising interest rates) will combine to push stock prices lower (usually toward the end of an economic expansion). The impact of falling commodity prices (and falling interest rates) will eventually begin to push stock prices higher (usually toward the latter part of an economic slowdown).

The usual sequence of events between the two markets will look something like this: A peak in commodity prices will be followed in time by a bottom in stock prices. However, for awhile, commodities and stocks will fall together. Then, stocks will start to trend higher. For a time, stocks will rise and commodities will continue to weaken. Then, commodities will bottom out and start to rally. For a time, commodities and stocks will trend upward together. Stocks will then peak and begin to drop. For awhile, stocks will drop while commodities continue to rally. Then, commodity prices will peak and begin to drop. This brings us back to where we began.

In other words, a top in commodities is followed by a bottom in stocks, which is followed by a bottom in commodities, which is followed by a top in stocks, which is followed by a top in commodities, which is followed by a bottom in stocks. These, of course, are general tendencies. An exception to this general tendency took place in 1987 and 1988. Stocks topped in August of 1987, and commodities topped in July of 1988. However, the bottom in stocks in the last quarter of 1987 preceded the final top in commodities during the summer of the following year. This turn of events violates the normal sequence. However, it could be argued that although stocks hit bottom in late 1987, the rally began to accelerate only after commodities started to weaken in the second half of 1988. It also shows that, while the markets do tend to follow the intermarket sequence described above, these are not hard and fast rules.

Another reason why it's so important to recognize the rotational sequence between commodities and stocks is to avoid misunderstanding the inverse relationship between these two sectors. Yes, there is an inverse relationship, but only after relatively long lead times. For long periods of time, both sectors can trend in the same direction.

FIGURE 6.14
COMMODITIES VERSUS EQUITIES FROM 1985 TO 1989. SOMETIMES COMMODITIES AND STOCKS WILL RISE AND FALL TOGETHER AND, AT OTHER TIMES, WILL SHOW AN INVERSE RELATIONSHIP. IT'S IMPORTANT TO UNDERSTAND THEIR ROTATIONAL SEQUENCE.

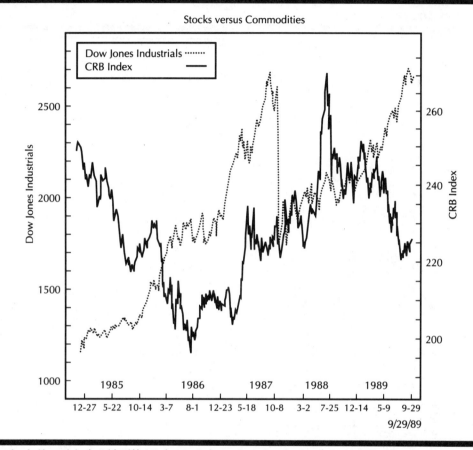

Stocks versus Commodities

GOLD AND THE STOCK MARKET

Usually when the conversation involves the relative merits of investing in commodities (tangible assets) versus stocks (financial assets), the focus turns to the gold market. The gold market plays a key role in the entire intermarket story. Gold is viewed as a safe haven during times of political and financial upheavals. As a result, stock market investors will flee to the gold market, or gold mining shares, when the stock market is in trouble. Certainly, gold will do especially well relative to stocks during times of high inflation (the 1970s for example), but will underperform stocks in times of declining inflation (most of the 1980s).

Gold plays a crucial role because of its strong inverse link to the dollar, its tendency to lead turns in the general commodity price level, and its role as a safe haven in times of turmoil. The importance of gold as a leading indicator of inflation will be discussed in more depth at a later time. For now, the focus is on the merits of gold as an investment relative to equities. Figure 6.15 compares the price of gold to

FIGURE 6.15
GOLD VERSUS THE STOCK MARKET FROM 1982 TO 1989. GOLD USUALLY DOES BEST IN AN INFLATIONARY ENVIRONMENT AND DURING BEAR MARKETS IN STOCKS. GOLD IS A LEADING INDICATOR OF INFLATION AND A SAFE HAVEN DURING TIMES OF ADVERSITY. STOCK MARKET INVESTORS WILL OFTEN FAVOR GOLD-MINING SHARES DURING PERIODS OF STOCK MARKET WEAKNESS.

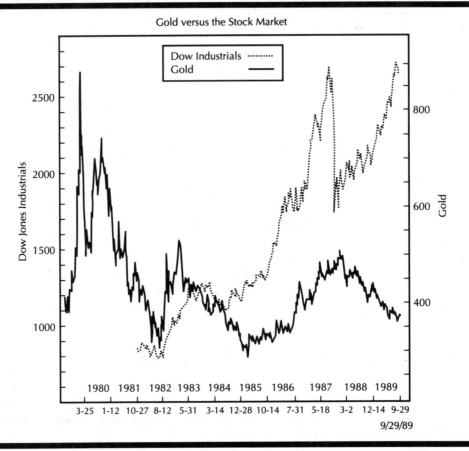

equities since 1982. Much of what was said in the previous section, in our comparison between commodities and stocks, holds true for gold as well. During periods of falling inflation, stocks outperform gold by a wide margin (1980 to 1985 and 1988 through the first half of 1989). During periods of rising inflation (the 1970s and the period from 1986 through the end of 1987), gold becomes a valuable addition to one's portfolio if not an outright alternative to stocks.

The period from 1988 through the middle of 1989 shows stocks and gold trending in opposite directions. This period coincided with general falling commodity prices and a rising dollar. Clearly, the wise place to be was in stocks and not gold. However, the sharp setback in the dollar in mid-1989 gave warning that things might be changing. Sustained weakness in the dollar would not only begin to undermine one of the bullish props under the stock market but would also provide support to the gold market, which benefits from dollar weakness.

GOLD—A KEY TO VITAL INTERMARKET LINKS

Since the gold market has a strong inverse link to the dollar, the direction of the gold market plays an important role in inflation expectations. A peak in the dollar in 1985 coincided with a major lowpoint in the gold market. The gold market top in December 1987 coincided with a major bottom in the dollar. The dollar peak in the summer of 1989 coincided with a major low in the gold market. The gold market leads turns in the CRB Index. The CRB Index in turn has a strong inverse relationship with a bond market. And, of course, bonds tend to lead the stock market. Since gold starts to trend upward prior to the CRB Index, it's possible to have a rising gold market along with bonds and stocks (1985–1987).

A major bottom in the gold market (which usually coincides with an important top in the dollar) is generally a warning that inflation pressures are just starting to build and will in time become bearish for bonds and stocks. A gold market top (which normally accompanies a bottom in the dollar) is an early indication of a lessening in inflation pressure and will in time have a bullish impact on bonds and stocks. However, it is possible for gold to drop along with bonds and stocks for a time.

It's important to recognize the role of gold as a *leading* indicator of inflation. Usually in the early stages of a bull market in gold, you'll read in the papers that there isn't enough inflation to justify the bull market since gold needs an inflationary environment in which to thrive. Conversely, when gold peaks out (in 1980 for example), you'll read that gold should not drop because of the rising inflation trend. Don't be misled by that backward thinking. *Gold doesn't react to inflation; it anticipates inflation.* That's why gold peaked in January of 1980 at a time of double-digit inflation and correctly anticipated the coming disinflation. That's also why gold bottomed in 1985, a year before the disinflation trend of the early 1980s had run its course. The next time gold starts to rally sharply and the economists say that there are no signs of inflation on the horizon, begin nibbling at some inflation hedges anyway. And the next time the stock market starts to look toppy, especially if the dollar is dropping, consider some gold mining shares.

INTEREST-RATE DIFFERENTIALS

The attractiveness of the dollar, relative to other currencies, is also a function of interest rate differentials with those other countries. In other words, if U.S. rates are high relative to overseas interest rates, this will help the dollar. If U.S. rates start to weaken relative to overseas rates, the dollar will weaken relative to overseas currencies. Money tends to flow toward those currencies with the highest interest rate yields and away from those with the lowest yields. This is why it's important to monitor interest rates on a global scale.

Any unilateral central bank tightening by overseas trading partners (usually to stem fears of rising domestic inflation) or U.S. easing will be supportive to overseas currencies and bearish for the dollar. Any unilateral U.S. tightening or overseas easing will strengthen the dollar. This explains why central bankers try to coordinate monetary policy to prevent unduly upsetting foreign exchange rates. In determining the impact on the dollar, then, it's not just a matter of which way interest rates are trending in this country but how they're trending in the United States relative to overseas interest rates.

SUMMARY

This chapter shows the strong link between the dollar and interest rates. The dollar has an important influence on the direction of interest rates. The direction of interest rates has a delayed impact on the direction of the dollar. The result is a circular relationship between the two. Short-term rates have more direct impact on the dollar than long-term rates. A falling U.S. dollar will eventually have a bearish impact on financial assets in favor of tangible assets. During times of severe stock market weakness, the dollar will usually fall as a result of Federal Reserve easing. Rising commodity prices will in time become bearish for stocks. Falling commodity prices usually precede an upturn in equities. Gold acts as a leading indicator of inflation and a safe haven during times of political and financial upheavals. The *normal* sequence of events among the various sectors is as follows:

- Rising *interest rates* pull the *dollar* higher.
- *Gold* peaks.
- The *CRB Index* peaks.
- *Interest rates* peak; *bonds* bottom.
- *Stocks* bottom.
- Falling *interest rates* pull the *dollar* lower.
- *Gold* bottoms.
- The *CRB Index* bottoms.
- *Interest rates* turn up; *bonds* peak.
- *Stocks* peak.
- Rising *interest rates* pull the *dollar* higher.

This chapter completes the direct comparison of the four market sectors—currencies, commodities, interest rate, and stock index futures. Of the four sectors, the one that has been the most neglected and the least understood by the financial community has been commodities. Because of the important role commodity markets play in the intermarket picture and their ability to anticipate inflation, the next chapter will be devoted to a more in-depth study of the commodity sector.

7

Commodity Indexes

One of the key aspects of intermarket analysis, which has been stressed repeatedly in the preceding chapters, has been the need to incorporate commodity prices into the financial equation. To do this, the Commodity Research Bureau Futures Price Index has been employed to represent the commodity markets. The CRB Index is the most widely watched barometer of the general commodity price level and will remain throughout the text as the major tool for analyzing commodity price trends. However, to adequately understand the workings of the CRB Index, it's important to know what makes it run. Although all of its 21 component markets are equally weighted, some individual commodity markets are more important than others. We'll consider the impact various commodities have on the CRB Index and why it's important to monitor those individual markets.

In addition to monitoring the individual commodity markets that comprise the CRB Index, it's also useful to consult the Futures Group Indexes published by the Commodity Research Bureau. A quick glance at these group indexes tells the analyst which commodity groups are the strongest and the weakest at any given time. Some of these futures groups have more impact on the CRB Index than others and merit special attention. The precious metals and the energy groups are especially important because of their impact on the overall commodity price level and their wide acceptance as barometers of inflation. I'll show how it's possible to view each group as a whole instead of just as individual markets. The relationship between the energy and precious metals sectors will be discussed to see if following one sector provides any clues to the direction of the other. Finally, movements in the energy and metals sectors will be compared to interest rates to see if there is any correlation.

There are several other commodity indexes that should be monitored in addition to the CRB Index. Although most broad commodity indexes normally trend in the same direction, there are times when their paths begin to differ. It is precisely at those times, when the various commodity indexes begin to diverge from one another, that important warnings of possible trend changes are being sent. To understand these divergences, the observer should understand how the various indexes are constructed.

First the CRB *Futures* Index will be compared to the CRB *Spot* Index. Analysts often confuse these two indexes. However, the CRB Spot Index is comprised of *spot* (cash) prices instead of *futures* prices and has a heavier industrial weighting than the CRB Futures Index. The CRB Spot Index is broken down into two other indexes, Spot *Foodstuffs* and Spot *Raw Industrials*. The Raw Industrials Index is especially favored by economic forecasters. Another index favored by many economists is the *Journal of Commerce (JOC) Industrial Materials Price Index*.

The debate as to which commodity index does a better job of predicting inflation centers around the relative importance of *industrial* prices versus *food* prices. Economists seem to prefer industrial prices as a better barometer of inflation and economic strength. However, the financial markets seem to prefer the more balanced CRB Futures Index, which includes both food and industrial prices. Although the debate won't be resolved in these pages, I'll try to shed some light on the subject.

COMMODITY PRICES, INFLATION, AND FED POLICY

Ultimately, inflation pressures are reflected in the Producer Price Index (PPI) and the Consumer Price Index (CPI). I'll show how monitoring trends in the commodity markets often provides clues months in advance as to which way the inflation winds are blowing. Since the Federal Reserve Board's primary goal is price stability, it should come as no surprise to anyone that the Fed watches commodity indexes very closely to help determine whether price pressures are intensifying or diminishing. What the Fed itself has said regarding the importance of commodity prices as a tool for setting monetary policy will be discussed.

HOW TO CONSTRUCT THE CRB INDEX

Since we've placed so much importance on the CRB Index, let's explain how it is constructed and which markets have the most influence on its movements. The Commodity Research Bureau Futures Price Index was first introduced in 1956 by that organization. Although it has undergone many changes in the ensuing 30 years, it is currently comprised of 21 active commodity markets. The key word here is *commodity. The CRB Index does not include any financial futures.* It is a *commodity* index, pure and simple. The calculation of the CRB Index takes three steps:

1. Each of the Index's 21 component commodities is *arithmetically* averaged using the prices for all of the futures months which expire on or before the end of the *ninth* calendar month from the current date. This means that the Index extends between nine and ten months into the future depending on where one is in the current month.

2. These 21 component arithmetic averages are then *geometrically* averaged by multiplying all of the numbers together and taking their 21st root.

3. The resulting value is divided by 53.0615, which is the *1967* base-year average for these 21 commodities. That result is then multiplied by an adjustment factor of .94911. (This adjustment factor is necessitated by the Index's July 20, 1987 changeover from 26 commodities averaged over 12 months to 21 commodities averaged over 9 months.) Finally, that result is multiplied by 100 in order to convert the Index into percentage terms:

$$\text{CRB Index} = \frac{\text{Current geometric average}}{\text{1967 geometric average (53.0615)}} \times .94911 \times 100$$

All of the 21 commodity markets that comprise the CRB Index are themselves traded as futures contracts and cover the entire spectrum of commodity markets. In alphabetical order, the 21 commodities in the CRB Index are as follows:

Cattle (Live), Cocoa, Coffee, Copper, Corn, Cotton, Crude Oil, Gold (New York), Heating Oil (No. 2), Hogs, Lumber, Oats (Chicago), Orange Juice, Platinum, Pork Bellies, Silver (New York), Soybeans, Soybean Meal, Soybean Oil, Sugar "11" (World), Wheat (Chicago)

Each of the 21 markets in the CRB Index carries equal weight in the preceding formula, which means that each market contributes 1/21 (4.7%) to the Index's value. However, although each individual commodity market has equal weight in the CRB Index, this does not mean that each commodity *group* carries equal weight. Some commodity *groups* carry more weight than others. The following breakdown divides the CRB Index by groups to give a better idea how the weightings are distributed:

MEATS: Cattle, hogs, porkbellies (14.3%)

METALS: Gold, platinum, silver (14.3%)

IMPORTED: Cocoa, coffee, sugar (14.3%)

ENERGY: Crude oil, heating oil (9.5%)

GRAINS: Corn, oats, wheat, soybeans, soybean meal, soybean oil (28.6%)

INDUSTRIALS: Copper, cotton, lumber (14.3%)

A quick glance at the preceding breakdown reveals two of the major criticisms of the CRB Index—first, the heavier weighting of the *agricultural* markets (62%) versus the *non-food* markets (38%) and, second, the heavy weighting of the *grain* sector (28.6%) relative to the other commodity groupings. The heavy weighting of the agricultural markets has caused some observers to question the reliability of the CRB Index as a predictor of inflation, a question which will be discussed later. The heavy grain weighting reveals why it is so important to follow the grain markets when analyzing the CRB Index, which leads us to our next subject—the impact various markets and market groups have on the CRB Index.

GROUP CORRELATION STUDIES

A comparison of how the various commodity groups correlate with the CRB Index from 1984 to 1989 shows that the Grains have the strongest correlation with the Index (84%). Two other groups with strong correlations are the Industrials (67%)*and the Energy markets (60%). Two groups that show weak correlations with the Index are the Meats (33%) and the Imported markets (−4%). The Metals group has a poor overall correlation to the CRB Index (15.98%). However, a closer look at the six years under study reveals that, in four of the six years, the metal correlations were actually quite high. For example, positive correlations between the Metals and the CRB Index were seen in 1984 (93%), 1987 (74%), 1988 (76%), and the first half of 1989 (89%). (Source: *CRB Index Futures Reference Guide*, New York Futures Exchange, 1989.)

Correlation studies performed for the 12-month period ending in October 1989 show that the grain complex remained the consistent leader during that time span

*Copper, cotton, crude oil, lumber, platinum, silver

and confirmed the longer-range conclusions discussed in the previous paragraph. In the 12 months from October 1988 to October 1989, the strongest individual comparisons with the CRB Index were shown by soybean oil (93%), corn (92.6%), soybeans (92.5%), soybean meal (91%), and oats (90%). The metals as a group also showed strong correlation with the CRB Index during the same time span: silver (86%), gold (77%), platinum (75%). (Source: Powers Associates, Jersey City, NJ)

GRAINS, METALS, AND OILS

The three most important sectors to watch when analyzing the CRB Index are the *grains, metals,* and *energy* markets. The oil markets earn their special place because of their high correlation ranking with the CRB Index and because of oil's importance as an international commodity. The metals also show a high correlation in most years. However, the special place in our analysis earned by the metals markets (gold in particular) is because of their role as a leading indicator of the CRB Index (discussed in Chapter 5) and their wide acceptance as leading indicator of inflation. The important place reserved for the grain markets results from their consistently strong correlation with the CRB Index.

Most observers who track the CRB Index are quite familiar with the oil and gold markets and follow those markets regularly. However, the CRB Index is often driven more by the grain markets, which are traded in Chicago, than by the gold and oil markets, which are traded in New York. A dramatic example of the grain influence was seen during the midwest drought of 1988, when the grain markets totally dominated the CRB Index for most of the spring and summer of that year. A thorough analysis of the CRB Index requires the monitoring of all 21 component markets that comprise the Index. However, special attention should always be paid to the *precious metals, energy,* and *grain* markets.

CRB FUTURES VERSUS THE CRB SPOT INDEX

The same six-year study referred to in the paragraph on "Group Correlation Studies" in Chapter 7 (p. 97) contained another important statistic, which has relevance to our next subject—a comparison of the CRB *Futures* Index to the CRB *Spot* Index. During the six years from 1984 to the middle of 1989, the correlation between these two CRB Indexes was an impressive 87 percent. In four out of the six years, the correlation exceeded 90 percent. What these figures confirm is that, despite their different construction, the two CRB Indexes generally trend in the same direction.

Despite the emphasis on the CRB Futures Index in intermarket analysis, it's important to look to other broad-based commodity indexes for confirmation of what the CRB Futures Index is doing. Divergences between commodity indexes usually contain an important message that the current trend may be changing. The other commodity indexes will sometimes lead the CRB Futures Index and, in so doing, can provide important intermarket warnings. Study of the CRB Spot Index also takes us into a deeper discussion of the relative importance of industrial prices.

HOW THE CRB SPOT INDEX IS CONSTRUCTED

First of all, the CRB Spot Index is made up of cash (spot) prices instead of futures prices. Second, it includes several commodities that are not included in the CRB

Futures Index. Third, it has a heavier industrial weighting. The 23 spot prices that comprise the CRB Spot Index are as follows in alphabetical order:

Burlap, butter, cocoa, copper scrap, corn, cotton, hides, hogs, lard, lead, print cloth, rosin, rubber, soybean oil, steel scrap, steers, sugar, tallow, tin, wheat (Minneapolis), wheat (Kansas City), wool tops, and zinc

There are *23* commodity prices in the CRB Spot Index, while the CRB Futures Index has *21*. Prices included in the CRB Spot Index that are not in the CRB Futures Index are burlap, butter, hides, lard, lead, print cloth, rosin, rubber, steel scrap, tallow, tin, wool tops, and zinc. One other significant difference is in the industrial weighting. Of the 23 spot prices included in the CRB Spot Index, 13 are industrial prices for a weighting of 56 percent. This contrasts with a 38 percent industrial weighting in the CRB Futures Index. It is this difference in the industrial weightings that accounts for the occasional divergences that exist between the Spot and Futures Indexes. To see why the heavier industrial weighting of the CRB Spot Index can make a major difference in its performance, divide the Spot Index into its two sub-indexes—The Spot *Raw Industrials* and the *Spot Foodstuffs*.

RAW INDUSTRIALS VERSUS FOODSTUFFS

In spite of their different composition, the CRB Futures and Spot Indexes usually trend in the same direction. To fully understand why they diverge at certain times, it's important to consult the two sub-indexes that comprise the CRB Spot Index—the Spot *Raw Industrials* and the Spot *Foodstuffs*. Significantly different trend pictures sometimes develop in these two sectors. For example, the Raw Industrial Index bottomed out in the summer of 1986, whereas the Foodstuffs didn't bottom out until the first quarter of 1987. The Foodstuffs, on the other hand, peaked in mid-1988 and dropped sharply for a year. The Raw Industrials continued to advance into the first quarter of 1989. While the Raw Industrials turned up first in mid-1986, the Foodstuffs turned down first in mid-1988.

By understanding how industrial and food prices perform relative to one another, the analyst gains a greater understanding into why some of the broader commodity indexes perform so differently at certain times. Some rely more heavily on industrial prices and some, like the CRB Futures Index, are more food-oriented. Many economists believe that industrial prices more truly reflect inflation pressures and strength or weakness in the economy than do food prices, which are more influenced by such things as agricultural subsidies, weather, and political considerations. Still, no one denies that food prices do play a role in the inflation picture. One popular commodity index goes so far as to exclude food prices completely. Since its creation in 1986, the Journal of Commerce (JOC) Index has gained a following among economists and market observers as a reliable indicator of commodity price pressures.

THE JOURNAL OF COMMERCE (JOC) INDEX

This index of 18 industrial materials prices was developed by the Center for International Business Cycle Research (CIBCR) at Columbia University and has been published daily since 1986. Its subgroupings include textiles, metals, petroleum products, and miscellaneous commodities. The components of the JOC Index were chosen specifically because of their success in anticipating inflation trends. The 18 commodities included in the JOC Index are broken down into the following subgroupings:

METALS: aluminum, copper scrap, lead, steel scrap, tin, zinc

TEXTILES: burlap, cotton, polyester, print cloth

PETROLEUM: crude oil, benzene

MISC: hides, rubber, tallow, plywood, red oak, old corrugated boxes

The JOC Index has been compiled back to 1948 on a monthly basis and, according to its creators, has established a consistent track record anticipating inflation trends. It can also be used to help predict business cycles, a subject which will be tackled in Chapter 13. One possible shortcoming in the JOC Index is its total exclusion of food prices. Why the exclusion of food prices can pose problems was demonstrated in 1988 and 1989 when a glaring divergence developed between food and industrial prices. This resulted in a lot of confusion as to which of the commodity indexes were giving the truer inflation readings.

VISUAL COMPARISONS OF THE VARIOUS COMMODITY INDEXES

This section shows how the various commodity indexes performed over the past few years and, at the same time, demonstrates why it's so important to know what commodities are in each index. It will also be shown why it's dangerous to exclude food prices completely from the inflation picture. Figure 7.1 compares the CRB Futures Index to the CRB Spot Index from 1987 to 1989. Historically, both indexes have normally traded in the same direction.

The CRB *Futures* Index peaked in the summer of 1988 at the tail end of the midwestern drought that took place that year. The Futures Index then declined until the following August before stabilizing again. The CRB *Spot* Index, however, continued to rally into March of 1989 before turning downward. From August of 1989 into yearend, the CRB Futures Index trended higher while the CRB Spot Index dropped sharply. Clearly, the two indexes were "out of sync" with one another. The explanation lies with the relative weighting of food versus industrial prices in each index.

FOODSTUFFS VERSUS RAW INDUSTRIALS

Figure 7.2 shows the Spot Foodstuffs and the Spot Raw Industrials Indexes from 1985 through 1989. The 23 commodities that are included in these two indexes are combined in the CRB Spot Index. An examination of the Raw Industrials and the Foodstuffs helps explain the riddle as to why the CRB Spot and the CRB Futures Indexes diverged so dramatically in late 1988 through the end of 1989. It also explains why the Journal of Commerce Index, which is composed exclusively of industrial prices, gave entirely different readings than the CRB Futures Price Index.

In the summer of 1986, Raw Industrials turned higher and led the upturn in the Foodstuffs by half a year. Both indexes trended upward together until mid-1988 when the Foodstuffs (and the CRB Futures Index) peaked and began a yearlong descent. The Raw Industrials rose into the spring of 1989 before rolling over to the downside. The Raw Industrials led at the 1986 bottom, while the Foodstuffs led at the 1988 peak.

FIGURE 7.1
A COMPARISON OF THE CRB *FUTURES* INDEX AND THE CRB *SPOT* INDEX FROM 1987 TO 1989. ALTHOUGH THESE TWO INDEXES HAVE A STRONG HISTORICAL CORRELATION, THEY SOMETIMES DIVERGE AS IN 1989. WHILE THE CRB SPOT INDEX HAS A HEAVIER *INDUSTRIAL* WEIGHTING, THE CRB FUTURES INDEX HAS A HEAVIER *AGRICULTURAL* WEIGHTING.

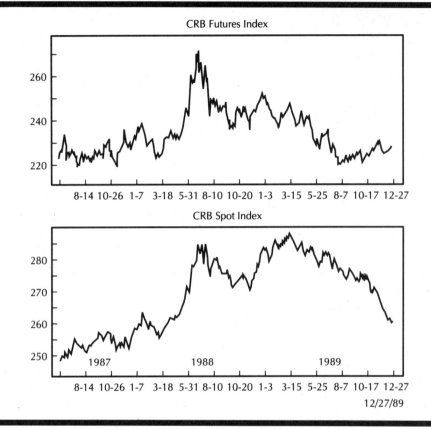

Reproduced with permission by Knight Ridder's Tradecenter. Tradecenter is a registered trademark of Knight Ridder's Financial Information.

Figure 7.3 puts all four indexes in proper perspective. The upper chart compares the CRB *Futures* and *Spot* Indexes. The lower chart compares the Spot Foodstuff and the Raw Industrial Indexes. Notice that *the CRB Futures Index tracks the Foodstuffs more closely*, whereas *the CRB Spot Index is more influenced by the Raw Industrials*. The major divergence between the CRB *Futures* and the CRB *Spot* Indexes is better explained if the observer understands their relative weighting of industrial prices relative to food prices and also keeps an eye on the two Spot sub-indexes.

THE JOC INDEX AND RAW INDUSTRIALS

Figure 7.4 shows the close correlation between the Raw Industrials Index and the Journal of Commerce Index. This should come as no surprise since both are composed exclusively of industrial prices. (One important difference between the two indexes is that the JOC Index has a 7.1 percent petroleum weighting whereas the Raw Industrials Index includes no petroleum prices. The CRB *Futures* Index, by contrast, has a 9.5

FIGURE 7.2

CRB SPOT FOODSTUFFS INDEX VERSUS THE CRB SPOT RAW INDUSTRIALS FROM 1985 TO 1989. INDUSTRIAL PRICES TURNED UP FIRST IN 1986. HOWEVER, FOOD PRICES PEAKED FIRST IN 1988. IT'S IMPORTANT WHEN MEASURING INFLATION TRENDS TO LOOK AT BOTH MEASURES.

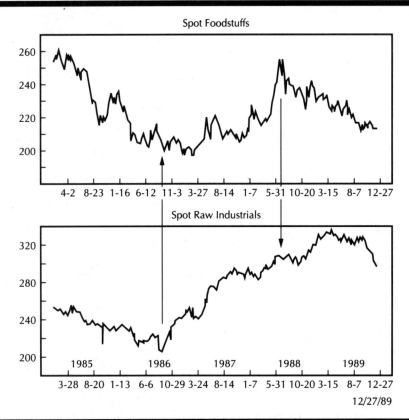

FIGURE 7.3
A COMPARISON OF THE CRB SPOT AND CRB FUTURES INDEXES (UPPER CHART) WITH THE
CRB SPOT RAW INDUSTRIALS AND CRB SPOT FOODSTUFFS (LOWER CHART). THE CRB FU-
TURES INDEX TRACKS THE FOODSTUFFS MORE CLOSELY, WHILE THE CRB SPOT INDEX IS
MORE CLOSELY CORRELATED WITH THE RAW INDUSTRIALS. THE CRB SPOT INDEX IS SUBDI-
VIDED INTO THE SPOT RAW INDUSTRIALS AND THE SPOT FOODSTUFFS.

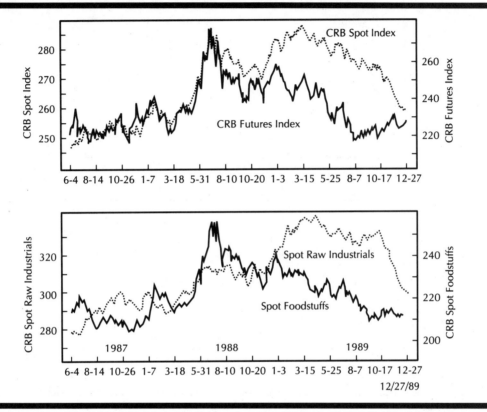

FIGURE 7.4

A COMPARISON OF THE CRB SPOT RAW INDUSTRIALS WITH THE JOURNAL OF COMMERCE (JOC) INDEX. SINCE BOTH INCLUDE ONLY INDUSTRIAL PRICES, THEY CORRELATE VERY CLOSELY.

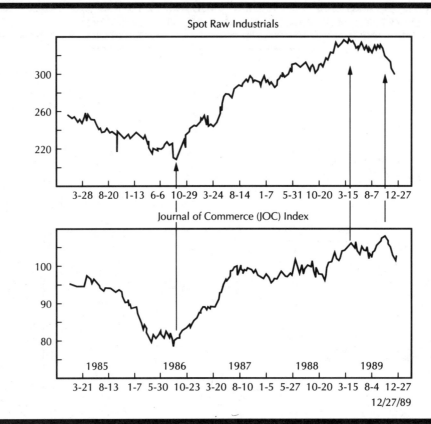

Spot Raw Industrials

Journal of Commerce (JOC) Index

12/27/89

percent energy weighting.) Notice how closely the two industrial indexes resemble each other. They both bottomed together in mid-1986 and peaked in 1989. The last recovery high in the JOC Index in late 1989, however, was not confirmed by the Raw Industrial Index, providing early warning that the JOC uptrend might be changing. That's another reason why it's so important to consult all of these indexes and not rely on just one or two. Having shown the important differences between food and industrial prices, now the *CRB Futures Index* will be compared with the *Journal of Commerce* Index.

THE CRB FUTURES INDEX VERSUS THE JOC INDEX

Figures 7.5 and 7.6 compare these two commodity indexes first from a longer view (1985 through 1989) and then a shorter view (mid-1988 to the end of 1989). Not surprisingly, the JOC Index rose faster in 1986 as industrial prices led the commodity advance. The more balanced CRB Index didn't accelerate upward until the following spring. In this case, the JOC Index was the stronger and gave an excellent leading signal that inflation pressures were awakening.

FIGURE 7.5
THE CRB FUTURES PRICE INDEX VERSUS THE JOURNAL OF COMMERCE (JOC) INDEX FROM 1985 TO 1989. SINCE THE CRB FUTURES INDEX INCLUDES FOOD PRICES WHILE THE JOC INDEX INCLUDES *ONLY* INDUSTRIAL PRICES, THESE TWO INDEXES OFTEN DIVERGE FROM EACH OTHER. IT'S IMPORTANT, HOWEVER, TO CONSIDER BOTH FOR A THOROUGH ANALYSIS OF COMMODITY PRICE TRENDS.

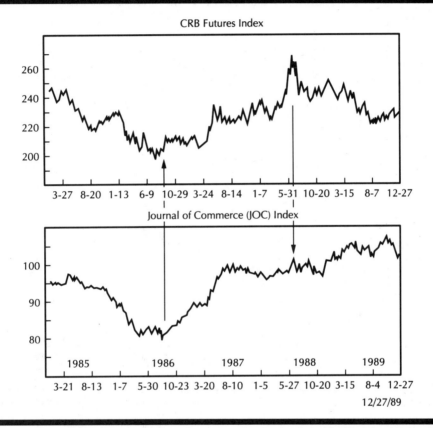

The picture gets cloudier from mid-1988 on. The CRB Index, heavily influenced by a major top in the grain markets, peaked in the summer of 1988. Futures prices declined until the following August before showing signs of stabilization. Meanwhile, the JOC Index continued to set new highs into the fall of 1989. Figure 7.6 shows 1989 in more detail. For most of that year, the CRB Index and the JOC Index trended in opposite directions. During the first half of 1989, the JOC Index strengthened while the CRB Index weakened. By the time the JOC Index started to weaken in October of 1989, the CRB Index was already beginning to rally.

Anyone consulting these two indexes for signs of which way inflation was going got completely opposite readings. The JOC Index was predicting higher inflation throughout most of 1989, while the CRB Index was saying that inflation had peaked in 1988. Going into the end of 1989, the JOC Index was predicting a slowdown of inflation, whereas the firmer CRB Index was predicting an uptick in inflation pressures. What is the intermarket trader to do at such times?

FIGURE 7.6
THE CRB FUTURES PRICE INDEX VERSUS THE JOURNAL OF COMMERCE (JOC) INDEX DURING 1988 AND 1989. BECAUSE OF THEIR DIFFERENT COMPOSITION, THESE TWO COMMODITY INDEXES TRENDED IN OPPOSITE DIRECTIONS DURING MOST OF 1989.

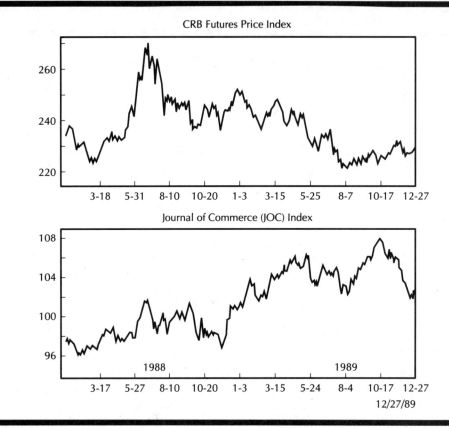

Reproduced with permission by Knight Ridder's Tradecenter. Tradecenter is a registered trademark of Knight Ridder's Financial Information.

Remember that the main purpose in performing intermarket analysis is not to do economic analysis, but to aid analysts in making trading decisions. The pertinent question is which of the two commodity indexes fit into the intermarket scenario better, and which one do the financial markets seem to be listening to. To help answer that question, refer to the most basic relationship in intermarket analysis — commodities versus interest rates. In previous chapters, the close positive link between commodity prices and interest rates was established. Compare interest rate yields to both of these commodity indexes to see if one has a better fit than the other.

INTEREST RATES VERSUS THE COMMODITY INDEXES

Figure 7.7 compares 30-year Treasury bond yields with the CRB Index. In Chapter 3 a similar chart was examined to demonstrate the strong fit between both measures. Although the fit is not perfect, there appears to be a close positive correlation between bond yields and the CRB Index. Both measures formed a "head and shoulders" bottom in 1986 and 1987. Except for the upward spike in interest rates in the fall of 1987, the

FIGURE 7.7
THE CRB INDEX VERSUS TREASURY BOND YIELDS FROM 1985 TO 1989. A STRONG VISUAL CORRELATION CAN BE SEEN BETWEEN THESE TWO MEASURES. DURING THE SECOND HALF OF 1988 AND MOST OF 1989, INTEREST RATES AND THE CRB INDEX DROPPED TOGETHER.

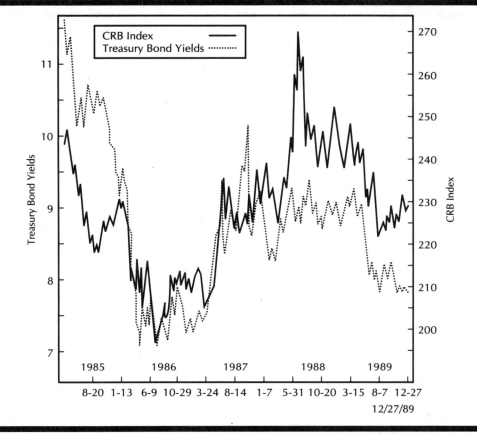

Reproduced with permission by Knight Ridder's Tradecenter. Tradecenter is a registered trademark of Knight Ridder's Financial Information.

peaks and troughs in bond yields were remarkably close to those in the CRB Index. An important peak in bond yields occurred in mid-1988 which corresponded closely with the major CRB top. Both measures then declined into August of 1989. Upward pressure in the CRB Index was beginning to pull bond yields higher as 1989 ended.

Figure 7.8 shows that the correlation between the JOC Index and bond yields was completely "out of sync" from mid-1988 to the end of 1989. While bond yields were declining on reduced inflation expectations, the JOC Index continued to set new recovery highs. The JOC Index was predicting higher inflation and continued economic growth while declining bond yields were predicting just the opposite.

Figure 7.9 compares all three measures. The upper chart compares the CRB Index and the JOC Index from the fall of 1988 to the end of 1989. The lower chart shows 30-year Treasury bond yields through the same time span. The chart shows a much stronger correlation between bond yields and the CRB Index. For most of 1989, bond yields trended in the opposite direction of the JOC Index. In the first half of the year, bond yields fell as the JOC Index continued to set new recovery highs. As the year ended, bond yields are showing signs of bouncing as the JOC Index is dropping.

FIGURE 7.8
THE JOURNAL OF COMMERCE (JOC) INDEX AND TREASURY BOND YIELDS FROM 1985 TO 1989. THESE TWO MEASURES CORRELATE CLOSELY UNTIL 1989. DURING THAT YEAR, TREASURY BOND YIELDS DROPPED SHARPLY WHILE THE JOC INDEX CONTINUED TO SET NEW HIGHS.

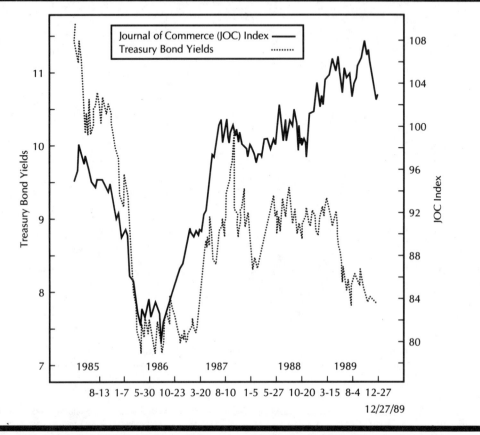

During that time span, the trader would have had little success trying to fit the JOC Index into his intermarket scenario. By contrast, the linkage between the CRB Index and bond yields appears to have held up quite well during that period.

THE CRB INDEX—A MORE BALANCED PICTURE

Inflation pressures subsided throughout 1989. At the producer level, inflation hovered around 1 percent in the second half of the year compared to more than 9 percent during the first half. As the Spot Foodstuffs Index shows, most of that decline in price pressures could be seen in the food markets and not the industrials. Going into the fourth quarter of 1989, food prices began to stabilize. At the wholesale level, food prices saw their strongest advance in two years. This pickup in food inflation occurred just as industrial prices were starting to weaken.

The evidence shown on the accompanying charts seems to support the inclusion of agricultural markets in the inflation picture. As always, the final judgment rests with the markets. It seems that the financial markets, and bonds in particular, respond

FIGURE 7.9
TREASURY BONDS YIELDS (BOTTOM CHART) COMPARED TO THE CRB FUTURES INDEX AND THE JOURNAL OF COMMERCE (JOC) INDEX (UPPER CHART) DURING 1989. DURING 1989, BOND YIELDS HAD A CLOSER CORRELATION TO THE CRB INDEX THAN TO THE JOC INDEX.

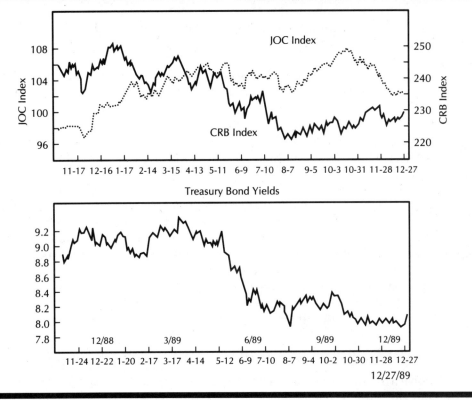

more closely to price trends in the more evenly-balanced CRB Index than in any of the indexes that rely exclusively on industrial prices. And this is our primary area of concern. All of the other commodity indexes have value and should be monitored in order to obtain a comprehensive picture of commodity price trends. However, I still prefer the CRB Futures Index as the primary commodity index for intermarket analysis.

THE CRB FUTURES GROUP INDEXES

To look "beneath the surface" of the CRB Futures Index, it's also useful to consult the CRB Futures Group Indexes published by the Commodity Research Bureau. These group indexes allow us to quickly determine which commodity groups are contributing the most to the activity in the CRB Index. The seven commodity sub-indexes are as follows:

ENERGY: Crude oil, heating oil, unleaded gasoline
GRAINS: Corn, oats (Chi.), soybean meal, wheat (Chi.)
IMPORTED: Cocoa, coffee, sugar "11"

INDUSTRIALS: Cotton, copper, crude oil, lumber, platinum, silver
OILSEED: Flaxseed, soybeans, rapeseed
MEATS: Cattle (live), hogs, porkbellies
METALS: Gold, platinum, silver

All of the commodities in the commodity group indexes are included in the CRB Futures Price Index with the exception of unleaded gasoline, flaxseed, and rapeseed. Also, notice that some commodities (crude oil, platinum, and silver) are included in two group indexes. The Commodity Research Bureau also publishes two financial Futures Group Indexes—Currency and Interest Rates. They include:

CURRENCY: British pound, Canadian dollar, Deutsche mark,
                  Japanese yen, Swiss franc
INTEREST RATES: Treasury Bills, Treasury Bonds, Treasury Notes

The main value in having these nine Futures Group Indexes available is the ability to study *groups* as opposed to *individual* markets. It's not unusual for one market, such as platinum in the Metals sector or heating oil in the Energy sector, to dominate a group for a period of time. However, more meaningful trends are established when the activity in one or two individual markets is confirmed by the group index. Group analysis also makes for quicker comparison between the nine sectors, including the commodity and financial groups. By adding any of the popular stock indexes to the group, the trader has before him the entire financial spectrum of currency, commodity, interest rate, and stock markets, which greatly facilitates intermarket comparisons.

THE CRB INDEX VERSUS GRAINS, METALS, AND ENERGY GROUPS

I mentioned earlier in the chapter that the three main groups to watch in the commodity sector are the *grains, metals,* and *energy* markets. Although some other individual markets may play an important role on occasion, these three groups have the most consistent influence over the CRB Index. Figures 7.10 to 7.12 compare the CRB Index to these three CRB group indexes in the five-year period from 1985 through 1989. Figure 7.10 reveals, in particular, how the upward spike in the grain markets in the spring and summer of 1988 marked the final surge in the CRB Index.

Figure 7.11 shows that the oil market bottom in 1986 was one of the major factors that started the general commodity rally that lasted for two years. A falling oil market in the first half of 1988 warned that the CRB rally was on shaky ground. An upward-trending oil market in the second half of 1989 quietly warned of growing inflation pressures in that sector, which began to pull the CRB Index higher during the final quarter of that year.

Figure 7.12 demonstrates the leading characteristics of the Precious Metals Index relative to the CRB Index. The strong metals rally in the spring of 1987 (influenced by the oil rally) helped launch the CRB bullish breakout. Falling metals prices during the first half of 1988 (along with oil prices) also warned that the CRB rally was too narrowly based. Stability in the metals sector during the summer of 1989 (partially as a result of the strong oil market) and the subsequent October–November 1989 rally in the precious metals played an important role in the CRB upturn during the second half of that year. To fully understand what's happening in the CRB Index, monitor all of the Futures Group Indexes. *But pay special attention to the grains, energy, and metals.*

FIGURE 7.10
THE CRB FUTURES PRICE INDEX VERSUS THE CRB GRAINS FUTURES INDEX FROM 1985 TO 1989. A STRONG HISTORICAL CORRELATION EXISTS BETWEEN THE GRAIN MARKETS AND THE CRB INDEX. THE 1988 PEAK IN THE CRB INDEX WAS CAUSED PRIMARILY BY THE GRAIN MARKETS.

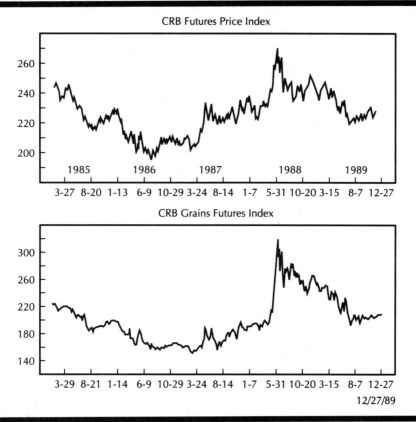

FIGURE 7.11
THE CRB FUTURES PRICE INDEX VERSUS THE CRB ENERGY FUTURES INDEX FROM 1985 TO 1989. THE ENERGY MARKETS ARE ALSO IMPORTANT TO THE CRB INDEX AND SHOULD BE GIVEN SPECIAL ATTENTION. THE 1986 BOTTOM IN THE CRB INDEX WAS CAUSED PRIMARILY BY THE BOTTOM IN OIL PRICES.

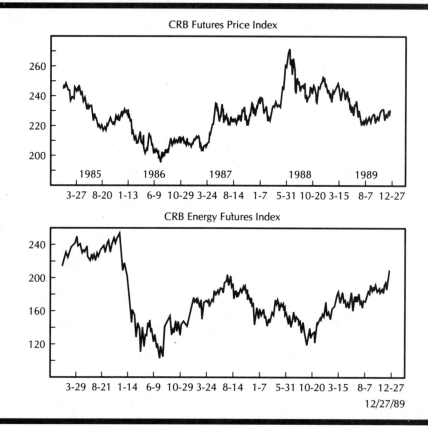

FIGURE 7.12
THE CRB FUTURES PRICE INDEX VERSUS THE CRB PRECIOUS METALS INDEX FROM 1985 TO 1989. THE PRECIOUS METALS GROUP IS ALSO IMPORTANT TO THE OVERALL TREND OF THE CRB INDEX. THE METALS MARKETS USUALLY LEAD THE CRB INDEX. THE LACK OF BULLISH CONFIRMATION BY THE METALS IN 1988 WAS A WARNING OF A PEAK IN THE CRB INDEX. A METALS RALLY IN LATE 1989 ALSO HELPED LAUNCH A CRB INDEX RALLY.

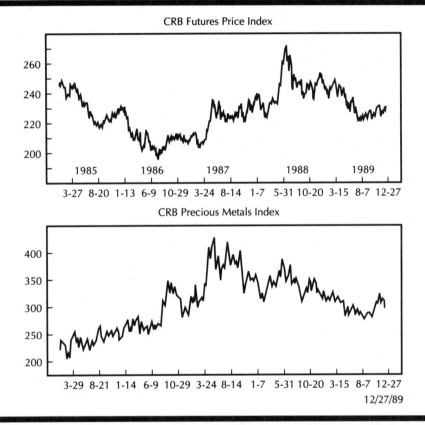

CRB Futures Price Index

CRB Precious Metals Index

12/27/89

Reproduced with permission by Knight Ridder's Tradecenter. Tradecenter is a registered trademark of Knight Ridder's Financial Information.

ENERGY VERSUS METALS MARKETS

I've already alluded to the interplay between the oil and precious metals markets. Although the fit between the two is far from perfect, it's useful to keep an eye on both. Since both are leading indicators of inflation, it stands to reason that major moves in one sector will eventually have an effect on the other. Figure 7.13 compares the CRB Energy Futures Index to the CRB Precious Metals Futures Index from 1985 through the end of 1989. Although they don't always trend in the same direction, they do clearly seem to impact on one another. Although the metals had been trending irregularly higher going into mid-1986, they didn't begin to soar until the summer of that year when the oil price collapse had been reversed to the upside.

Both sectors dropped through the second half of 1987 and most of 1988, although the 1987 peak occurred in the precious metals markets first. Oil prices rose through most of 1989. However, it wasn't until the second half of 1989, as the oil rally gathered more momentum, that the inflationary implications of rising oil prices began to have a bullish impact on precious metals. And, of course, if both of those sectors are moving

FIGURE 7.13
THE CRB ENERGY FUTURES INDEX VERSUS THE CRB PRECIOUS METALS FUTURES INDEX FROM 1985 TO 1989. SINCE THESE TWO COMMODITY GROUPS ARE LEADING INDICATORS OF IN-FLATION, THEY USUALLY IMPACT ON EACH OTHER. THE METALS RALLY IN 1986 WAS HELPED BY A BOTTOM IN OIL. BOTH PEAKED TOGETHER IN MID-1987. BOTH RALLIED TOGETHER TOWARD THE END OF 1989.

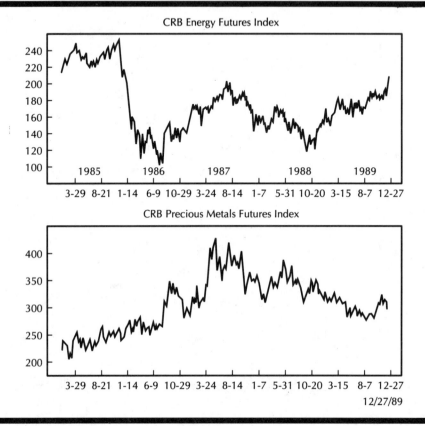

in tandem, their combined effect will have a profound influence on the CRB Index. It's always a good idea for metals traders to watch the oil charts, and vice versa.

THE INTERMARKET ROLES OF GOLD AND OIL

There are times when the gold and oil futures markets, either in tandem or separately, become the dominant markets in the intermarket picture. This is partly because the financial community watches both markets so closely. The price of gold is quoted on most media business stations and is widely watched by investors. For short periods of time, either of these two markets will have an effect on the price of bonds. Of the two, however, oil seems to be more dominant.

In the fall of 1989, surging gold prices (partially the result of a sagging dollar and stock market weakness) sent renewed inflation fears through the financial markets and helped keep a lid on bond prices. Unusually cold weather in December of 1989 pushed oil prices sharply higher (led by heating oil) and caused some real fears in the financial community (bond traders, in particular) of a possible uptick in inflation. *The bond market seems especially sensitive to trends in oil futures.* The trend in gold and oil also plays a decisive role in the attractiveness of gold and oil shares, which will be discussed in Chapter 9.

METALS AND ENERGY FUTURES VERSUS INTEREST RATES

If precious metals and oil prices are so important in their own right, and if they have such a dominant influence on the CRB Index, do they correlate with interest rates? This is always our acid test. You can judge for yourself by studying Figures 7.14 and 7.15. The bottom in bond yields in 1986 was very much influenced by rallies in both oil and metals. Conversely, tops in the metals and oil in mid-1987 preceded the top in bond yields by a few months. As 1989 ended, upward pressure in the metals and oils was able to check the decline in bond yields and began to pull bond yields higher.

FIGURE 7.14
TREASURY BOND YIELDS (BOTTOM CHART) VERSUS THE CRB PRECIOUS METALS FUTURES INDEX FROM 1985 TO 1989. SINCE PRECIOUS METALS ARE LEADING INDICATORS OF INFLATION, THEY HAVE AN IMPACT ON INTEREST RATE TRENDS. METALS PEAKED FIRST IN 1987 AND THEN BOTH MEASURES DROPPED UNTIL THE FOURTH QUARTER OF 1989.

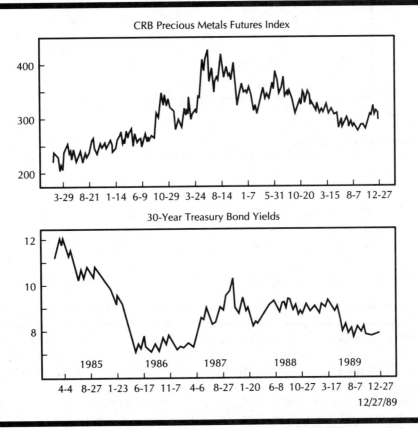

FIGURE 7.15

TREASURY BOND YIELDS (BOTTOM CHART) VERSUS THE CRB ENERGY FUTURES INDEX (UPPER CHART) FROM 1985 TO 1989. ENERGY PRICES ALSO INFLUENCE INTEREST RATE TRENDS. BOTH TURNED UP IN 1986. OIL PRICES TURNED DOWN FIRST IN 1987. A BULLISH BREAKOUT IN ENERGY PRICES IN LATE 1989 IS BEGINNING TO PULL INTEREST RATE YIELDS HIGHER.

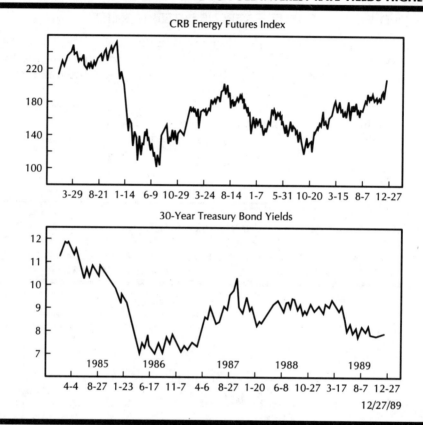

CRB Energy Futures Index

30-Year Treasury Bond Yields

12/27/89

The moral seems to be this: For longer-range intermarket analysis, the CRB Index is superior to either the metals or oil. However, there are short periods when either of these two markets, or both, will play a dominant role in the intermarket analysis. Therefore, it's necessary to monitor the gold and oil markets at all times.

COMMODITIES AND FED POLICY

A couple of years ago, then Treasury Secretary James Baker called for the use of a commodity basket, including gold, as an indicator to be used in formulating monetary policy. Fed Governors Wayne Angell and Robert Heller also suggested using commodity prices to fine-tune monetary policy. Studies performed by Mr. Angell and the Fed supported the predictive role of commodity prices in providing early warnings of inflation trends.

In February of 1988, Fed Vice Chairman Manuel Johnson confirmed in a speech at the Cato Institute's monetary conference that the Fed was paying more attention to fluctuations in the financial markets—specifically movements in the dollar, commodities, and interest rate differentials (the yield curve)—in setting monetary policy. A couple of weeks later, Fed Governor Angell added that movements in commodity prices had historically been a good guide to the rate of inflation, not just in the United States but globally as well.

Such admissions by the Fed Governors were significant for a number of reasons. The Fed recognized, in addition to the reliability of commodity markets as a leading indicator of inflation, the importance of the interplay between the various financial markets. The discounting mechanism of the markets was also given the mantle of respectability. The Fed seemed to be viewing the marketplace as the ultimate critic of monetary policy. Fed governors were learning to listen to the markets instead of blaming them. As added confirmation that some Fed members had become avid commodity watchers, the recorded minutes of several Fed meetings included reference to activity in the commodity markets.

Rising commodity prices are associated with an increase in inflation pressures and typically lead to Fed tightening. Falling commodity prices often precede an easier monetary policy. Sometimes activity in the commodity markets make it more difficult for the Fed to pursue its desired monetary goals. During the second half of 1989, the financial community was growing impatient with the Federal Reserve for not driving down interest rates faster to stave off a possible recession.

One of the factors that prevented a more aggressive Fed easing at the end of 1989 was the relative stability in the commodity price level and the fourth quarter rallies in the precious metals and oil markets (Figure 7.16). To make matters worse, an arctic cold snap in December of 1989 caused oil futures (especially heating oil) to skyrocket and raised fears that early 1990 would see a sharp uptick in the two most widely-watched inflation gauges, the Producer Price Index (PPI) and the Consumer Price Index (CPI). The reasons for those fears, and the main reason the Fed watches commodity prices so closely, is because sooner or later significant changes in the commodity price level translate into changes in the PPI and the CPI, which brings us to the final point in this discussion: The relationship between the CRB Index, the Producer Price Index, and the Consumer Price Index.

THE CRB INDEX VERSUS THE PPI AND THE CPI

Most observers look to popular inflation gauges like the Consumer Price Index (CPI) and the Producer Price Index (PPI) to track the inflation rate. The problem with these measures, at least from a trading standpoint, is that they are lagging indicators. The PPI measures 2700 prices at the producer level and is a measure of wholesale price trends. The CPI is constructed from 400 items, including retail prices for both goods and services, as well as some interest-related items (about one-half of the CPI is made up of the price of services and one-half of commodities). Both indexes are released monthly for the preceding month. (I'm referring in this discussion to the CPI-W, which is the Consumer Price Index for Urban Wage Earners and Clerical Workers.)

The CRB Index measures the current trading activity of 21 raw materials every 15 seconds. (A futures contract on the CRB Index was initiated in 1986 by the New York Futures Exchange, which also provides continuous updating of CRB Index futures prices.) Inasmuch as commodity markets measure prices at the earliest stage of production, it stands to reason that commodity prices represented in the CRB Index should lead wholesale prices which, in turn, should lead retail prices. The fact that CRB Index prices are available instantaneously on traders' terminal screens can also create an immediate impact on other markets.

FIGURE 7.16
A SURGE IN OIL PRICES DURING THE FOURTH QUARTER OF 1989, SIGNALING HIGHER IN-FLATION, HAD A BEARISH INFLUENCE ON BOND PRICES AND HELPED PUSH INTEREST RATE YIELDS HIGHER.

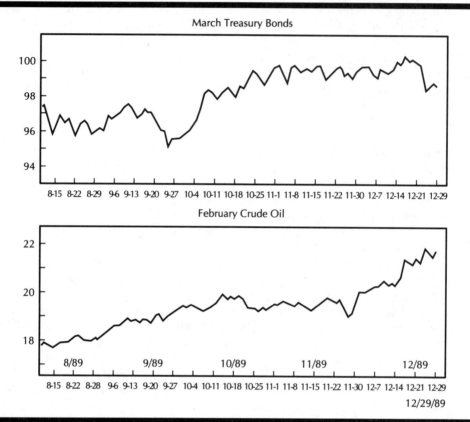

Reproduced with permission by Knight Ridder's Tradecenter. Tradecenter is a registered trademark of Knight Ridder's Financial Information.

Despite their different construction and composition, there is a strong statistical correlation between all three measures. Comparing annual rates of change for the CPI and the PPI against cash values of the CRB Index also reveals a close visual correlation (see Figures 7.17 and 7.18). The PPI is more volatile than the CPI and is the more sensitive of the two. The CRB, representing prices at the earliest stage of production, tracks the PPI more closely than it does the CPI. Over the ten years ending in 1987, the CRB showed a 71 percent correlation with the PPI and a 68 percent correlation with the CPI. During that same period, the CRB led turns in the PPI by one month on average and the CPI by eight months. (Source: *CRB Index White Paper: An Investigation Into Non-Traditional Trading Applications for CRB Index Futures*, New York Futures Exchange, 1988, prepared by Powers Research, Inc. Jersey City, NJ.)

From the early 1970s through the end of 1987, six major turning points were seen in the inflation rate, measured by annual rates of change in the CPI. The CRB Index led turns in the CPI four times out of the six with an average lead time of eight months. The two times when the CRB Index lagged turns in the CPI Index (1977 and

FIGURE 7.17
THE CRB FUTURES PRICE INDEX VERSUS ANNUAL RATES OF CHANGE FOR THE CONSUMER PRICE INDEX (CPI-W) AND THE PRODUCER PRICE INDEX (PPI) FROM 1971 TO 1987. (*SOURCE: CRB INDEX WHITE PAPER: AN INVESTIGATION INTO NON-TRADITIONAL TRADING APPLICATIONS FOR CRB INDEX FUTURES*, PREPARED BY POWERS RESEARCH, INC., 30 MONTGOMERY STREET, JERSEY CITY, NJ 07302, MARCH 1988.)

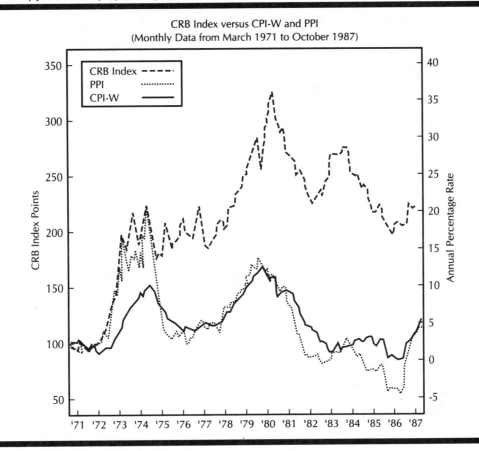

CRB Index versus CPI-W and PPI
(Monthly Data from March 1971 to October 1987)

Reproduced with permission of the New York Futures Exchange.

1980), the lag time averaged seven and a half months. The 1986 bottom in the CRB Index, which signaled the end of the disinflation of the early 1980s, led the upturn in the CPI by five months.

What these statistics, and the accompanying charts suggest, is that the CRB Index can be a useful guide in helping to anticipate changes in the PPI and CPI, often with a lead time of several months. Where the CRB Index lags behind the CPI (as happened in 1980 when the CRB peak occurred seven months after the downturn in the CPI), the commodity action can still be used as confirmation that a significant shift in the inflation trend has taken place. (Gold peaked in January of 1980, correctly signaling the major top in the CPI in March of that year and the CRB Index in November.) A rough guide used by some analysts is that a 10 percent move in the CRB Index is followed within six to eight months by a 1 percent move in the CPI in the same direction.

FIGURE 7.18

**A COMPARISON OF 12-MONTH RATES OF CHANGE BETWEEN THE CRB FUTURES PRICE INDEX
AND THE CONSUMER PRICE INDEX (CPI) FROM 1970 TO 1989. (*SOURCE:* CRB COMMODITY
YEAR BOOK 1990, COMMODITY RESEARCH BUREAU, 75 WALL STREET, NEW YORK, NY 10005.)**

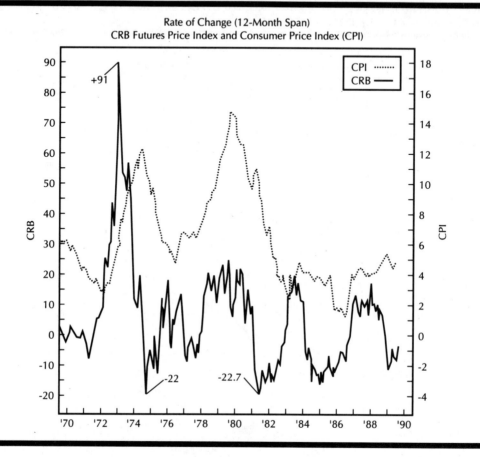

Rate of Change (12-Month Span)
CRB Futures Price Index and Consumer Price Index (CPI)

THE CRB, THE PPI, AND CPI VERSUS INTEREST RATES

The study cited earlier also shows why it's dangerous to rely on PPI and CPI numbers
to trade bonds. The same study suggests that the CRB Index is a superior indicator
of interest rate movements. In the 15 years from 1973 to 1987, the CRB Index showed
an 80 percent correlation with ten-year Treasury yields, while the PPI and CPI had
correlations of 70 percent and 57 percent, respectively. From 1982 to 1987, the CRB
had a correlation with Treasury yields of 90 percent, whereas the PPI and CPI had
correlations with interest rates of 64 percent and −67 percent, respectively. (In previous chapters, the strong *negative* correlation of the CRB Index to Treasury bond
prices was discussed.)

    In every instance, correlations between the CRB Index and constant yields to
maturity on ten-year Treasury securities are consistently higher than either of the
other two inflation measures. Bond traders seem to pay more attention to the CRB
Index, which provides instant inflation readings on a minute-by-minute basis, and
less attention to the PPI and CPI figures which, by the time they're released on a
monthly basis, represent numbers which are several months old.

SUMMARY

This chapter took a close look at the various commodity indexes. We compared the CRB *Futures* Index to the CRB *Spot* Index, and showed that the CRB Spot Index can be further subdivided into the *Spot Raw Industrials* and the *Spot Foodstuff* Indexes. Although the CRB Spot Index is more influenced by the Raw Industrials, the CRB Index has a closer correlation with the Foodstuffs. We compared the *Journal of Commerce (JOC) Index*, which is comprised solely of industrial prices, to the more balanced CRB Futures Index, and showed that the latter Index correlates better with interest rates. We discussed why it's dangerous to exclude food prices completely from the inflation picture. Although it's important to keep an eye on all commodity indexes, it's also necessary to know the composition of each.

The nine CRB Futures sub-groups were considered as another way to monitor the various market sectors and to make intermarket comparisons. Special attention should be paid to the *grain, metals,* and *oil* sectors when analyzing the CRB Index. *Metals* and *oil* prices are also important in their own right and often play a dominant role in intermarket analysis.

The Federal Reserve Board keeps a close watch on commodity price trends while formulating monetary policy. This is because significant price trends in the commodity price level eventually have an impact on the Producer Price Index (PPI) and the Consumer Price Index (CPI).

8

International Markets

The chapters on the intermarket field have concentrated so far on the domestic picture. We've examined the interrelationships between the four principal financial sectors—currencies, commodities, interest rates, and equities. The purpose was to show that the trader should always look beyond his particular area of interest. Since each of the four financial sectors is tied to the other three, a complete technical analysis of any one sector should include analysis of the other three. The goal is to consider the broader environment in which a particular market is involved. Let's carry the intermarket approach a step further and add an international dimension to the analysis.

The primary goal in this chapter will be to put the U.S. stock market into a global perspective. This will be accomplished by including as part of the technical analysis of the U.S. market an analysis of the other two largest world markets, the British and Japanese stock markets. I'll show how following the overseas markets can provide valuable insights into the U.S. stock market and why it's necessary to know what's happening overseas.

How global inflation and interest rate trends impact on world equity markets will be considered. By comparing these three world economic measures, the same principles of intermarket analysis that have been used on a domestic level can be applied on a global scale. I'll show why these global intermarket comparisons suggested that the world stock markets entered the 1990s on very shaky ground.

The world's second largest equity market is located in Japan. Going into 1990, intermarket analysis in that country showed a weakening currency and rising inflation. Monetary tightening to combat inflation pushed interest rates higher and bond prices lower—a potentially lethal combination for the Japanese stock market. I'll show how an intermarket analysis of the Japanese situation held bearish implications for the Japanese stock market and the potentially negative implications that analysis carried for the U.S. stock market.

WORLD STOCK MARKETS

Figures 8.1 through 8.5 compare the world's three largest stock markets—United States, Japan, and Britain—in the five-year period from 1985 through the end of 1989. The main purpose of the charts, which overlay all three markets together, is simply to show that global markets generally trend in the same direction. This shouldn't come as a surprise to anyone. On a domestic level, individual stocks are influenced by bull and bear markets in the stock market as a whole. Not all stocks go up or down at the same speed or even at exactly the same time, but all are influenced by the overriding trend of the market. The same is true on an international level. The world experiences *global* bull and bear markets.

Although the stock markets of individual countries may not rise or fall at exactly the same speed or time, all are influenced by the global trend. A stock investor in the United States wouldn't consider buying an individual stock without first determining the direction of the U.S. stock market as a whole. In the same way, an analysis of the U.S. stock market wouldn't be complete without determining whether the global equity trend is in a bullish or bearish mode. (It's worth noting here that global trends are also present for interest rates and inflation.)

Figure 8.1 shows the generally bullish trend from 1985 through the end of 1989, with the downward interruption in all three markets in the fall of 1987. Figure 8.2

FIGURE 8.1
A COMPARISON OF THE JAPANESE, AMERICAN, AND BRITISH STOCK MARKETS FROM 1985 THROUGH 1989.

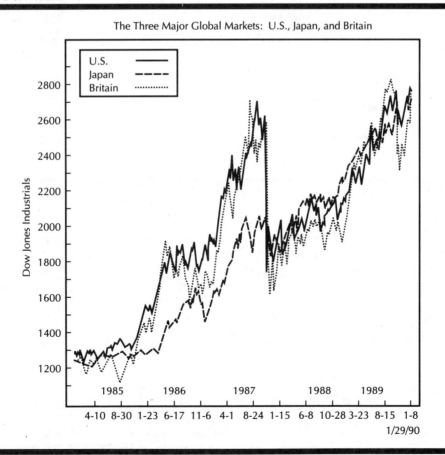

The Three Major Global Markets: U.S., Japan, and Britain

FIGURE 8.2

THE WORLD'S THREE LARGEST STOCK MARKETS RESUMED UPTRENDS TOGETHER IN EARLY 1987 AND COLLAPSED TOGETHER IN THE FALL OF THE SAME YEAR.

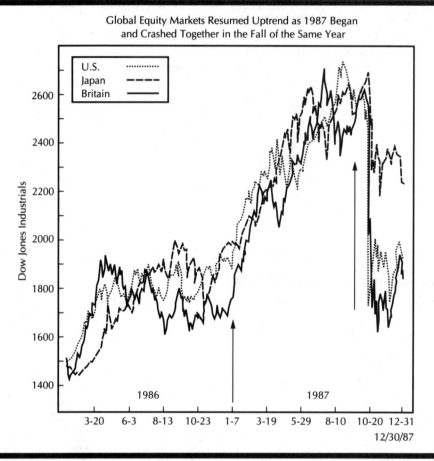

Global Equity Markets Resumed Uptrend as 1987 Began and Crashed Together in the Fall of the Same Year

focuses on the events of 1986 and 1987. As 1987 began, all three markets were completing a period of consolidation and resuming their major bull trends. In the second half of 1987, all three markets underwent serious downside corrections. Figure 8.3 focuses on the 1987 top in the global markets and holds two important messages:

- All three equity markets collapsed in 1987.
- Britain peaked first, while Japan peaked last.

THE GLOBAL COLLAPSE OF 1987

The first important message is that all world markets experienced severe selloffs in the second half of 1987. When events in the United States are examined on a global perspective, one can see that the U.S. experience was only one part of a much bigger picture. The preoccupation with such things as *program trading* as the primary cause of the U.S. selloff becomes harder to justify as an adequate explanation. If *program trading* caused the U.S. selloff, how do we explain the collapse in the other world

FIGURE 8.3
AT THE 1987 PEAK, THE BRITISH STOCK MARKET PEAKED IN JULY, THE AMERICAN MARKET IN AUGUST, AND THE JAPANESE STOCK MARKET IN OCTOBER. BRITAIN HAS HAD A LONG HISTORY OF LEADING THE U.S. MARKET AT PEAKS.

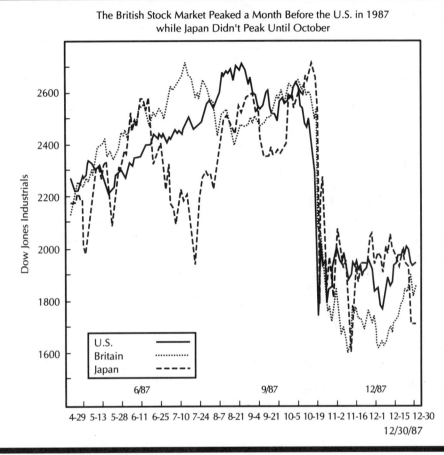

The British Stock Market Peaked a Month Before the U.S. in 1987
while Japan Didn't Peak Until October

markets that didn't have *program trading* at the time? Clearly, there were and are much larger economic forces at work on the world stage. In Chapter 14, I'll have more to say about *program trading*.

The second message is the chronological sequence of the three tops. The British stock market peaked in July of 1987, a full month prior to the U.S. peak which occurred in August. The British market has a tendency to lead the U.S. market at peaks. (In the fall of 1989, the British stock market started to drop at least a month prior to a severe selloff in U.S. stocks in mid-October. Sixty years earlier, the 1929 collapse in the U.S. market was foreshadowed by a peak in the British stock market *a full year earlier.*) In 1987, the Japanese market didn't hit its peak until October, when the more serious global collapse actually took place.

Figure 8.4 shows the Japanese market leading the world markets upward from their late 1987 bottoms. Figure 8.5 shows that the global markets again corrected downward in October 1989. After a global rally that lasted into the end of that year, the new decade of the 1990s was greeted by signs that global stocks might be rolling over to the downside once again.

FIGURE 8.4
**A COMPARISON OF THE THREE STOCK MARKETS FOLLOWING THE 1987 GLOBAL COLLAPSE.
THE JAPANESE MARKET RECOVERED FIRST AND PROVIDED MUCH-NEEDED STABILITY TO
WORLD STOCK MARKETS.**

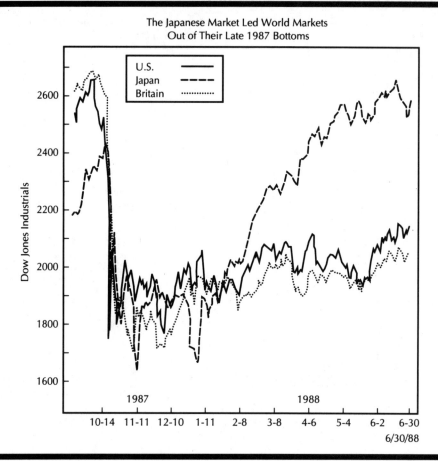

The Japanese Market Led World Markets
Out of Their Late 1987 Bottoms

FIGURE 8.5
ALL MARKETS SUFFERED A MINI-CRASH IN OCTOBER 1989 AND THEN RECOVERED INTO YEAREND. THE BRITISH MARKET STARTED TO DROP SHARPLY IN SEPTEMBER, LEADING THE U.S. DROP BY ABOUT A MONTH. THE FOURTH-QUARTER RECOVERY INTO NEW HIGHS IN JAPAN BOUGHT GLOBAL BULL MARKETS SOME ADDITIONAL TIME. ALL MARKETS ARE START-ING TO WEAKEN AS 1990 IS BEGINNING.

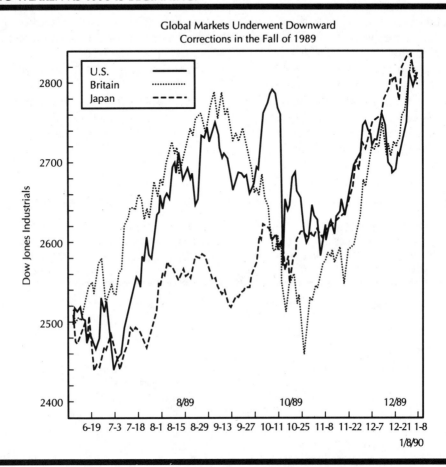

Global Markets Underwent Downward
Corrections in the Fall of 1989

BRITISH AND U.S. STOCK MARKETS

Figures 8.6 through 8.10 provide a visual comparison of the British and the U.S. stock markets from 1985 into the beginning of 1990. Although the charts are not exactly alike, there is a strong visual correlation. Given their strong historical ties, it can be seen why it's a good idea to keep an eye on both. As is often the case with intermarket comparisons, clues to one market's direction can often be found by studying the chart of a related market. I've already alluded to the tendency of the British market to lead the U.S. stock market at tops. In Figure 8.6, three examples of this phenomenon can be seen in the three peaks that took place in early 1986, late 1987, and late 1989. (Going back a bit further in time, U.S. stock market peaks in 1929, 1956, 1961, 1966, 1972, and 1976 were preceded by tops in British stocks.)

Figure 8.7 compares the British and American markets during 1986. The peak in the British market in the spring of 1986, and its ensuing correction, coincided with a period of consolidation in the U.S. market. The breaking of a major down trendline by the British market in December of that year correctly signaled resumption of the American uptrend shortly thereafter.

FIGURE 8.6

A COMPARISON OF THE BRITISH AND AMERICAN STOCK MARKETS FROM 1985 THROUGH 1989. SINCE BOTH MARKETS DISPLAY STRONG HISTORICAL CORRELATION, THEY SHOULD BE MONITORED FOR SIGNS OF CONFIRMATION OR DIVERGENCE. THE BRITISH MARKET LED THE U.S. MARKET AT THE LAST THREE IMPORTANT PEAKS IN 1986, 1987, AND 1989.

1/8/90

FIGURE 8.7
A COMPARISON OF THE BRITISH AND AMERICAN STOCK MARKETS DURING 1986. THE BRITISH PEAK IN THE SPRING OF 1986 AND ITS UPSIDE BREAKOUT IN DECEMBER OF THE SAME YEAR COINCIDED WITH A MAJOR CONSOLIDATION PERIOD IN AMERICAN EQUITIES.

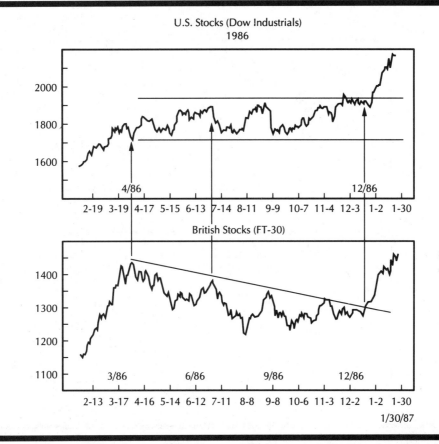

Figure 8.8 shows the British market hitting its peak in July of 1987, preceding the American top by a month. In the fourth quarter of that year, the British market completed a "double bottom" reversal pattern, which provided an early signal that the global equity collapse had run its course. Figure 8.9 shows both markets undergoing consolidation patterns before resuming their uptrends together in January of 1989.

Figure 8.10 shows the value of market comparisons and the use of divergence analysis. The British *Financial Times Stock Exchange 100 share index (FTSE)* peaked in mid-September of 1989 and started to drop sharply. The American *Dow Jones Industrial Average* actually set a new high in early October. Any technical analyst who spotted the serious divergence between these two global stock indexes should have known that something was seriously wrong and shouldn't have been too surprised at the mini-crash that occurred in New York on October 13, 1989. Figure 8.10 also shows that the rebound in the American market that carried to yearend in 1989 also began with the upside penetration of a down trendline in the British market. Both markets ended the decade on an upswing.

FIGURE 8.8
A COMPARISON OF THE BRITISH AND AMERICAN STOCK MARKETS DURING 1987. THE BRITISH MARKET PEAKED A MONTH BEFORE AMERICAN STOCKS IN THE SUMMER OF 1987 AND COMPLETED A *DOUBLE BOTTOM REVERSAL PATTERN* AS 1987 CAME TO AN END.

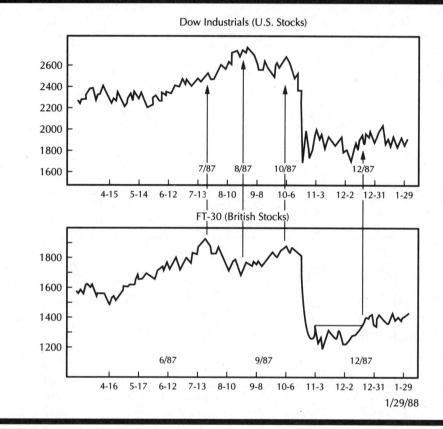

FIGURE 8.9
A COMPARISON OF THE BRITISH AND AMERICAN STOCK MARKETS IN 1988 AND EARLY 1989. AFTER CONSOLIDATING SIMULTANEOUSLY THROUGH THE SECOND HALF OF 1988, BOTH MARKETS RESUMED THEIR MAJOR BULL TRENDS AS 1989 BEGAN.

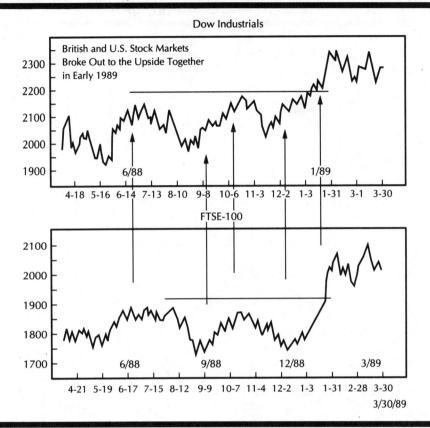

FIGURE 8.10

A COMPARISON OF THE BRITISH AND AMERICAN STOCK MARKETS DURING 1989 AND EARLY 1990. THE MINI-COLLAPSE IN U.S. STOCKS DURING OCTOBER 1989 WAS FORESHADOWED A MONTH EARLIER BY A FALLING BRITISH MARKET. AFTER RALLYING INTO YEAREND, BOTH MARKETS HAVE BROKEN UP TRENDLINES IN THE NEW DECADE.

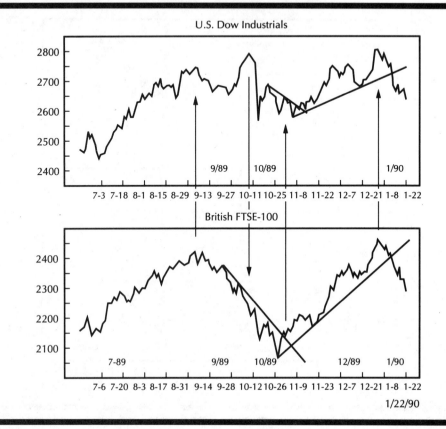

U.S. AND JAPANESE STOCK MARKETS

Figure 8.11 through 8.15 provide a comparison of the American market (utilizing the *Dow Jones Industrial Average*) and the Japanese market (utilizing the *Nikkei 225 Stock Average*). The fit between these two markets isn't as tight as that between the American and British markets. Still, there's no question that they have an impact on one another. Figure 8.11 demonstrates the global bull market from 1985 through 1989 as reflected in the world's two largest stock markets.

In late 1986, the Japanese market underwent a downward correction while the U.S. market was consolidating (Figure 8.12). In the fourth quarter of that year, the Nikkei 225 Average broke a down trendline in early November and began another upward climb. The alert American chartist might have taken that bullish signal in the Japanese market as an early warning of more upward movement in American shares.

We've already mentioned the fact that the American market peaked in August of 1987, two months prior to the peak in Japan. Figure 8.13 shows, however, that the real

FIGURE 8.11
A COMPARISON OF THE JAPANESE AND AMERICAN STOCK MARKETS FROM 1985 THROUGH 1989. ALTHOUGH THE FIT BETWEEN THESE TWO MARKETS ISN'T AS TIGHT AS THAT BETWEEN THE AMERICAN AND BRITISH MARKETS, THE AMERICAN MARKET IS VERY MUCH INFLUENCED BY MARKET TRENDS IN JAPAN.

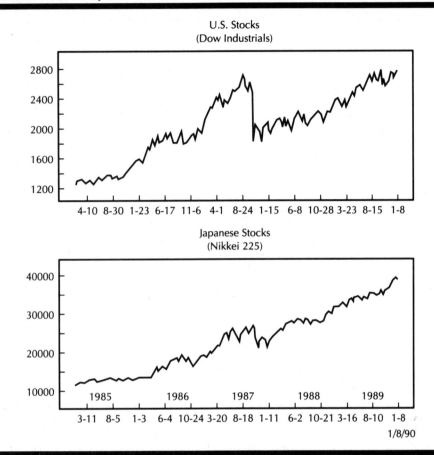

global collapse began after the Japanese market began to roll over to the downside in October of that year. This same chart shows the Nikkei 225 Average completing a major "double bottom" in February of 1988. This major "buy" signal in Japan turned out to be an excellent early indication that the global uptrend was in the process of resuming following the late-1987 collapse. Figure 8.14 shows an upside breakout in Japanese stocks in November of 1988, leading a similar bullish breakout in the States almost two months later.

Figure 8.15 compares events in the United States and Japan in 1989. Both markets hit peaks in October and then stabilized. The events of that month show how aware the world had become of global linkages. The Dow Jones Industrial plunged almost 200 points on Friday, October 13th. The world watched through the weekend to see how Japan would open on Monday morning (Sunday evening in New York). The fear was that continued weakness in Japan could start a worldwide selling panic. Fortunately, the market stabilized in Japan. The ensuing Japanese rally calmed worldwide jitters and helped spark a global bounce that carried to yearend.

FIGURE 8.12
IN THE FOURTH QUARTER OF 1986, THE JAPANESE STOCK MARKET (REPRESENTED BY THE NIKKEI 225 STOCK AVERAGE) ENDED ITS CORRECTION AND PROVIDED AN EARLY WARNING THAT THE AMERICAN UPTREND WAS ABOUT TO RESUME.

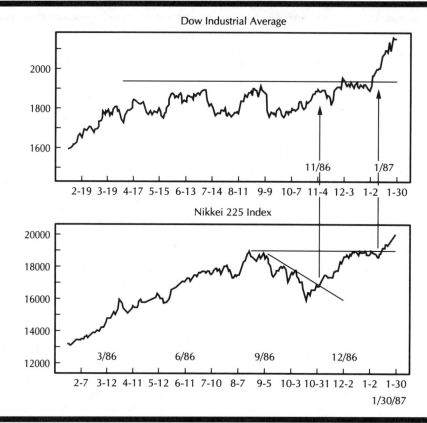

In mid-November of 1989, the Japanese market reached a crucial barrier, which was the peak set two months earlier. A failure at that important resistance level would carry bearish implications on a global scale. Figure 8.15 shows that the bullish breakout into new highs by the Nikkei 225 Average in late November coincided exactly with an upside breakout in the American market, which carried the Dow Jones Industrial Average all the way to a retest of its October highs. The ability of the Japanese market to rally to new high ground bought the global bull market some additional time.

While the Japanese stock market was resuming its bull trend, developments in other sectors of the Japanese market were sending danger signals as 1989 ended. The yen was weakening, inflation in Japan was rising (largely owing to the jump in oil prices), interest rates were rising, and Japanese bond prices were weakening. From an intermarket perspective, things were beginning to look dangerous for Japanese equities.

Figure 8.16 divides the Japanese markets into the four sectors utilized for intermarket analysis—currencies, commodities, bonds, and stocks. The chart on the upper

FIGURE 8.13
THE JAPANESE STOCK MARKET DIDN'T PEAK UNTIL OCTOBER OF 1987 (TWO MONTHS AFTER THE U.S. MARKET HIT ITS HIGH). HOWEVER, THE SELLOFF IN JAPAN COINCIDED WITH THE GLOBAL SELLING PANIC THAT ENSUED. AS 1988 BEGAN, THE NIKKEI 225 STOCK AVERAGE COMPLETED A MAJOR *DOUBLE BOTTOM* AND POINTED THE WAY HIGHER FOR THE REST OF THE GLOBAL MARKETS.

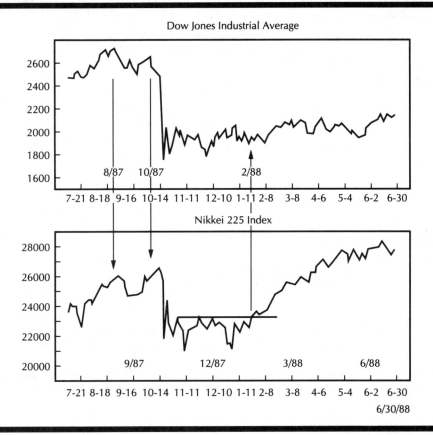

left shows the Japanese yen weakening relative to the U.S. dollar as 1990 began. Weakness in the yen helped boost inflation pressures in Japan. To make matters worse, an upward spike in oil prices (lower left) as 1989 ended intensified fears of Japanese inflation. In an effort to control inflation and help stabilize the yen, Japanese interest rates were raised. (Japanese central bankers had raised their discount rate three times in succession, activating the "three-steps-and-a-stumble" rule, which was discussed in Chapter 4). The chart on the lower right shows a dramatic plunge in the price of Japanese bonds. The collapse in Japanese bonds in January of 1990 began to pull Japanese stocks lower (upper right).

The Japanese market dropped in eight of the first eleven trading days of the new decade, losing 5 percent of its value. In just over two weeks, the Nikkei 225 Average gave back about a third of the previous year's gains. The yield on the ten-year government bond soared to its highest level since November 1985. Japanese inflation

FIGURE 8.14
A BULLISH BREAKOUT BY THE NIKKEI 225 IN NOVEMBER OF 1988 OCCURRED TWO MONTHS BEFORE THE AMERICAN MARKET RESUMED ITS UPTREND IN JANUARY OF 1989.

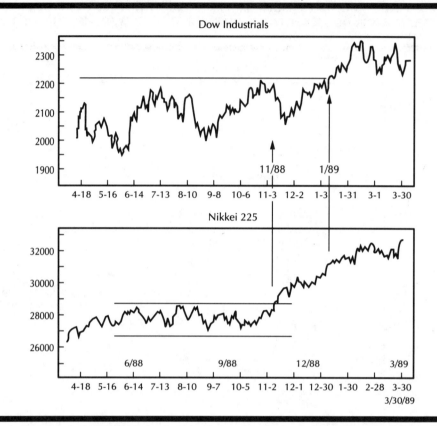

FIGURE 8.15
THE JAPANESE AND AMERICAN MARKETS CORRECTED DOWNWARD TOGETHER IN OCTOBER 1989. HOWEVER, STABILITY IN JAPAN PREVENTED ADDITIONAL GLOBAL WEAKNESS. THE SETTING OF NEW HIGHS IN JAPAN IN NOVEMBER OF 1989 BOUGHT THE GLOBAL BULL MARKETS SOME ADDITIONAL TIME. BOTH MARKETS ARE DROPPING TOGETHER AS 1990 IS BEGINNING.

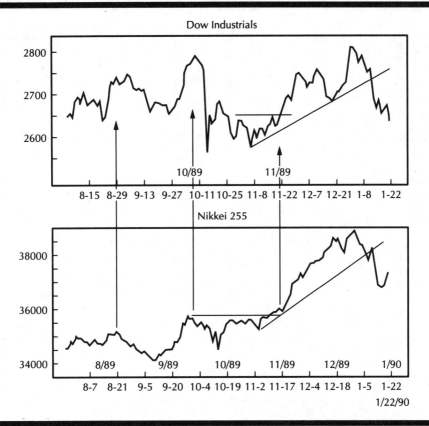

FIGURE 8.16

THE FOUR MARKET SECTORS IN JAPAN — THE JAPANESE YEN (UPPER LEFT), CRUDE OIL (LOWER LEFT), JAPANESE BONDS (LOWER RIGHT), AND THE NIKKEI 225 STOCK AVERAGE (UPPER RIGHT). AS 1989 ENDED, THE WEAKER YEN AND HIGHER OIL PRICES RAISED INFLATION FEARS IN JAPAN. HIGHER INTEREST RATES TO COMBAT INFLATION ARE PUSHING BOND PRICES LOWER WHICH, IN TURN, ARE HAVING A BEARISH IMPACT ON JAPANESE EQUITIES.

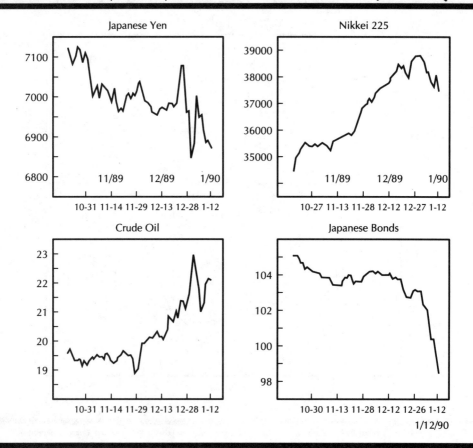

had risen to 3 percent, which is low by our standards but higher than the Japanese government's target of 2 percent. Besides its weakness relative to the U.S. dollar, the Japanese yen had lost 15 percent against the West German mark in the previous three months. The combined affect of these bearish intermarket factors weighed heavily on the Japanese market. On Friday, January 12, 1990, the Nikkei 225 slid 653 points for its eighth worst performance ever. This bearish action in Tokyo stocks, caused mainly by the collapsing Japanese bond market, sent bearish ripples across the globe (Figure 8.17.)

In London that same day, the FTSE-100 (pronounced Footsie) lost 37.8 points, its largest loss in two months. In New York, the Dow Industrials tumbled over 71 points. In addition to the bearish overseas action that Friday morning, the New York market had troubles of its own. The producer price index for December was 0.7 percent, which pushed the U.S. wholesale inflation rate for 1989 up to 4.8 percent, the highest inflation number since 1981. The major culprit behind the surge in the

FIGURE 8.17

THE COLLAPSE IN JAPANESE BONDS (UPPER LEFT) AS 1990 BEGINS IS PULLING JAPANESE STOCKS DOWN (LOWER LEFT) WHICH, IN TURN, IS SENDING BEARISH RIPPLES THROUGH LONDON (LOWER RIGHT) AND NEW YORK (UPPER RIGHT) STOCK MARKETS.

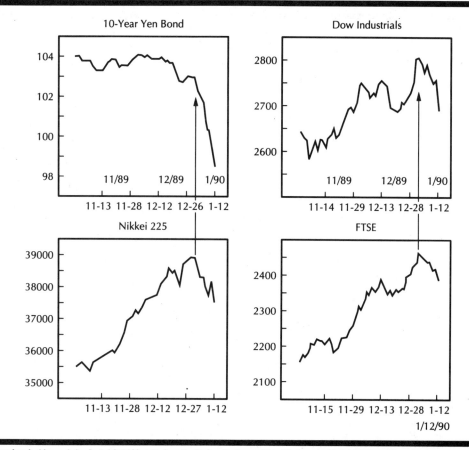

U.S. inflation rate was the upward spike in the price of oil the previous month. It seemed clear that the world markets were struggling with two major themes as the 1990s began—accelerating inflation and higher interest rates—both factors holding potentially bearish implications for global equities.

GLOBAL INTEREST RATES

Figure 8.18 compares the bond prices for the United States, Japan, and Britain for the last three months of 1989 and the first two weeks of 1990. All three bond markets are weakening together. Japanese bond *prices* are relatively higher than both the United States and Britain (meaning Japanese *yields* are lower than the United States and Britain) but are quickly trying to narrow the spread. British bond prices are lower than the other two (meaning British bond *yields* are actually higher than the United States and Japan). Figure 8.19 shows that British bonds had already been dropping for some time and revealed a bearish divergence with U.S. bonds.

FIGURE 8.18
A COMPARISON OF JAPANESE, AMERICAN, AND BRITISH BOND MARKETS. ALL THREE ARE DROPPING TOGETHER AS 1989 ENDS AND 1990 BEGINS. WEAKNESS ABROAD IS HAVING A BEARISH IMPACT ON U.S. TREASURY BONDS. IT'S IMPORTANT TO WATCH GLOBAL TRENDS WHEN ANALYZING THE U.S. BOND MARKET.

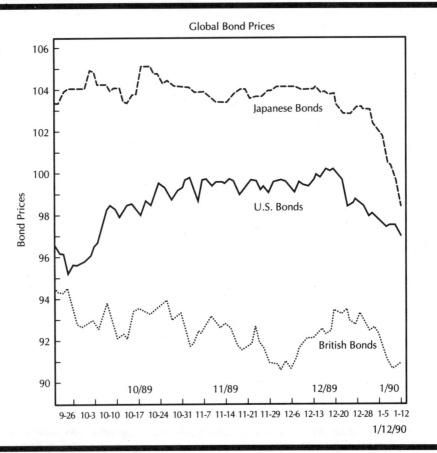

Global Bond Prices

An examination of world interest rates showed a rising global trend. As a result, world bond *prices* were coming under additional downward pressure. The U.S. bond market appeared to be out of line with other global bond markets. As the new decade began, the sharp drop in global bond prices finally began to pull U.S. bond prices lower.

The U.S. Treasury bond market was fighting a losing battle on many fronts at the start of 1990. Internationally, U.S. bond prices were trying to buck a global trend toward falling bond prices. Domestically, the bond market was struggling with rising inflation (commodity markets had recently set a six-month high) and a falling dollar. In the previous section, we showed the value of watching global stock market trends for insight into the U.S. market. The same lesson holds true for bonds. It's important to watch global bond markets for clues to the U.S. bond market. As important as the domestic U.S. markets are, they don't operate in a vacuum.

FIGURE 8.19
BRITISH BONDS HAVE BEEN DROPPING THROUGH MOST OF 1989 (BECAUSE OF HIGHER BRITISH INFLATION) AND ARE SHOWING A BEARISH DIVERGENCE WITH AMERICAN TREASURY BONDS AT THE BEGINNING OF 1990. THE WEAKER BRITISH BOND MARKET IS PULLING U.S. BONDS LOWER. TECHNICAL ANALYSIS OF U.S. BONDS SHOULD INCLUDE TECHNICAL ANALYSIS OF FOREIGN BOND MARKETS.

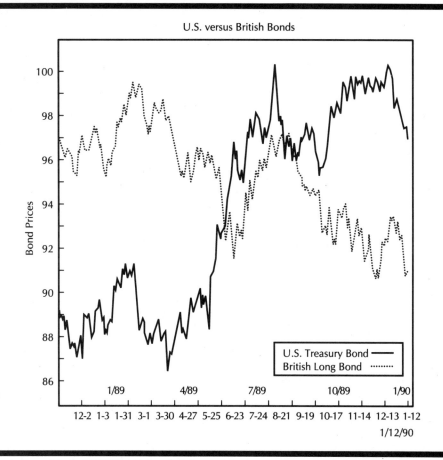

U.S. versus British Bonds

Bond Prices

U.S. Treasury Bond ———
British Long Bond ·········

12-2 1-3 1-31 3-1 3-30 4-27 5-25 6-23 7-24 8-21 9-19 10-17 11-14 12-13 1-12

1/12/90

GLOBAL BONDS AND GLOBAL INFLATION

Figure 8.20 shows the interplay between U.S. and Japanese bond prices (two charts on the left) and the U.S. and Japanese stock markets (two charts on the right) during the fourth quarter of 1989 and the first two weeks of 1990. It can be seen that intermarket comparisons can be applied on many different levels. Compare global stock prices to one another. Notice both stock markets beginning to weaken. Then compare global bond prices to one another. Notice both bond markets beginning to weaken. Compare bonds to stocks both on a global and on a domestic level. If we accept that U.S. stock prices are influenced by U.S. bond prices, then what influences U.S. bond prices becomes very important. If world bond prices are showing signs of moving lower, chances are U.S. bond prices will follow. Technical analysis of global bond trends becomes a part of the analysis of the U.S. bond market.

FIGURE 8.20

AMERICAN STOCKS (LOWER RIGHT) ARE BEING PULLED DOWNWARD BY JAPANESE STOCKS (UPPER RIGHT) AND A WEAKER U.S. BOND MARKET (LOWER LEFT) BOTH OF WHICH ARE BEING PULLED LOWER BY JAPANESE BONDS (UPPER LEFT) AT THE START OF 1990.

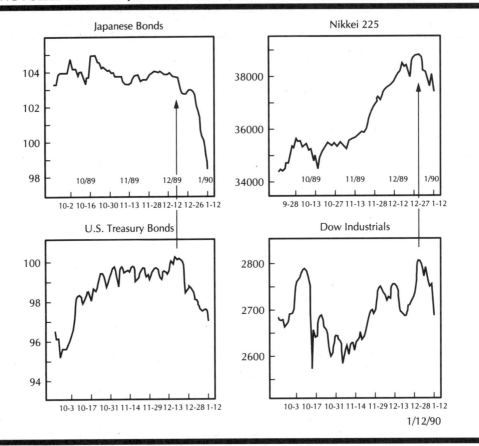

1/12/90

U.S. stock prices are influenced in two ways by global markets. First, by a direct comparison with overseas stock markets, such as Britain and Japan (which are influenced by their own domestic bond markets). And second, by U.S. bond prices which are themselves influenced by global bond markets. Discussion of the bond market and global interest rates naturally leads to the question of global inflation.

It's important to keep an eye on world inflation trends. This is true for two reasons. Inflation rates in the major industrialized countries usually trend in the same direction. Some turn a little ahead of others, and some are laggards. Some rise or fall faster than others. But, sooner or later, each country falls into line and joins the global trend. Global inflation peaked as the 1980s began. Japan, the United States, and Italy peaked in early 1980. Britain's inflation rate peaked a few months earlier, in late 1979. Canada, France, and West Germany turned down in 1981. Six years later, in 1986, global inflation began to creep higher again. Inflation bottomed during that year in the U.S., Japan, West Germany, France, Britain, and Italy (see Figure 8.21).

Since all countries are influenced by global inflation trends, it's important to monitor what's happening around the globe to get a better fix on the inflation trend

FIGURE 8.21
A COMPARISON OF GLOBAL INFLATION RATES FROM 1977 THROUGH 1989. (CHART COURTESY OF *BUSINESS CONDITIONS DIGEST*, U.S. DEPARTMENT OF COMMERCE, BUREAU OF ECONOMIC ANALYSIS, DECEMBER 1989.)

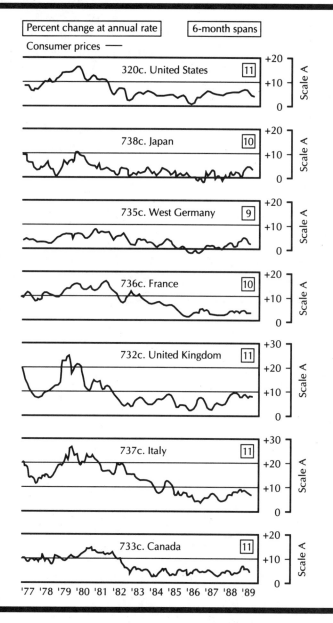

in each individual country. If one country gets out of line with the others, it's only a matter of time before it gets back into line. The second reason it's so important to monitor inflation around the world is because the direction of inflation ultimately determines the direction of interest rates, which is critical to bond and stock market forecasting and trading. As you might suspect, in order to anticipate global inflation trends, it's important to study movements in world commodity markets.

GLOBAL INTERMARKET INDEXES

Figure 8.22 (courtesy of the *Pring Market Review*, P.O. Box 329, Washington, CT 06794) compares three global measures—World Short Rates (plotted inversely), the World Stock Index (calculated by Morgan Stanley Capital International, Geneva) and the Economist Commodity Index. This type of chart allows for intermarket comparisons of these three vital sectors on a global scale. The world money market rates are plotted inversely to make them move in the same direction as money market prices.

When world money market prices are rising (meaning short-term rates are falling), this is bullish for global stocks. When world money market prices are falling (meaning short-term rates are rising), it is considered bearish for global stocks. *Money market prices usually lead stock prices at major turning points.* As the chart shows, the global bull market in stocks that began in 1982 was supported by rising money market prices. However, since 1987 global stock prices have risen to new highs, while money

---

FIGURE 8.22
THIS CHART COMPARES WORLD SHORT RATES (PLOTTED INVERSELY), THE MORGAN STANLEY CAPITAL INTERNATIONAL WORLD STOCK INDEX (MIDDLE LINE), AND THE ECONOMIST COMMODITY PRICE INDEX (BOTTOM LINE). INTERMARKET ANALYSIS CAN BE PERFORMED ON A GLOBAL SCALE. (CHART COURTESY OF *PRING MARKET REVIEW*, PUBLISHED BY THE INTERNATIONAL INSTITUTE FOR ECONOMIC RESEARCH, P.O. BOX 329, WASHINGTON, CT 06794.)

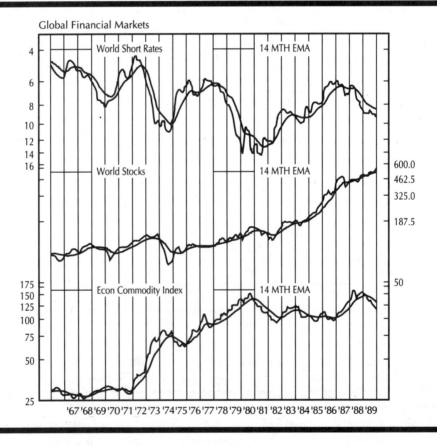

market prices have been dropping. This divergence, if it continues, holds bearish implications for global stock prices.

The lines in Figure 8.22 that accompany each index are 14-month exponential moving averages. Major turning points are signalled when an index crosses above or below its moving average line or when the moving average line itself changes direction. As 1989 ended, the chart shows stocks in a bullish moving average alignment, while money market prices are bearish—a dangerous combination. The chart also shows the generally inverse relationship between the two upper lines, representing world financial markets, and the lower line, representing global commodity price trends, which is the *Economist Commodity Price Index*.

THE ECONOMIST COMMODITY PRICE INDEX

For analysis of commodity price trends on a global scale, the most useful index to watch is the Economist Commodity Price Index (published by *The Economist* magazine, P.O. Box 58524, Boulder, CO 80322). This index is comprised of 27 commodity markets and is about equally weighted between food (49.8%) and industrial prices (50.2%). The commodities are assigned different weightings, which are determined by imports into the European market in the 1984–1986 period.

The markets with the heaviest weightings are copper, aluminum, cotton, timber, coffee, and the soybean complex. The composite index is subdivided into foods and industrials. The industrials portion is further subdivided into metals and non-food agriculturals. The index uses a base year of 1985 = 100. *The Economist Commodity Price Index does not include any precious metals (gold, platinum, and silver); nor does it include any oil markets.* The exclusion of those two markets may help explain the bearish position of the Economist Index in 1989.

Figure 8.22 shows that as 1989 ended, the global commodity index is dropping along with money market prices (rising short-term rates). This is an unusual alignment, given the historical inverse relationship between those two barometers. As the chart shows, when commodity prices are falling, world money prices are generally rising. How do we explain the discrepancy in 1989? The inflation scare that gripped the global markets as 1989 ended and 1990 began was centered around the strong rally in the world price of gold (which is a leading indicator of inflation) and the sharp global advance in the price of oil.

Weakness in the Economist Commodity Index in late 1989 might be partially explained by its exclusion of gold and oil prices from its composition. This brings us back to a point made in Chapter 7, namely, that it's always a good idea to keep an eye on what gold and oil are doing. The jump in those two widely-watched commodity markets as 1989 ended sent inflation jitters around the globe and caused global tightening by central bankers.

To add to the inflation concerns, the British inflation rate for 1989 was 7.8 percent, up from 4.9 percent the previous year, while the Japanese wholesale inflation rate for 1989 showed its first advance in 7 years. In the United States, it was reported in early January 1990, that the U.S. inflation rate for 1989 had risen to 4.6 percent, its highest level in eight years, with an even higher wholesale inflation rate of 4.8 percent. The British government had already raised the base interest rate from 7.5 percent to 15 percent from mid-1988 to October of 1989. There was fear that another rate hike was in the offing. Japanese central bankers had raised interest rates three times since the previous May. There was talk of more tightening in Tokyo as the yen weakened and inflation intensified.

That bad news on the inflation front as the new decade began postponed any additional monetary easing by the U.S. Federal Reserve Board, at least for the time being. In mid-January of 1990, Fed Vice Chairman Manuel Johnson and Fed Governor Wayne Angell, both of whom were mentioned in the previous chapter, stated that any further Fed easing would be put on hold. Wayne Angell specifically mentioned the need for commodity prices to start dropping as a requirement for further Fed easing. Advances in key commodity markets had heightened fears of a global shift to higher inflation and were clearly influencing monetary decisions made by central bankers around the world, including our own Federal Reserve Board. Figures 8.23 and 8.24 show the upward pressure on global interest rates as the new decade began. Figure 8.25 reveals a strong visual correlation between global equity markets, many of which were setting new highs as 1989 ended.

SUMMARY

This chapter extended our intermarket analysis to the international realm. It showed that trends in commodity prices (inflation), interest rates, and stocks are visible on

FIGURE 8.23
FOREIGN SHORT RATES HAVE BEEN RISING AROUND THE GLOBE SINCE 1988 BUT STARTED TO ACCELERATE UPWARD IN JAPAN IN 1989. (CHART COURTESY *PRING MARKET REVIEW*.)

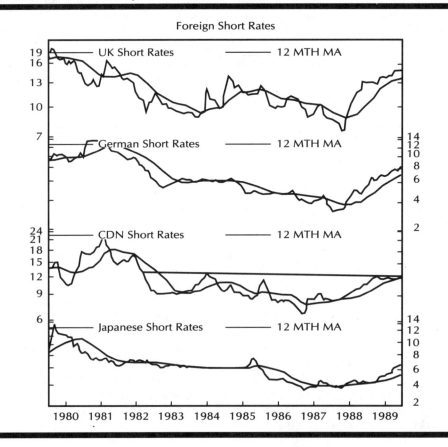

FIGURE 8.24
GLOBAL BOND YIELDS ARE TRENDING HIGHER IN 1989, LED BY GERMAN RATES. BRITISH AND JAPANESE YIELDS ARE JUST BREAKING OUT FROM BASING PATTERNS. RISING GLOBAL RATES EVENTUALLY PULL AMERICAN RATES HIGHER. (CHART COURTESY OF _PRING MARKET REVIEW_.)

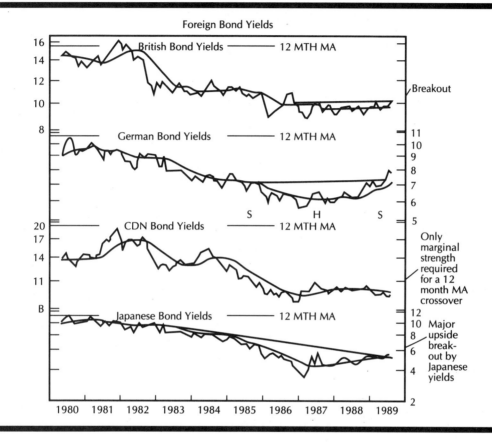

a global scale. International currency trends are also important. Global indexes are available that allow intermarket comparisons among the the major financial sectors. *All world markets are interrelated.* The U.S. market, as important as it is, doesn't operate in a vacuum. Intermarket analysis can and should be done on a global scale. Overseas stock markets, especially those in Japan and England, should be monitored for signs of confirmation or divergence with the U.S. stock market. Overseas bond markets should also be watched for clues as to which way global interest rates are moving. To gain insights into global interest rates, it's also necessary to watch world commodity trends. For that purpose, the Economist Commodity Index can be used along with certain key commodities, such as gold and oil.

The study of gold and oil leads us to the next stop on the intermarket journey, and that is the study of industry groups. Two global themes that were seen as the 1980s ended were strength in asset-backed stocks, such as gold mining and energy shares, which benefit from rises in those commodities, and weakness in interest-sensitive stocks, which are hurt when bond prices fall (and interest rates rise). The relevance of intermarket analysis for stock groups will be examined in the next chapter.

FIGURE 8.25

A COMPARISON OF SEVEN WORLD STOCK MARKETS FROM 1977 THROUGH 1989. IT CAN BE SEEN THAT BULL MARKETS EXIST ON A GLOBAL SCALE. WORLD STOCK MARKETS GENERALLY TREND IN THE SAME DIRECTION. IT'S A GOOD IDEA TO FACTOR OVERSEAS STOCK MARKETS INTO TECHNICAL ANALYSIS OF DOMESTIC EQUITIES. (CHART COURTESY OF *BUSINESS CONDITIONS DIGEST*.)

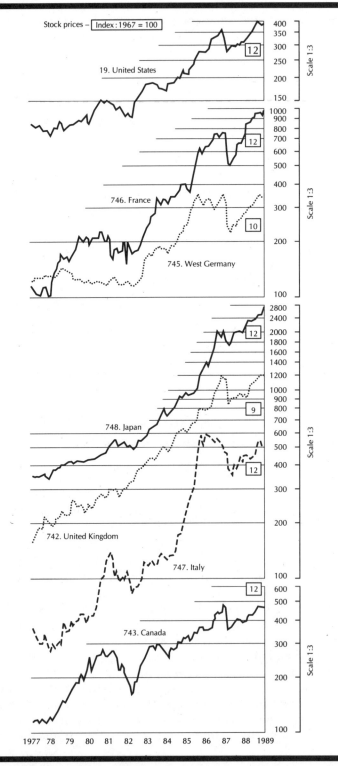

9

Stock Market Groups

It's often been said that the stock market is a "market of stocks." It could also be said that the stock market is a "market of stock *groups*." Although it's true that most individual stocks and most stock groups rise and fall with the general market, they may not do so at the same speed or at exactly the same time. Some stock groups will rise faster than others in a bull market, and some will fall faster than others in a bear market. Some will tend to lead the general market at tops and bottoms and others will tend to lag. In addition, not all of these groups react to economic news in exactly the same way.

Many stocks groups are tied to specific commodity markets and tend to rise and fall with that commodity. Two obvious examples that will be examined in this chapter are the *gold mining* and *energy* stocks. Other examples would include copper, aluminum, and silver mining shares. These commodity stocks tend to benefit when commodity prices are rising and inflation pressures are building. On the other side of the coin are *interest-sensitive* stocks that are hurt when inflation and interest rates are rising. *Bank* stocks are an example of a group of stocks that benefit from declining interest rates and that are hurt when interest rates are rising. In this chapter, the focus will be on *savings and loan* stocks and *money center* banks. Other examples include regional banks, financial services, insurance, real estate, and securities brokerage stocks.

The stock market will be divided into those stocks that benefit from rising inflation and rising interest rates and those that are hurt by such a scenario. The working premise is relatively simple. In a climate of rising commodity prices and rising interest rates, inflation stocks (such as precious metals, energy, copper, food, and steel) should do better than financially-oriented stocks such as banks, life insurance companies, and utilities. In a climate of falling inflation and falling interest rates, the better plays would be in the financial (interest-sensitive) stock groups.

STOCK GROUPS AND RELATED COMMODITIES

This discussion of the intermarket group analysis touches on two important areas. First, I'll show how stock groups are affected by their related commodity markets, and vice versa. Sometimes the stock group in question will lead the commodity market, and sometimes the commodity will lead the stock group. A thorough technical analysis of either market should include a study of the other. *Gold mining shares usually lead the price of gold.* Gold traders, therefore, should keep an eye on what gold mining shares are doing for early warnings as to the direction the gold market might be taking. Stock traders who are considering the purchase or sale of gold mining shares should also monitor the price of gold.

The second message is that intermarket analysis of stock groups yields important clues as to where stock investors might want to be focusing their attention and capital. If inflation pressures are building (commodity prices are rising relative to bond prices), emphasis should be placed on inflation stocks. If bond prices are strengthening relative to commodity prices (a climate of falling interest rates and declining inflation), emphasis should be placed on interest-sensitive stocks.

THE CRB INDEX VERSUS BONDS

In Chapter 3, the commodity/bond relationship was identified as the most important in intermarket analysis. The fulcrum effect of that relationship tells which way inflation and interest rates are trending. One way to study this relationship of commodities to bonds is to plot a relative strength ratio of the Commodity Research Bureau Price Index over Treasury bond prices. If the CRB Index is rising relative to bond prices, this means inflation pressures are building and higher interest rates will be the likely result, providing a negative climate for the stock market. If the CRB/bond relationship is weakening, this would suggest declining inflation and falling interest rates, a climate beneficial to stock prices.

Now this same idea will be used in the group analysis. However, this time that relationship will help determine whether to commit funds to inflation or interest-sensitive stocks. There's another bonus involved in this type of analysis and that is the tendency for interest-sensitive stocks to lead other stocks.

In Chapter 4, the ability of bonds to lead the stock market was discussed at some length. Rising bond prices are positive for stocks, whereas falling bonds are usually negative. Interest-sensitive stocks are closely linked to bonds. Interest-sensitive stocks are often more closely tied to the bond market than to the stock market. As a result, *turns in interest-sensitive stocks often precede turns in the market as a whole.*

What tends to happen at market tops is that the bond market will start to drop. The bearish influence of falling bond prices (and rising interest rates) pulls interest-sensitive stocks downward. Eventually, the stock market will also begin to weaken. This downturn in the stock averages will often be accompanied by an upturn in certain tangible asset stock groups, such as energy and gold mining shares.

GOLD VERSUS GOLD MINING SHARES

The intermarket analysis of stock groups will begin with the gold market. This is a logical point to start because of the key role played by the gold market in intermarket analysis. To briefly recap some points made earlier regarding the importance of gold, the gold market usually trends in the opposite direction of the U.S. dollar; the gold market is a leading indicator of the CRB Index; gold is viewed as a leading indicator of inflation; gold is also viewed as a safe haven in times of political and financial turmoil.

A dramatic example of the last point was shown in the fourth quarter of 1989 and the first month of 1990 as gold mining shares became the top performing stock group at a time when the stock market was just beginning to experience serious deterioration. There is a strong positive link between the trend of gold and that of gold mining shares. A technical analysis of one without the other is unwise and unnecessary. The accompanying charts show why.

One of the key premises of intermarket analysis is the need to look to related markets for clues. Nowhere is that more evident than in the relationship between the price of gold itself and gold mining shares. As a rule, *they both trend in the same direction.* When they begin to diverge from one another, an early warning is being given that the trend may be changing. Usually one will lead the other at important turning points. Knowing what is happening in the leader provides valuable information for the laggard. Many people assume that commodity prices, being the more sensitive and the more volatile of the two, lead the related stock group. It may be surprising to learn, then, that *gold mining shares usually lead the price of gold.* However, that's not always the case. In 1980, gold peaked eight months before gold shares. In 1986, gold led again.

Figure 9.1 compares the price of gold futures (upper chart) with an index of gold mining shares (source: Standard and Poors). The period covered in the chart is from

---

FIGURE 9.1

A COMPARISON OF GOLD AND GOLD MINING SHARES FROM 1985 INTO EARLY 1990. BOTH MEASURES USUALLY TREND IN THE SAME DIRECTION. GOLD LED GOLD SHARES HIGHER IN 1986. HOWEVER, GOLD SHARES TURNED DOWN FIRST IN THE FALL OF 1987 AND TURNED UP FIRST IN THE FALL OF 1989.

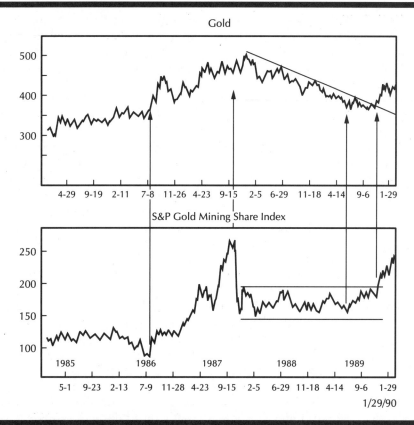

the middle of 1985 into January of 1990. There are three points of particular interest on the chart. Going into the summer of 1986, gold was going through a basing process (after hitting a low in the spring of 1985). Gold shares, however, where drifting to new lows. In July of 1986, gold prices turned sharply higher (influenced by a rising oil market and bottom in the CRB Index). That bullish breakout in gold marked the beginning of a bull market in gold mining shares. In this case, the price of gold clearly led the gold mining shares.

From the summer of 1986 to the end of 1987, the price of gold appreciated about 40 percent, while gold stocks rose over 200 percent. This outstanding performance gave gold stocks the top ranking of all stock groups in 1987. However, gold stocks took a beating in October 1987 and became one of the worst performing stock groups through the following year. Late in 1987, a bearish divergence developed between the price of bullion and gold stocks and, in this instance, gold stocks led the price of gold. From the October peak, the S&P gold index lost about 46 percent of its value. The price of gold, however, after an initial selloff in late October, firmed again and actually challenged contract highs in December.

While gold was threatening to move into new highs, gold stocks barely managed a 50 percent recovery. This glaring divergence between gold and gold stocks was a clear warning that odds were against the gold rally continuing. Gold started to drop sharply in mid-December, and gold stocks dropped to new bear market lows. Back in 1986, gold led gold stocks higher. At the 1987 top, gold stocks led gold lower. It becomes increasingly clear that an analysis of either market is incomplete without a corresponding analysis of the other.

As 1989 unfolded, it was becoming evident that an important bullish divergence was developing between gold and gold shares. As gold continued to trend lower, gold shares appeared to be forming an important basing pattern. During September 1989, the gold index broke through overhead resistance, correctly signaling that a new uptrend had begun in gold mining shares. Shortly thereafter, gold broke a two-year down trendline and started an uptrend of its own.

Figure 9.2 is an overlay chart of gold and gold shares over the same five years; it shows gold shares leading gold at the 1987 top and the 1989 bottom. Figure 9.3 provides a closer view of the 1989 bottom and shows that, although the gold market was forming the second trough of a "double bottom" during October, gold mining shares were already rallying strongly (the last trough in the gold mining shares was hit in June 1989, four months earlier). It's worth noting, however, that the real bull move in gold mining shares didn't shift into high gear until gold completed its "double bottom" at the end of October. Something else happened in October of 1989 that helped catapult the rally in gold and gold mining shares: That was a sharp selloff in the stock market.

As so often happens, events in one sector impact on another. On Friday, October 13, 1989, the Dow Jones Industrial Average dropped almost 200 points. In the ensuing weeks, some frightened money flowing out of stocks found its way into the bond market in a "flight to quality." A large portion of that money, however, found its way into gold and gold mining shares. Gold-oriented mutual funds also experienced a large inflow of capital. Figure 9.4 shows the S&P gold mining share index (upper chart) and a ratio of the gold mining index divided by the S&P 500 stock index (lower chart).

Figure 9.4 shows that, on a relative strength basis, gold shares actually began to outperform the S&P 500 index in June of 1989 after underperforming stocks during the preceding year. However, it wasn't until the end of October and early November

FIGURE 9.2
ANOTHER COMPARISON OF GOLD AND THE S&P GOLD MINING INDEX FROM 1985 TO JANUARY OF 1990. AT THE 1987 PEAK, GOLD SHARES SHOW A MAJOR BEARISH DIVERGENCE WITH GOLD. IN LATE 1989, GOLD SHARES TURNED UP BEFORE GOLD.

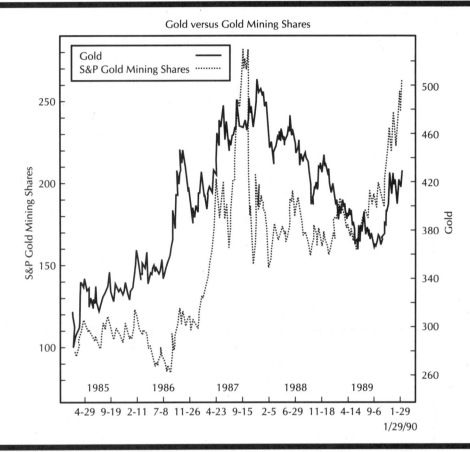

Gold versus Gold Mining Shares

that an important down trendline in the ratio was broken and gold stocks really began to shine. From the fall of 1989 through January of 1990, gold stocks outperformed all other stock market sectors. Gold mutual funds became the big winners of 1989. Gold had once again proven its role as a safe haven in times of financial turmoil. Figure 9.5 shows the bullish breakout in the gold shares coinciding with the October 1989 peak in the stock market.

Another intermarket factor that helped launch the bull move in gold was a sharp selloff in the dollar immediately following the mini-crash of October 1989. The week after the October stock market selloff, the U.S. dollar gapped downward and soon began a downtrend (Figure 9.6). Stock market weakness forced the Federal Reserve to lower interest rates in an effort to stem the stock market decline. Lower interest rates (and expectations of more Fed easing to come) caused the flight of funds into T-bills and T-bonds and pushed the dollar into a deep slide (lower interest rates are bearish for the dollar). This slide in the dollar, in turn, helped fuel the strong rally in gold and gold mining stocks.

FIGURE 9.3
**A CLOSER LOOK AT GOLD VERSUS GOLD STOCKS FROM 1987 THROUGH THE END OF 1989.
GOLD SHARES SHOWED A MAJOR BULLISH DIVERGENCE WITH GOLD IN 1989 AND COR-
RECTLY ANTICIPATED THE BULLISH BREAKOUT IN GOLD FUTURES IN THE AUTUMN.**

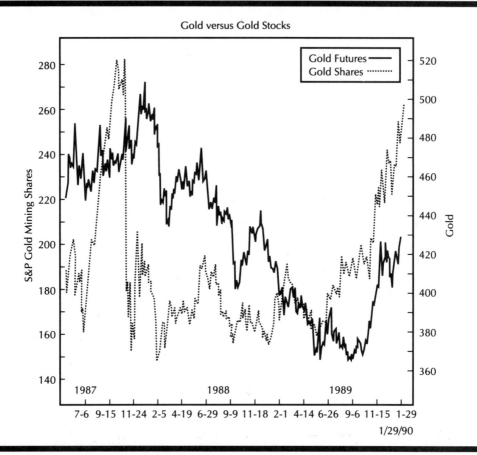

Gold versus Gold Stocks

FIGURE 9.4
THE UPPER CHART SHOWS THE BASING ACTIVITY AND BULLISH BREAKOUT IN THE S&P GOLD MINING INDEX. THE BOTTOM CHART IS A RATIO OF GOLD STOCKS DIVIDED BY THE S&P 500 STOCK INDEX AND SHOWS GOLD OUTPERFORMING THE MARKET FROM THE SUMMER OF 1989. GOLD SHARES REALLY BEGAN TO GLITTER IN NOVEMBER.

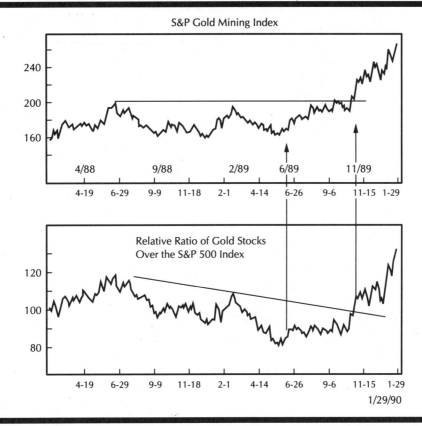

FIGURE 9.5
**GOLD SHARES VERSUS THE S&P 500 STOCK INDEX. THE STOCK MARKET PEAK IN OCTOBER
1989 HAD A LOT TO DO WITH THE FLIGHT OF FUNDS INTO GOLD MINING SHARES. GOLD
AND GOLD MINING SHARES ARE A HAVEN IN TIMES OF FINANCIAL TURMOIL.**

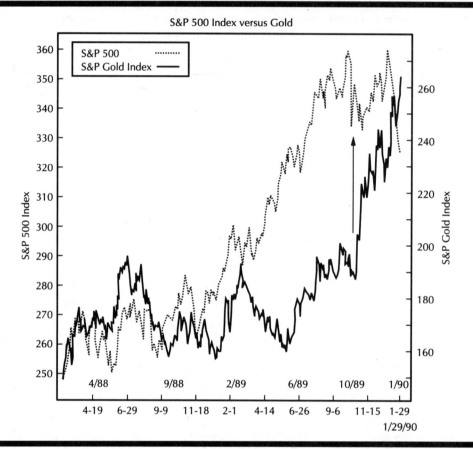

FIGURE 9.6
A GLANCE AT ALL FOUR SECTORS IN THE FALL OF 1989. AFTER THE MINI-COLLAPSE IN THE DOW INDUSTRIALS (UPPER RIGHT) ON OCTOBER 13, 1989, T-BILLS (LOWER RIGHT) RALLIED IN A FLIGHT TO QUALITY AND FED EASING. LOWER INTEREST RATES CONTRIBUTED TO A SHARP DROP IN THE DOLLAR (UPPER LEFT), WHICH FUELED THE STRONG RALLY IN GOLD (LOWER LEFT).

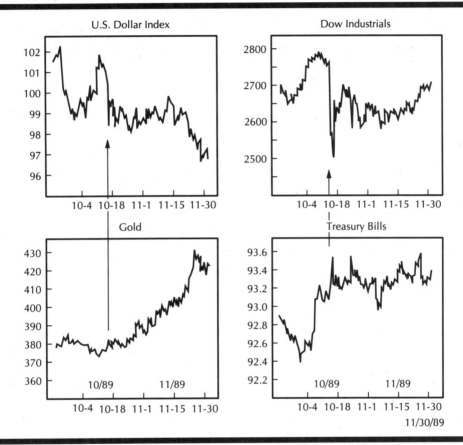

WHY GOLD STOCKS OUTSHINE GOLD

During 1987 gold rose only 40 percent while gold shares gained 200 percent. From the fall of 1989 to January 1990, gold shares rose 50 percent while gold gained only about 16 percent. The explanation lies in the fact that gold shares offer leverage arising from the fact that mining profits rise more sharply than the price of the gold itself. If it costs a company $200 an ounce to mine gold and gold is trading at $350, the company will reap a profit of $150. If gold rises to $400, it will appreciate in value by only 15 percent ($50/$350), whereas the company's profits will appreciate by 33 percent ($50/$150). Figure 9.7 shows some gold mining shares benefiting from the leveraged affect of rising gold prices.

OIL VERSUS OIL STOCKS

Another group that turned in a strong performance as 1989 ended was the energy sector. Oil prices rose strongly in the fourth quarter and contributed to the rising

---

FIGURE 9.7

GOLD VERSUS THREE GOLD MINING STOCKS. GOLD STOCKS APPEAR TO BE LEADING THE PRICE OF GOLD HIGHER AS 1990 IS BEGINNING.

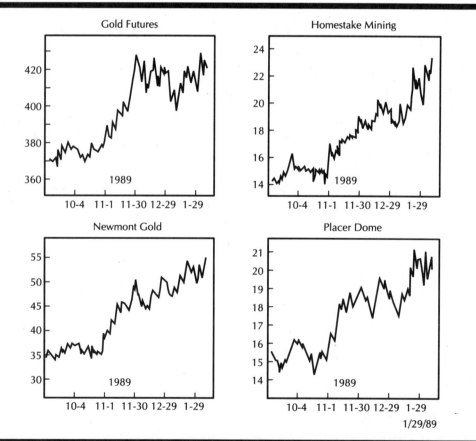

1/29/89

prices of oil shares. Rising oil prices help domestic and international oil companies as well as other energy-related stocks like oilfield equipment and service stocks, and oil drilling stocks. The discussion here will be limited to the impact of crude oil futures prices on the international oil companies. The basic premise is the same; Namely, that there is a strong relationship between the price of oil and oil shares. To do a complete technical analysis of one, it is necessary to do a technical analysis of the other.

Figures 9.8 and 9.9 compare the price of crude oil to an index of international oil company shares (source: Standard and Poors) from 1985 to the beginning of 1990. While oil shares have been much stronger than the price of oil during those five years, the charts clearly show that turning points in the price of crude have had an important impact on the price of oil shares. The arrows in Figure 9.8 pinpoint where major turning points in the price of oil coincide with similar turning points in oil shares. Important bottoms in oil shares in 1986, late 1987, late 1988, and late 1989 coincide with rallies in crude oil. Peaks in oil shares in 1987 and early 1988 coincide with peaks in oil prices.

FIGURE 9.8
A COMPARISON OF CRUDE OIL FUTURES AND THE S&P INTERNATIONAL OIL INDEX FROM 1985 INTO EARLY 1990. ALTHOUGH OIL SHARES HAVE OUTPERFORMED THE PRICE OF OIL, TURNING POINTS IN OIL FUTURES HAVE HAD A STRONG INFLUENCE OVER SIMILAR TURNING POINTS IN OIL SHARES.

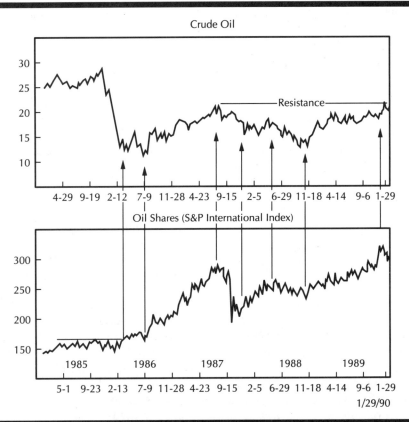

FIGURE 9.9
ANOTHER LOOK AT CRUDE OIL FUTURES VERSUS INTERNATIONAL OIL STOCKS. A STRONG POSITIVE CORRELATION CAN BE SEEN BETWEEN BOTH INDEXES. IT'S A GOOD IDEA TO WATCH BOTH.

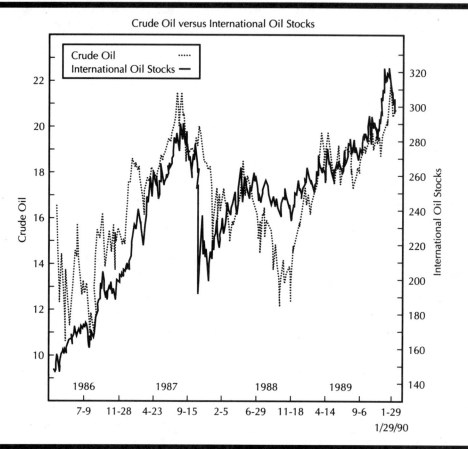

Crude Oil versus International Oil Stocks

Figure 9.8 also shows oil prices challenging major overhead resistance near $23.00 as 1990 begins. The inability of oil to clear that important barrier is causing profit-taking in oil shares. Figure 9.9 uses an overlay chart to compare both markets over the same five years. The strong positive correlation is clearly visible.

Figure 9.10 provides a closer look at oil and oil shares in 1988 and 1989. While the two charts are not identical, it can be seen that turning points in the price of oil had an impact on oil shares. The breaking of down trendlines by crude oil at the end of 1988 and again in the fall of 1989 helped launch strong rallies in oil shares. Figure 9.11 provides an even closer look at the second half of 1989 and January of 1990. In this case, oil shares showed a leading tendency. In November of 1989, oil shares resolved a "symmetrical triangle" on the upside. This bullish signal by oil shares led a similar bullish breakout by crude oil a couple of weeks later. A "double top" appeared in oil shares as oil was spiking up to new highs in late December of that year. This "double top" warned that a top in crude oil prices might be at hand.

FIGURE 9.10
A COMPARISON OF OIL AND INTERNATIONAL OIL SHARES IN 1988 AND 1989. UPSIDE BREAK-
OUTS IN OIL PRICES COINCIDED WITH RALLIES IN OIL SHARES.

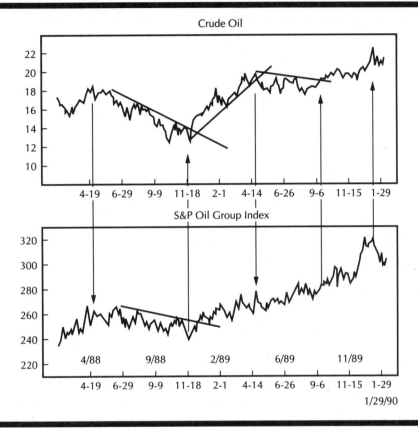

As January of 1990 ended, both oil and oil shares are again trying to rally together. Figure 9.12 compares oil prices to individual oil companies—Texaco, Exxon,
and Mobil. The "double top" referred to earlier can be seen in the Exxon and Mobil charts. The late December top in Texaco occurred at about the same time as
that in crude oil. As January is ending, crude oil is rallying for a challenge of contract highs. All three oil companies appear to be benefiting from the rally in oil futures, but are clearly lagging well behind oil as the commodity is retesting overhead
resistance.

ANOTHER DIMENSION IN DIVERGENCE ANALYSIS

What these charts show is that a technical analysis of the price of crude oil can
shed light on prospects for oil-related stocks. At the same time, analysis of oil shares
often aids in analysis of oil itself. The principles of confirmation and divergence
are carried to another dimension when the analysis of stock groups such as oil and
gold are compared to analysis of their related commodities. The analyst is never sure

FIGURE 9.11
IN NOVEMBER 1989, A BULLISH BREAKOUT IN OIL SHARES PRECEDED A SIMILAR BREAKOUT BY OIL PRICES A COUPLE OF WEEKS LATER. AS OIL SPIKED UPWARD IN DECEMBER 1989, OIL STOCKS FORMED A "DOUBLE TOP," WARNING OF A POSSIBLE PEAK IN OIL.

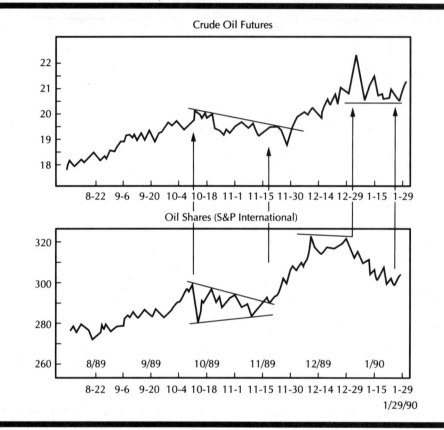

FIGURE 9.12
CRUDE OIL FUTURES VERSUS THREE INTERNATIONAL OIL COMPANIES IN THE FOURTH QUARTER OF 1989 AND EARLY 1990. TEXACO APPEARS TO BE TRACKING OIL VERY CLOSELY. EXXON AND MOBIL TURNED DOWN BEFORE OIL BUT ARE BENEFITTING FROM THE BOUNCE IN OIL FUTURES.

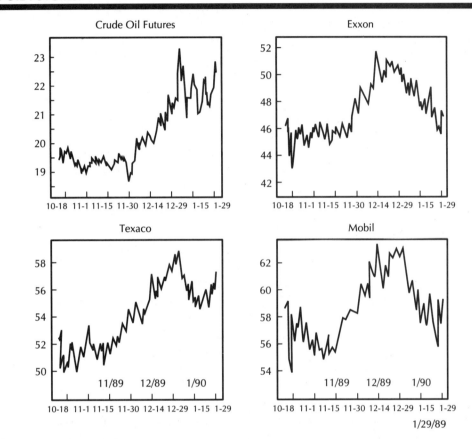

FIGURE 9.13

THE UPPER CHART COMPARES INTERNATIONAL OIL SHARES TO THE S&P 500 STOCK INDEX FROM JANUARY 1989 TO JANUARY 1990. THE BOTTOM CHART IS A RELATIVE STRENGTH RATIO OF OIL SHARES DIVIDED BY THE S&P 500 INDEX. THE S&P OIL INDEX OUTPERFORMED THE MARKET FROM SEPTEMBER 1989 TO JANUARY 1990.

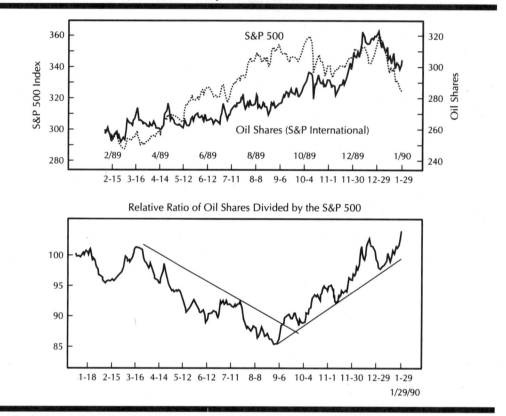

which one will lead, or which one will provide the vital clue. The only way to know is to follow both.

Figure 9.13 compares international oil shares to the broad market during 1989. The upper chart plots the S&P oil share index versus the S&P 500 stock index. The bottom chart is a ratio of oil shares divided by stocks. As the bottom chart shows, oil stocks outperformed the broad market by a wide margin during the fourth quarter of 1989 and the first month of 1990. Clearly, the place to be as the old year ended was in oil stocks (along with precious metals). *One place not to be was in interest-sensitive stocks.*

INTEREST-SENSITIVE STOCKS

On January 31, 1990, *Investor's Daily* ranked its 197 industry groups for the prior six months. The six best-performing groups were all commodity related: Gold Mining (1), Food—Sugar Refining (2), Silver Mining (3), Oil & Gas—Field Services (4), Oil & Gas—Offshore Drilling (5), Oil & Gas—International Integrated (6). Four other oil groups ranked in the top 20 on the basis of relative strength. In sharp contrast, *bank* stocks and *savings & loan* stocks were ranked at the lower end of the list. *Money center* banks were ranked 193 out of a possible 197 for the last five months of 1989 and the first month of 1990. *Savings & loan* shares did a bit better but still came in a relatively weak 147 out of 197 groups. Although most commodity stocks ranked in the top 10 percent, most bank stocks ranked in the bottom 25 percent during those six months.

That wasn't the case throughout all of 1989, however. Earlier that year, financial stocks had been the better performers, whereas gold and oil shares languished. What changed toward the end of 1989 was a pickup in inflation pressures and a swing toward higher interest rates. To make matters worse, the dollar and stocks came under heavy downward pressure in the autumn of 1989, fueling inflation fears and a flight from financial stocks to gold and energy shares. The very same forces that helped inflation stocks, rising inflation and rising interest rates, hurt interest-sensitive stocks like savings and loans and money center banks. The sharp drop in interest-sensitive stocks that began in October of 1989 also warned that the broader market might be in some trouble.

SAVINGS AND LOANS VERSUS THE DOW

Figure 9.14 compares the S&P Savings and Loan Group Index to the Dow Jones Industrial Average from 1985 through the beginning of 1990. The tendency of the S&L group to lead the broad market at tops can be seen both in the second half of 1987 and the last quarter of 1989. The S&L Index formed a major "head and shoulders" topping pattern throughout 1986 and 1987. As stocks were rallying to new highs in the summer of 1987, the S&Ls were forming a "right shoulder" as part of a topping pattern. That bearish divergence was a warning that the stock market rally might be in danger. To the far right of Figure 9.14, the sharp breakdown in the S&Ls in the last quarter of 1989 again warned of impending weakness in the broad market. Figure 9.15 gives a closer view of the 1989 peak. Even though the Dow Industrials rallied for a challenge of the October peak in December 1989, S&Ls and other interest-sensitive stocks continued to drop sharply, sending a bearish warning that the stock market rally was suspect.

SAVINGS AND LOANS VERSUS BONDS

Figure 9.16 compares the S&L group index to Treasury bonds. The arrows pinpoint the turning points in the S&L group relative to bond prices. Notice that bond price movements have an important influence on S&L share prices. During 1986 and 1987, the S&L group was caught in between the upward pull of rising stock prices and the downward pull of a falling bond market. By the time the S&Ls were forming their "right shoulder" peak in the summer of 1987, bonds had already begun their collapse. It seems clear that the more bearish bond market (and the accompanying rise in interest rates) hit the interest-sensitive sector before it hit the general market. The bond market therefore became a leading indicator for the interest-sensitive stocks which, in turn, became a leading indicator for the stock market as a whole.

Figure 9.16 shows the bond market rally stalling in the fourth quarter of 1989 and finally turning lower in an apparent "double top." The loss of upward momentum in bonds and the subsequent rise in interest rates contributed to the sharp selloff in financial stocks. In this case, however, the actual price slide appears to have begun in the interest-sensitive stocks with bonds following.

FIGURE 9.14

THE S&P SAVINGS AND LOAN INDEX VERSUS THE DOW INDUSTRIALS FROM 1985 TO THE END OF 1989. THE S&Ls TURNED DOWN BEFORE THE DOW IN 1987 AND AGAIN IN THE FALL OF 1989. THE S&L INDEX WAS FORMING THE THIRD PEAK IN A "HEAD AND SHOULDERS" TOP IN AUGUST 1987 AS STOCKS WERE REACHING NEW HIGHS. INTEREST-SENSITIVE STOCKS USUALLY PEAK BEFORE THE DOW.

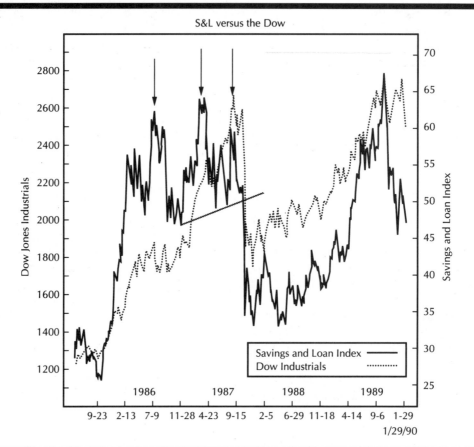

Reproduced with permission by Knight Ridder's Tradecenter. Tradecenter is a registered trademark of Knight Ridder's Financial Information.

FIGURE 9.15
THE S&L STOCKS PEAKED IN OCTOBER 1989 ALONG WITH THE DOW. HOWEVER, THE DE-CEMBER RALLY IN THE DOW WASN'T CONFIRMED BY THE S&L STOCKS. THIS NEGATIVE DI-VERGENCE WAS A BEARISH WARNING FOR THE BROAD MARKET.

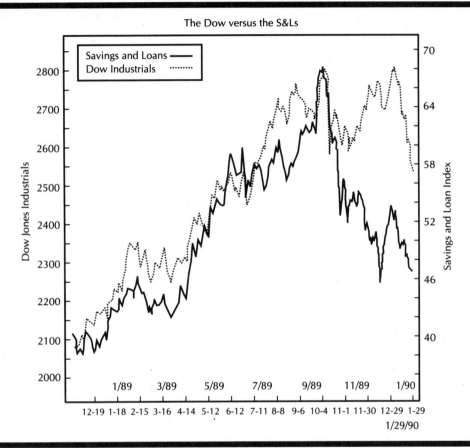

The Dow versus the S&Ls

FIGURE 9.16
**THE S&L STOCKS SHOW A STRONG CORRELATION WITH TREASURY BONDS. THE DOWN-
WARD PULL OF BONDS IN 1987 CONTRIBUTED TO THE TOPPING ACTION IN THE S&L IN-
DEX. IN THE FALL OF 1989, THE RALLY FAILURE IN BONDS HAD A LOT TO DO WITH THE
SUBSEQUENT COLLAPSE IN THE S&Ls.**

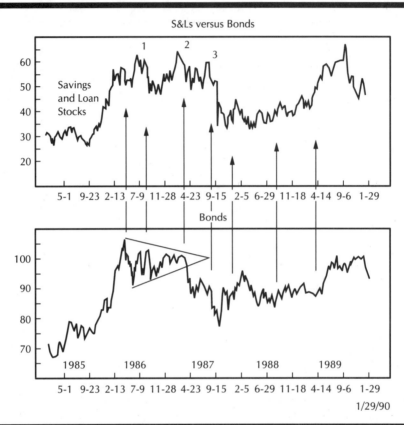

SAVINGS AND LOANS VERSUS THE CRB INDEX

If the bond market trends in the same direction as interest-sensitive stocks, the CRB
Index should move inversely to both. Figure 9.17 compares the S&Ls to the CRB Index.
A rising CRB should be bearish for S&Ls; a falling CRB Index should be bullish. And
this is what Figure 9.17 shows. Figure 9.17 reveals the CRB Index tracing out a "head
and shoulders" bottom in 1986 and 1987, whereas the S&Ls are tracing out a "head
and shoulders" top. However, the patterns are not synchronous. The "left shoulder" in
the S&Ls in 1986 coincides with the middle trough (the head) in the CRB Index. The
third trough (the "right shoulder") in the CRB Index in the spring of 1987 coincides
with the middle peak (the head) in the S&Ls. The "right shoulder" in the S&Ls in
August of 1987 occurs well after the CRB Index has completed its basing pattern and
is linked to the stock market peak that month. Still, it appears that a lot of the action
in the S&Ls can be attributed to weakness in bonds and strength in the CRB Index.

The S&Ls remained under pressure from the summer of 1987 to the summer
of 1988. During that same time, the CRB Index continued to rally. In the summer
of 1988, the CRB Index peaked out and began a yearlong descent. During that same

FIGURE 9.17
THE S&L INDEX SHOWS A STRONG NEGATIVE CORRELATION WITH THE CRB INDEX FROM 1985 TO 1990. THE 1987 TOP IN THE S&Ls MIRRORED A SIMILAR BOTTOM IN THE CRB INDEX. THE MID-1988 PEAK IN THE CRB HELPED LAUNCH THE S&L RALLY. THE PEAK IN THE S&Ls IN THE AUTUMN OF 1989 COINCIDED WITH THE BREAKING OF A DOWN TRENDLINE BY THE CRB INDEX.

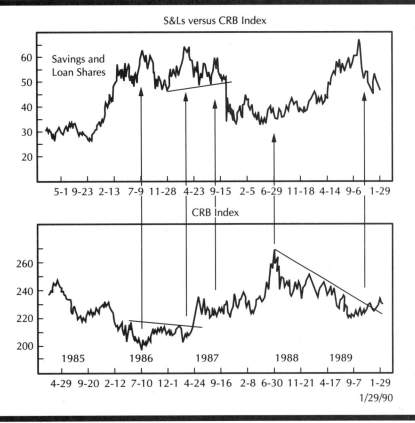

year, the S&Ls rallied sharply. In the fall of 1989, it can be seen that the peak in the S&L stocks occurred at about the same time that the CRB Index was breaking its yearlong down trendline. Since the S&Ls are so closely tied to the bond market, and the bond market moves inversely to the CRB Index, it shouldn't be surprising to discover a strong inverse relationship between the S&Ls and the CRB Index.

MONEY CENTER BANKS VERSUS THE NYSE COMPOSITE INDEX

Another group that suffered from rising interest rates as the 1980s came to a close was the *Money Center* banks. Figure 9.18 compares the S&P Money Center Group Index with the New York Stock Exchange Composite Index through 1989 and the beginning of 1990. Up until October 1989, Money Center banks had easily kept pace with the stock market. Both peaked together in October of that year. However, as the NYSE Index rallied into early January, the Money Center bank shares continued to plummet. Part of the reason for that sharp selloff is the same as for the S&Ls and other interest-sensitive stocks—falling bond prices (rising interest rates) and firming

FIGURE 9.18
**MONEY CENTER BANKS VERSUS THE NYSE COMPOSITE INDEX. INTEREST-SENSITIVE MONEY
CENTER BANKS ALSO DROPPED SHARPLY FROM OCTOBER 1989 INTO JANUARY OF 1990.
FINANCIAL STOCKS FELL UNDER THE WEIGHT OF RISING INTEREST RATES AND FALLING
BOND PRICES. THIS WEAKNESS HELPED PULL THE MARKET LOWER.**

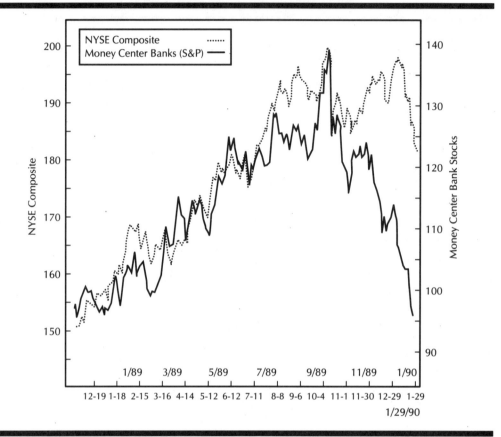

commodity prices (especially oil). The weakness in the Money Center stocks also
provided another warning to the stock market technician that the attempt by the
broad stock market averages to recover to new highs was not likely to succeed, at
least not until the interest-sensitive stocks started to stabilize.

GOLD STOCKS VERSUS MONEY CENTER STOCKS

Figure 9.19 shows a couple of other ways to monitor the relationship between inflation
and disinflation stocks. The upper chart compares the S&P Gold Group Index to the
S&P Money Center Group Index. Up to the fall of 1989, the Money Center banks were
outperforming gold stocks by a wide margin. From October of 1989 on, however,
that relationship changed abruptly and dramatically. As the Money Center banks
collapsed, gold stocks began to rally sharply. Part of the explanation for this dramatic
shift between commodity and interest-sensitive stocks is seen in the bottom chart
which plots the ratio between the CRB Index and bonds.

FIGURE 9.19
THE UPPER CHART COMPARES GOLD STOCKS TO MONEY CENTER STOCKS AS 1989 ENDED. SOME MONEY FLEEING FINANCIAL STOCKS WENT TO GOLD SHARES. THE BOTTOM CHART IS A RATIO OF THE CRB INDEX DIVIDED BY TREASURY BONDS. THE BASING PATTERN IN THE RATIO SINCE AUGUST OF 1989 AND THE SUBSEQUENT UPSIDE BREAKOUT CONFIRMED THE SHIFT TOWARD STRONGER COMMODITIES AND WEAKER BONDS. THIS BENEFITTED INFLATION STOCKS, SUCH AS GOLD AND OIL, AND HURT INTEREST-SENSITIVE STOCKS.

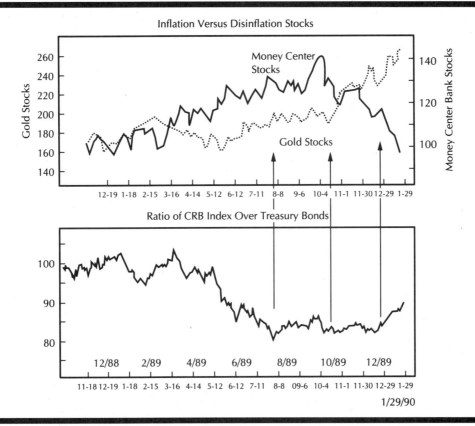

As long as the CRB/bond ratio was falling earlier in the year, odds favored the interest-sensitive stocks. The CRB/bond ratio bottomed in August of 1989 and continued to stabilize through the fourth quarter. In December, the ratio broke out to the upside and confirmed that a trend change had, in fact, taken place. The pendulum, which had favored bond prices for a year, now showed commodity prices in the ascendancy. That crucial shift explains the dramatic move away from interest-sensitive stocks toward commodity stocks. And, in doing so, this shift also warned of the uptick in interest rates which began to push stock prices lower.

SUMMARY

This chapter showed the relevance of intermarket comparisons between various futures markets and related stock groups. It discussed how many stock groups are tied to specific commodity markets (such as oil, gold, silver, copper, aluminum, and sugar). Since those commodities and their related stock groups usually trend in the same direction, their relative performance should be studied and compared. Interest-sensitive

FIGURE 9.20
LONDON COPPER PRICES VERSUS PHELPS DODGE, THE LARGEST COPPER PRODUCER IN THE UNITED STATES. THE MAJOR "DOUBLE TOP" IN COPPER IN THE AUTUMN OF 1989 AND ITS SUBSEQUENT COLLAPSE COINCIDED WITH A SHARP DROP IN THE PRICE OF PHELPS DODGE. THE ARROWS SHOW THAT RALLIES IN THE PRICE OF COPPER HAVE BEEN BENEFICIAL TO PHELPS DODGE SHARE PRICES.

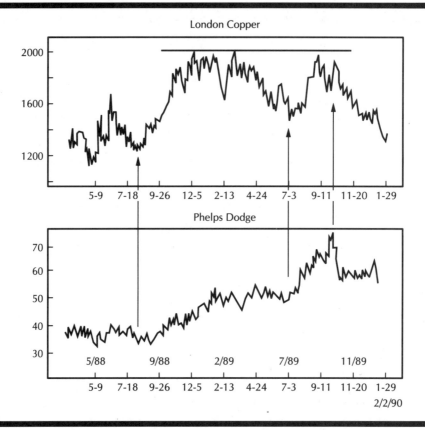

Reproduced with permission by Knight Ridder's Tradecenter. Tradecenter is a registered trademark of Knight Ridder's Financial Information.

stocks, such as savings and loans and money center banks, usually trend in the same direction as the bond market and in the opposite direction of commodity markets. By monitoring the CRB Index/bond ratio, the intermarket trader is able to tell whether money should be placed in inflation (commodity) or disinflation (interest-sensitive) stocks. Because of their close relationship to bonds, interest-sensitive stocks have a tendency to lead the stock market at major tops and bottoms.

Not all commodity groups trend in the same direction. Copper and aluminum shares weakened in the second half of 1989 as copper and aluminum prices fell (along with most industrial prices) (see Figure 9.20). Copper weakness in late 1989 was also tied to stock market weakness as fear of recession intensified. Chapter 13 will discuss the role of copper as an economic forecaster and its relation to the stock market. That chapter will also discuss in more depth the relative performance of commodity and interest-sensitive stocks at major cyclical turning points.

Another interest-sensitive group mentioned briefly in this chapter is the utilities. In Chapter 10, we'll examine how intermarket analysis affects the Dow Jones Utility Average and the usefulness of the Dow Utilities as a leading indicator of the Dow Jones Industrial Average.

10

The Dow Utilities as a Leading Indicator of Stocks

Dow Theory is based on the comparison of two Dow Jones averages—the Dow Jones Transportation Average and the Dow Jones Industrial Average. One of the basic tenets of Dow Theory is that these two averages should trend in the same direction. In other words, they should confirm each other's trend. Many analysts pay less attention to the third average published in the daily pages of the Wall Street Journal—*the Dow Jones Utility Average*. Yet, *the Dow Utilities have a respectable record of anticipating turns in the Dow Industrials.*

This leading tendency of utility stocks is based on their relatively close ties to the bond market, which also is a leading indicator of stocks. The Dow Utilities provide another link in the intermarket chain between the bond market and the stock market. Because they are so interest-sensitive, utilities usually reflect interest rate changes (as reflected in the bond market) before those changes are reflected in the broader market of stocks. Since they are impacted by the direction of interest rates and inflation, utilities are also affected by such things as the trend of the dollar and commodity prices. For these reasons, the Dow Utilities are a part of the intermarket picture.

DOW UTILITIES VERSUS THE DOW INDUSTRIALS

Before looking at a comparison of the Dow Utilities relative to the Dow Industrials in more recent times, let's consider their relationship over a longer time span. Since 1970, five major turns in the Dow Industrials were preceded by a turn in the Dow Utilities.

1. The November 1972 peak in the utilities preceded a similar peak in the Dow Industrials two months later in January of 1973. Both averages dropped into the second half of 1974.
2. In September 1974, a bottom in the utilities preceded a bottom in the industrials three months later in December. Both averages rallied for two years.

3. The utilities hit another peak in January of 1981, preceding a top in the industrials three months later in April. Both averages declined together into 1982.

4. The utilities bottomed in July of 1982, preceding a major bottom in the industrials one month later in August. Both averages rallied together until 1987.

5. In January of 1987, the utilities hit a major top, leading the peak in the industrials seven months later in August 1987.

During these two decades, the Dow Utilities failed to lead a major turn in the Dow Industrials only three times. In March of 1980, both averages bottomed together. In 1970 the industrials bottomed one month before the utilities. In 1977 the industrials peaked about six months before the utilities. Of the eight major turns since 1970, the utilities led the industrials five times, turned at the same time once, and lagged only twice. The leading tendency of the Dow Utilities at market tops is especially impressive.

Research provided by John G. McGinley, Jr. (*Technical Trends*, P.O. Box 792, Wilton, CT 06897) shows that the Dow Utilities have led the Dow Industrials at every peak since 1960 with only one exception—the 1977 peak. During those 30 years, the Dow Utilities peaked ahead of the Dow Industrials by an average of three months, although the actual lead time varied from ten months to one month. Part of the explanation as to why the utility stocks lead the industrial stocks can be found in the relatively close correlation between the utility stocks and the bond market, which will be discussed later. Consider now the more recent record of how the utilities have performed relative to the broad market.

Figures 10.1 and 10.2 compare the relative performance of the Dow Jones Utility Average (upper chart) and the Dow Jones Industrial Average (lower chart) since 1983. As the various charts are examined, a long view will be given. Then a closer view of the more recent action will be given and some other intermarket comparisons will be incorporated to include bonds and commodities. Figure 10.1 shows both averages generally rising and falling together. As long as the two averages are moving in the same direction, they are merely confirming each other's trends. It's when one of them begins to diverge from the other that we begin to take notice. Figure 10.2 provides a closer view of the 1987 top.

The Dow Utilities hit its peak in January of 1987 and started to weaken. (It will be demonstrated later that part of the reason for this weakness in the utilities was tied to similar weakness in the bond market.) The selloff in the Dow Utilities set up a major negative divergence with the Dow Industrials which continued to rally for another seven months. As the industrials were hitting their peak in August, the utilities were just forming a "right shoulder" in a "head and shoulders" topping pattern (in the previous chapter, we discussed a similar topping pattern in the interest-sensitive *savings and loan* stocks). Although the lead time in 1987 was a relatively long seven months, the peak in the Dow Utilities provided plenty of warning that the rally in stocks was approaching a dangerous stage and warned stock market technicians to be especially alert to any technical signs of a breakdown in the stock averages.

Both averages rallied together into the second half of 1989. As 1989 ended, however, another divergence developed, except this time, the Dow Utilities rallied to new highs while the Dow Industrials failed to do so. (Both averages were in the process of re-challenging their all-time highs that were set in 1987). Given their normal historical relationship, the rally to new highs in the utilities could be viewed as a positive development. Many technicians took the view that the outlook for the

FIGURE 10.1

A COMPARISON OF THE DOW JONES UTILITY AVERAGE AND THE DOW JONES INDUSTRIAL AVERAGE FROM 1983 THROUGH 1989. GENERALLY, BOTH AVERAGES TREND IN THE SAME DIRECTION. TREND CHANGES ARE USUALLY SIGNALED WHEN THEY DIVERGE. IN 1987, THE DOW UTILITIES PEAKED SEVEN MONTHS BEFORE THE DOW INDUSTRIALS.

Dow Jones Utility Average

Dow Jones Industrial Average

2/7/90

industrials would remain healthy as long as the utilities remained strong. Figure 10.3 gives a closer view of market events at the end of 1989.

Figure 10.3 compares the Dow Utilities to the Dow Industrials during the fourth quarter of 1989 and the first two months of 1990. Both averages sold off in mid-October and then rallied together into the beginning of January. Although the two charts are closely related, the utilities did manage to rally to new highs while the industrials were unable to clear their October peak. On a short-term basis, however, the last rally attempt by the industrials was not confirmed by the utilities. The utilities completed a "double top" and broke down during the first week of 1990. The industrials broke down a week later.

Toward the end of January, the utilities also started to stabilize a few days before the industrials. In both instances, the utilities led the industrials by a few days to a week. The ability of the utilities to stabilize above their October lows was significant. A violation of those lows by the Dow Utilities would have been viewed by technicians as a particularly bearish development for the stock market as a whole.

FIGURE 10.2
IN AUGUST 1987, AS THE DOW INDUSTRIALS WERE HITTING THEIR MAJOR PEAK, THE UTILITIES (WHICH PEAKED IN JANUARY) WERE FORMING A "RIGHT SHOULDER" IN A TOPPING PATTERN, THEREBY CREATING A BEARISH DIVERGENCE. BOTH RALLIED TOGETHER INTO THE SECOND HALF OF 1989. AS 1989 ENDED, THE UTILITY RALLY WASN'T CONFIRMED BY THE INDUSTRIALS.

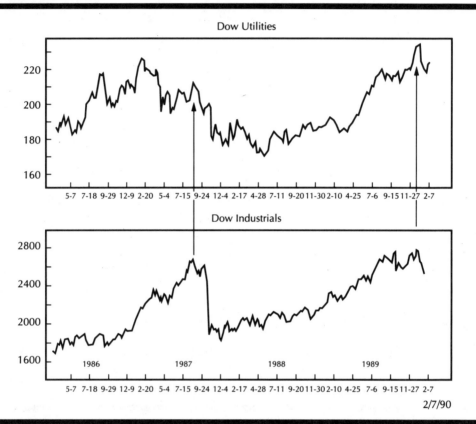

2/7/90

FIGURE 10.3
IN THE FIRST WEEK OF 1990, THE DOW UTILITIES COMPLETED A "DOUBLE TOP" FORMATION AND BROKE AN UP TRENDLINE, PRECEDING A SIMILAR BREAKDOWN BY THE DOW INDUSTRIALS A WEEK LATER. AS JANUARY 1990 ENDED, THE UTILITIES STABILIZED A FEW DAYS EARLIER THAN THE INDUSTRIALS.

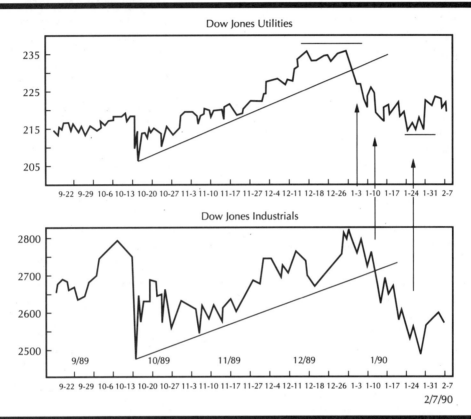

BONDS LEAD UTILITIES AT TOP

As revealed in Figure 10.3, the Dow Utilities peaked in the new year about a week ahead of the Dow Industrials. Expanding the focus, it is evident what intermarket forces pulled the Dow Utilities lower. Figure 10.4 compares the Dow Utilities to Treasury bond futures during the same time span. First of all, notice that *the rally in the utilities during the fourth quarter of 1989 was not confirmed by the bond market.* As the utilities rallied to new highs, the bond market stayed in a trading range. During the final week of 1989, bonds broke down and hit a two-month low. *This breakdown in bonds preceded the breakdown in the utilities by a week.* Toward the right side of the chart, the utilities are stabilizing while the bonds are probing for a bottom. The rally in the interest-sensitive utilities appears to be hinting that bonds are also due for a rally.

Widen the intermarket circle now to include commodities. Figure 10.5 shows that the breakdown in bonds during the final week in 1989 (which contributed to the

FIGURE 10.4
DURING THE LAST WEEK IN DECEMBER OF 1989, BOND FUTURES SET A TWO-MONTH LOW, PRECEDING THE BREAKDOWN IN THE UTILITIES A WEEK LATER. BONDS USUALLY LEAD THE DOW UTILITIES. AS JANUARY 1990 ENDED, THE RALLY IN THE UTILITIES PROVIDED SOME STABILITY TO THE BOND MARKET.

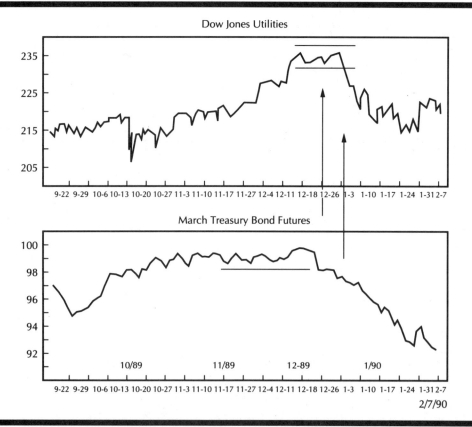

FIGURE 10.5
**THE BREAKDOWN IN BOND FUTURES THE LAST WEEK OF 1989 COINCIDED WITH A BULLISH
BREAKOUT IN THE COMMODITY RESEARCH BUREAU FUTURES PRICE INDEX (LOWER CHART).
THE RALLY IN THE CRB INDEX FROM LATE SUMMER OF 1989 PREVENTED THE BOND MARKET
FROM RESUMING ITS UPTREND.**

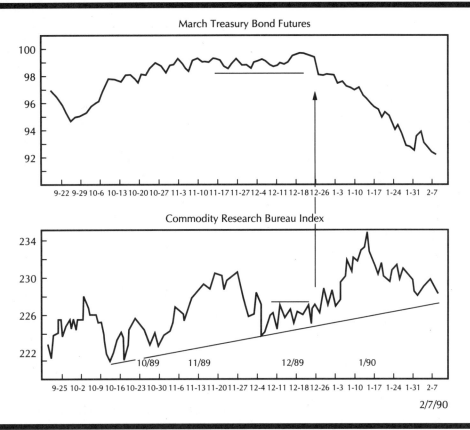

selloff in the utilities a week later) coincided with an upside breakout in the CRB
Index. As the bottom chart shows, the rise in commodity prices (which usually trend
in the opposite direction of bonds) was a primary reason that bonds were unable
to set new highs during the fourth quarter. The bullish breakout in the CRB Index
during the last week of the year finally pushed bond prices into a slide.

Figure 10.6 shows the main culprit that caused the commodity rally and the bond
and utilities to tumble. Crude oil prices (sparked by a virtual explosion in heating
oil) rallied sharply during December 1989. Probably more than any other factor, the
ensuing rally in oil prices sent inflation jitters through the financial markets (and
around the world) and contributed to the selloff in bonds. This oil rally hit bonds in
another way. Japan imports all of its oil. The jump in oil during December (combined
with a weak yen) pushed Japan's inflation rate sharply higher and caused a collapse
in Japanese bond prices. As discussed in Chapter 8, downward pressure on global
bond markets also pulled U.S. bonds lower. To the far right of both charts in Figure
10.6, the oil market has started to weaken, which is relieving downward pressure on
bonds (and the Dow Utilities and, in turn, the Dow Industrials).

FIGURE 10.6
**THE BULLISH BREAKOUT IN CRUDE OIL FUTURES IN MID-DECEMBER 1989 WAS A MAJOR
FACTOR IN THE BREAKDOWN IN BONDS. THE OIL RALLY CAUSED GLOBAL BOND MARKETS
(ESPECIALLY IN JAPAN) TO TUMBLE, WHICH ALSO HELPED PULL U.S. BOND PRICES LOWER.**

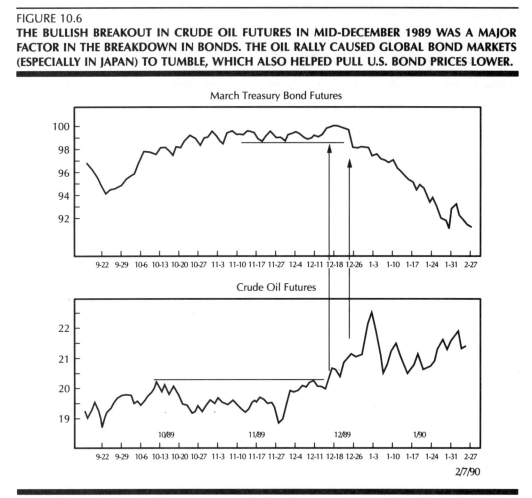

A LONGER VIEW OF UTILITIES AND BONDS

The previous discussion showed the ripple effect that usually occurs among the
financial sectors. As 1989 ended, commodities (oil in particular) started to rally;
bonds started to drop; a week later the interest-sensitive utilities followed bonds
lower; a week later the broader stock market followed bonds and the utilities lower.
The key to understanding the relationship between the Dow Utilities and the Dow
Industrials lies in the recognition of the close relationship between the utilities and
bonds. As a general rule, the bond market (which is especially inflation-sensitive)
turns first. Utilities, being especially interest-sensitive, turn in the same direction as
bonds before the general market does. The general market, as reflected in the Dow
Jones Industrial Average, usually is the last to turn.

Figures 10.7 and 10.8 compare the Dow Jones 20 Bond Average to the Dow Jones
Utility Average. It can be seen that bonds and utilities are closely correlated. Both
peaked during the first half of 1987 several months before stocks, which didn't top
until August. (Although the Dow Jones 20 Bond Average set new highs in early
1987, Treasury bonds failed to do so, thereby forming a negative divergence with

FIGURE 10.7
**THERE IS A STRONG VISUAL CORRELATION BETWEEN THE DOW JONES UTILITY AVERAGE
(SOLID LINE) AND THE DOW JONES 20 BOND AVERAGE (DOTTED LINE). BOTH TURNED
DOWN TOGETHER IN THE FIRST HALF OF 1987 AND THEN RALLIED TOGETHER INTO THE
SECOND HALF OF 1989. AS 1989 ENDED, BOTH WEAKENED.**

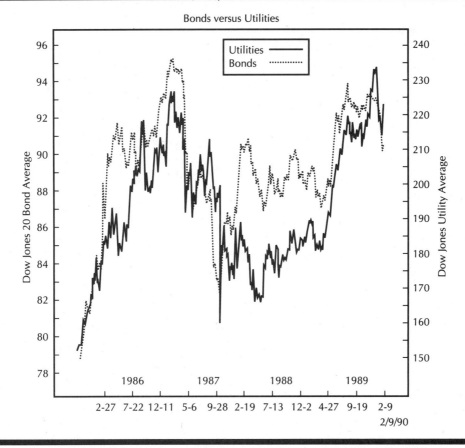

the utilities.) Both rallied together to the fourth quarter of 1989. At the 1989 top, bonds formed a "double top" and failed to confirm the rally to new highs by the utilities (see Figure 10.8).

THE CRB INDEX VERSUS BONDS AND UTILITIES

If the Dow Utilities trend in the same direction as bonds, they should trend in the opposite direction of commodity prices. Figure 10.9 compares Treasury bonds and utilities (upper chart) to the CRB Index (lower chart). The upper chart shows the negative divergence between Treasury bonds and the Dow Utilities in early 1987 and again in late 1989. The bearish action in bonds pulled the utilities lower. However, the bearish action in both bonds and utilities is closely correlated with rallies in the CRB Index. The final top in the Dow Utilities and the final peak in the bonds in early 1987 coincided with a trough in the CRB Index. The breakdown in the two financial markets in the spring of 1987 coincided with an upside breakout in the CRB Index.

FIGURE 10.8
A CLOSER LOOK AT THE DOW UTILITIES (SOLID LINE) VERSUS THE DOW JONES 20 BOND AVERAGE (DOTTED LINE) IN 1989. THE BOND MARKET FAILED TO ESTABLISH A NEW HIGH DURING THE FOURTH QUARTER, FORMED A "DOUBLE TOP" FORMATION, AND CREATED A BEARISH DIVERGENCE WITH THE DOW UTILITY AVERAGE.

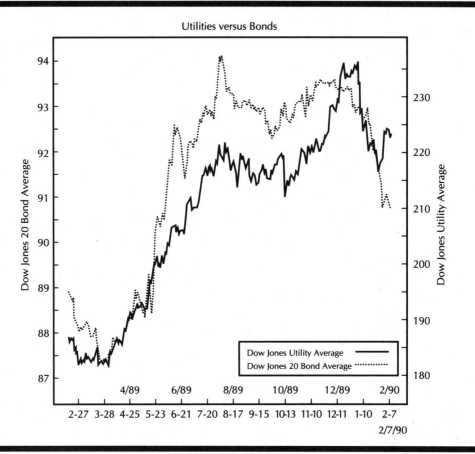

Reproduced with permission by Knight Ridder's Tradecenter. Tradecenter is a registered trademark of Knight Ridder's Financial Information.

FIGURE 10.9
WEAKNESS IN TREASURY BONDS AND UTILITIES IN EARLY 1987 AND LATE 1989 (UPPER CHART) IS LINKED TO STRENGTH IN THE CRB INDEX (BOTTOM CHART). THE RALLY IN TREASURY BONDS AND UTILITIES FROM MID-1988 IS LINKED TO THE PEAK IN THE CRB INDEX. BOTH FINANCIAL AVERAGES TREND IN THE OPPOSITE DIRECTION OF THE CRB INDEX. TREASURY BONDS FAILED TO CONFIRM THE RALLY TO NEW HIGHS BY THE UTILITIES AT BOTH THE 1987 AND THE 1989 PEAKS.

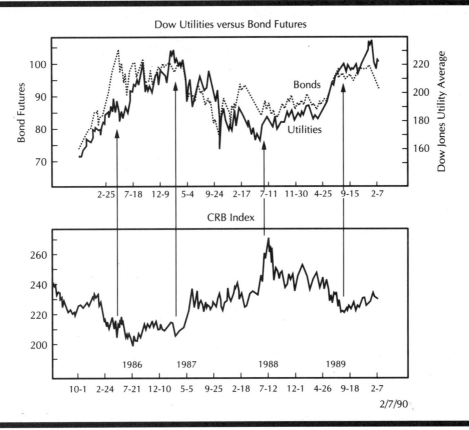

The CRB peak in mid-1988 helped launch the rallies in bonds and utilities that lasted for a year. Finally, the CRB bottom in the autumn of 1989 began the topping process in bonds and utilities. We've established that utilities are positively linked to bonds, and that bonds are negatively linked to commodities. It follows, then, that *the Dow Utilities are also negatively linked to commodities.* Any significant rally in the commodity markets will push interest rates higher and bond prices lower, which is bearish for the utilities. Downtrending commodity markets will be bullish for bonds and eventually for utilities as well.

BONDS, UTILITIES, AND THE DOW INDUSTRIALS

The final comparison links bonds, the Dow Utilities, and the Dow Industrials. Figure 10.10 shows all three markets over the last five years. The upper chart overlays Treasury bonds and the Dow Jones Utility Average. The bottom chart plots the Dow Jones Industrial Average. The chart shows that the utilities are closely linked to bonds,

---

FIGURE 10.10
BONDS AND UTILITIES (UPPER CHART) USUALLY LEAD THE STOCK MARKET (BOTTOM CHART) AT IMPORTANT TURNING POINTS. IN THE FIRST HALF OF 1987, BONDS AND UTILITIES TURNED DOWN AND PROVIDED A WARNING THAT THE STOCK MARKET RALLY HAD REACHED A DANGEROUS STAGE.

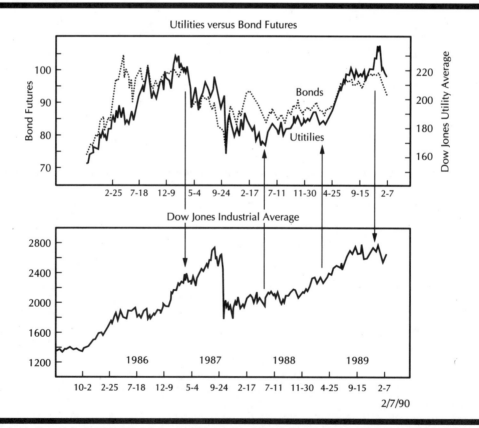

and that both bonds and utilities usually lead turns in the broader market. The 1987 peaks provide an excellent example of that interplay. The Dow Jones Utility Average has become a part of the intermarket analysis and takes its place in the analysis of the U.S. dollar, commodity prices, bonds, and stocks. Its proper place lies between bonds and the industrial stock market averages. Utilities provide another vehicle for determining the impact inflation and interest rate trends are having on the stock market as a whole. Analysis of the utilities also provides another way to measure interest-sensitive stock groups, a topic discussed in Chapter 9.

SUMMARY

The Dow Jones Utility Average (which includes 15 utility stocks) is the most widely-watched utility index. Because utility stocks are so interest rate-sensitive, they usually are impacted by interest rate changes before the general market. As a result, utilities usually follow the lead of bond prices and, in turn, usually lead the Dow Industrials at important turns. With one exception, (1977), the Dow Utilities have peaked ahead of the Dow Industrials every time since 1960 with an average lead time of three months. The Dow Utilities have more of an impact on the industrials during times when stocks are especially sensitive to interest rates. The reasons the utilities are so interest-sensitive are because of their heavy borrowing needs and their relatively high dividends (which compete directly with yields in money market funds and certificates of deposit). The defensive qualities of utilities make them especially attractive during economic downturns and also explain their relatively strong performance at stock market bottoms.

Although most of the 15 stocks are electric utilities (which are more interest-sensitive), some gas companies are included, which can be influenced by changes in natural gas prices. At market peaks, in particular, natural gas companies have a tendency to lag behind the electric utility stocks. The explosion in energy prices toward the end of 1989, and the relatively strong performance of gas companies during that fourth quarter, may partially explain why the Dow Utility Average set new highs as 1989 ended.

Because of their strong link to bonds and their tendency to lead the stock market, the utility stocks fit into the growing intermarket arsenal. The stock market is influenced by the utility stocks, which are influenced by the bond market and interest rates. Bonds and interest rates are influenced by commodity trends which, in turn, are affected by the trend of the U.S. dollar. Given their impressive record as a leading indicator of the Dow Industrials, I suspect that if Charles Dow were alive today, he'd make the Dow Utilities an integral part of his Dow Theory.

11

Relative-Strength Analysis
of Commodities

In stock market work, *relative-strength* analysis is very common. Portfolio managers move their money into those stock groups they believe will lead the next stock market advance or, in a down market, will decline less than the other groups. In other words, they're looking for those stock groups or stocks that will *outperform* the general market on a relative basis. The group rotation process is scrutinized to determine which stock groups are leaders and which are laggards. Stock groups and individual stocks are compared to some objective benchmark, usually the Standard and Poor's 500 stock index. A ratio is calculated by dividing the stock group or the individual stock by the S&P 500 index. If the *relative-strength* (RS) line is rising, the other entity is outperforming the general market. If the *relative-strength* (RS) line is declining, the stock group or stock is underperforming the market.

There are two major advantages to the use of relative-strength analysis as a technical trading tool. First, another confirming technical indicator is created on the price chart. If technical traders see a breakout on their price chart or some technical evidence that an item is beginning a move, they can look to the relative-strength line for added confirmation. *Bullish action on the price chart should be confirmed by a rising relative-strength line.* Divergence can play a role as well. A price move on the chart that is not confirmed by the RS line can create a divergence with the price action and warn of a possible trend change.

The second advantage lies in the ability to *rank* various items according to relative strength. By *normalizing* the relative-strength numbers in some fashion, traders can rank the various groups or individual items from the strongest to the weakest. This will enable them to focus their attention on those items with the greatest relative strength (if they're looking to buy) or the lowest relative strength (if they're looking to sell). In this chapter, the same principles of relative-strength analysis will be applied to the commodity markets. Since the chapter will be dealing with commodity markets instead of stocks, the Commodity Research Bureau Futures Index will be employed.

All that is required for relative-strength analysis is the availability of some objective benchmark that commodity groups and individual commodities can be measured against. The logical choice is the CRB Index, which includes all of the commodities we'll be looking at (with the exception of gasoline). There are several ways commodity traders can employ relative-strength analysis to facilitate trade selection. To begin, a group selection approach will be used.

GROUP ANALYSIS

Utilizing the seven commodity sub-indices provided by the Commodity Research Bureau, we'll determine which groups have turned in the best performance on a relative-strength basis. The use of group analysis simplifies the trade selection process and helps commodity traders determine which commodity sectors are turning in the strongest or the weakest performances. Buying should be concentrated in the strongest sectors and selling in the weakest. After isolating the best group candidates, the relative-strength comparisons within those groups will be considered. The relative performance between the two leading groups will also be compared to see which is the best bet. Group analysis doesn't always tell the whole story, however.

INDIVIDUAL RANKINGS

Individual market comparisons can also help isolate which markets are turning in the best relative-strength performance. In this section the individual markets will be ranked by relative performance over two time periods to see which ones qualify as the best buying or selling candidates. The reason for using two time periods is to see if a market's relative ranking is improving or deteriorating. Suggestions will be made about how traders might incorporate this information into their overall trading plans.

RATIO ANALYSIS

Ratio analysis is generally employed in relative-strength analysis. (*Relative-strength* analysis in this context refers to the comparison of two entities, utilitizing price ratios, and is not to be confused with the *Relative Strength Index*, which is an oscillator developed by Welles Wilder.) Ratio charts allow comparisons between any two entities regardless of how they are priced. Some commodities are priced in cents per bushel, dollars per ounce, or cents per pound. The CRB Index is priced in points. Ratio analysis allows for universal comparisons. The ability to compare any two entities is especially important when making comparisons between different financial sectors, such as the CRB Index (commodities), foreign currencies, Treasury bonds, and stock index futures, a subject that will be discussed in Chapter 12. However, there's still something else needed.

RELATIVE-STRENGTH RATIOS

When one entity is divided by another, a value or quotient is the result. These values can be plotted on a chart and compared with other values or ratio lines. However, the actual value will be influenced by the price of the numerator. Assuming a constant denominator, if the commodity in the numerator has a higher value than another commodity, the resulting quotient will also be higher. Therefore, a more objective method is required in order to compare the ratio values. A *relative* ratio does two things. First, it creates a *ratio* by dividing one entity (such as a commodity) by another entity (such as the CRB Index). It then creates an *index* with a starting value of 100, which begins at any time interval chosen by the trader.

This study will be using time spans of 25 and 100 trading days in the examples, although any period could have been chosen. The computer will give each ratio a starting value of 100 for any time period chosen. By doing so, it is possible to compare relative values. For example, one ratio may show a value of 110 over the selected time span. Another may show a ratio of 90. This means that the ratio of 110 increased by 10 percent during the time span chosen. The ratio of 90 declined by 10 percent during the same period. The market with a ratio of 110 outperformed the market with 90 and will have a higher relative-strength ranking. The relative ratio lines will look the same as ordinary ratio lines on the chart. The major advantage of the *relative ratio* is the ability to *compare* the actual ratio values on an objective basis and then to rank them according to relative performance.

GROUP COMPARISON

Compare the relative performance of the seven CRB Group Indexes in the 100 days spanning October 1989 to mid-February 1990. By using a relative ratio and choosing a 100 day time period, it is possible to determine a relative ranking of the seven groups over the latest five-month period.*

1. Energy (104.46)
2. Precious Metals (104.38)
3. Livestock & Meats (102.82)
4. Imported (97.03)
5. Industrials (95.97)
6. Oilseeds (95.54)
7. Grains (95.39)

Before even looking at a chart, some useful information is available. It is known that, during the previous 100 trading days, the *energy* and *precious metal* groups turned in the best relative performance, whereas the *grains* were the weakest. (Gold and energy stocks were also the two best performing stock market groups during this same time period.) The premise of relative-strength analysis is similar to that of trend analysis—that trends persist. The basic assumption is that if one is looking for markets with bullish potential, a logical place to start is with those markets that have demonstrated superior relative performance. There's no guarantee that superior performance will continue, but it provides a place to start. The next step is to analyze the ratio charts themselves.

COMMODITY GROUP RATIO CHARTS

Figures 11.1 through 11.3 plot the two leading groups (energy and precious metals) and the weakest group (the grains). Each Figure shows the actual commodity group index in the upper chart and the relative ratio line in the lower chart. The time span on all the charts is 100 trading days. The *relative ratio* simply divides the group index in question by the CRB Index. Chart analysis can then be applied to the group index itself and the ratio line. As a rule, they should trend in the same direction.

*See Chapter 7 for an explanation of the CRB Group Indexes.

FIGURE 11.1
THE UPPER CHART SHOWS THE CRB ENERGY GROUP INDEX OVER 100 DAYS. THE LOWER CHART IS A *RELATIVE RATIO* OF THE ENERGY GROUP INDEX DIVIDED BY THE CRB INDEX. RATIO LINES CAN BE COMPARED TO THE ACTUAL INDEX FOR SIGNS OF DIVERGENCE. TREND-LINES CAN BE EMPLOYED ON THE RATIO ITSELF. AFTER BEING THE BEST-PERFORMING COMMODITY GROUP IN LATE 1989, ENERGY FUTURES LOST GROUND IN EARLY 1990.

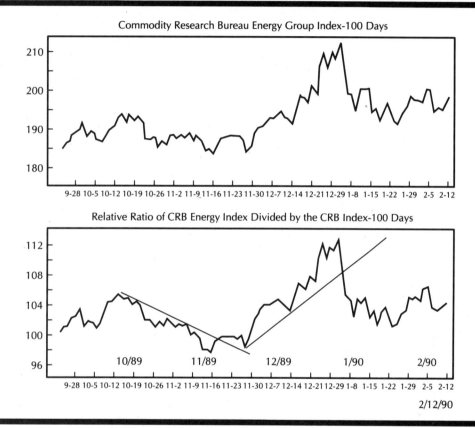

Commodity Research Bureau Energy Group Index-100 Days

Relative Ratio of CRB Energy Index Divided by the CRB Index-100 Days

2/12/90

FIGURE 11.2
**A COMPARISON OF THE CRB PRECIOUS METALS GROUP INDEX (UPPER CHART) AND A REL-
ATIVE RATIO OF THE PRECIOUS METALS INDEX (LOWER CHART) DIVIDED BY THE CRB INDEX
OVER 100 DAYS. PRECIOUS METALS WERE THE SECOND STRONGEST COMMODITY GROUP IN
THE FOURTH QUARTER OF 1989. THE BREAKING OF THE UP TRENDLINE IN LATE DECEMBER
SIGNALED THAT THE PRECIOUS METALS' RELATIVE STRENGTH WAS SLIPPING.**

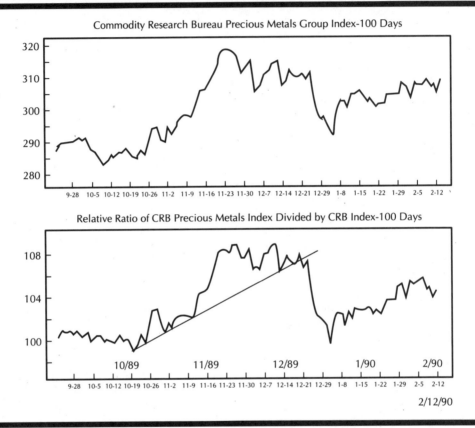

Commodity Research Bureau Precious Metals Group Index-100 Days

Relative Ratio of CRB Precious Metals Index Divided by CRB Index-100 Days

2/12/90

FIGURE 11.3
THE CRB GRAIN GROUP INDEX (UPPER CHART) IS COMPARED TO A RELATIVE RATIO OF THE GRAIN INDEX DIVIDED BY THE CRB INDEX (BOTTOM CHART) OVER 100 DAYS. GRAINS WERE THE WEAKEST COMMODITY GROUP AS 1990 BEGAN BUT ARE SHOWING SIGNS OF STABILIZING. IN LATE 1989, THE RATIO TURNED DOWN BEFORE THE ACTUAL CRB GRAIN INDEX.

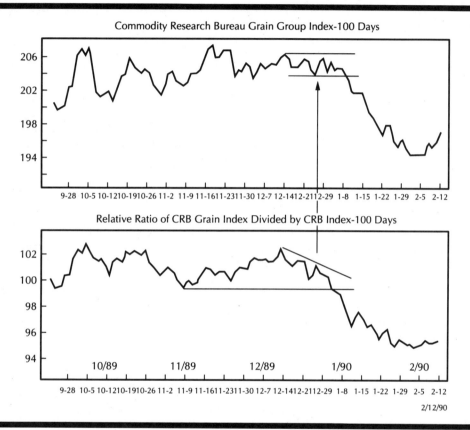

ENERGY GROUP ANALYSIS

Having identified the two strongest groups, the trader should look within each group for the best performing individual commodities. Figures 11.4 through 11.6 plot the relative performance of the three energy markets: crude oil, unleaded gasoline, and heating oil. The energy group turned in the best performance, with a 100-day relative ratio of 104.46. This means the group as a whole gained 4.46 percent during the previous 100 days relative to the CRB Index. The rankings among the three energy markets are:

1. Crude oil (112.24)
2. Gasoline (111.39)
3. Heating oil (103.11)

These rankings would suggest that long positions be placed with crude oil as opposed to the products, assuming that the trader is bullish on the group. If the trader is bearish on energy prices, the products would qualify as better short-sale candidates.

FIGURE 11.4
CRUDE OIL FUTURES (UPPER CHART) COMPARED TO A CRUDE OIL/CRB INDEX RATIO (BOTTOM CHART) OVER 100 DAYS. THE BULLISH BREAKOUT IN CRUDE OIL IN LATE NOVEMBER OF 1989 WAS CONFIRMED BY SIMILAR BULLISH ACTION IN THE OIL/CRB RATIO. BOTH ARE TESTING UP TRENDLINES.

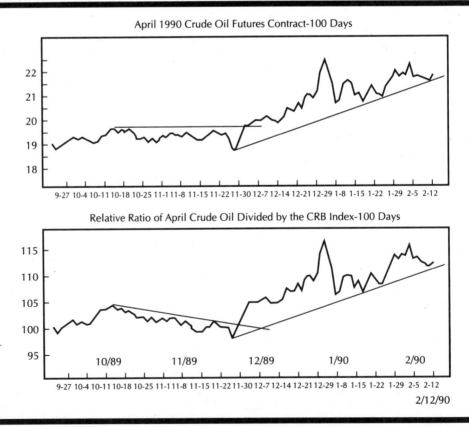

FIGURE 11.5

UNLEADED GASOLINE FUTURES (UPPER CHART) COMPARED TO A GASOLINE/CRB INDEX RATIO (LOWER CHART). BOTH CHARTS ARE SIMILAR. ANY VIOLATION OF THE LOWER TRADING BANDS WOULD BE BEARISH FOR GASOLINE. GASOLINE FUTURES OUTPERFORMED THE CRB INDEX BY 11 PERCENT IN THE PREVIOUS 100 DAYS BUT LOST 10 PERCENT FROM THEIR JANUARY PEAK RELATIVE TO THE CRB INDEX.

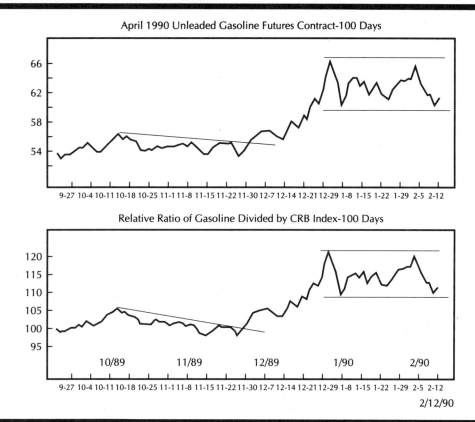

April 1990 Unleaded Gasoline Futures Contract-100 Days

Relative Ratio of Gasoline Divided by CRB Index-100 Days

2/12/90

FIGURE 11.6
HEATING OIL FUTURES (UPPER CHART) COMPARED TO A HEATING OIL/CRB INDEX RATIO (BOTTOM CHART). HEATING OIL HAS BEEN THE WEAKEST OF THE ENERGY MARKETS DURING THE LAST 100 TRADING DAYS. IF THE ENERGY MARKETS BREAK DOWN, HEATING OIL MAY BE THE BEST SHORT-SELLING CANDIDATE BECAUSE OF ITS WEAK RELATIVE-STRENGTH RANKING.

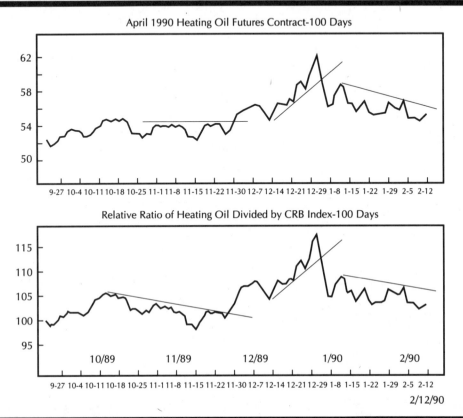

PRECIOUS METALS GROUP ANALYSIS

Figures 11.7 through 11.9 plot the three precious metals (gold, platinum, and silver) in order of their own performance relative to the CRB Index. Over the past 100 days, these are the relative rankings of the three precious metals:

1. Gold (109.20)
2. Platinum (105.40)
3. Silver (95.92)

The relative ratio for gold appreciated by 9.2 percent over the past 100 days, and platinum by 5.4 percent. The silver ratio actually lost 4.08 percent. These rankings suggest that of the three, gold is the strongest, platinum is the second strongest, and silver, a weak third. This technique would suggest that primary emphasis should be

FIGURE 11.7

GOLD FUTURES (UPPER CHART) COMPARED TO A GOLD/CRB INDEX RATIO (BOTTOM CHART). GOLD HAS OUTPERFORMED THE CRB INDEX BY 9 PERCENT DURING THE PREVIOUS 100 DAYS BUT IS LOSING MOMENTUM. THE RATIO LINE HAS ALREADY BROKEN A MINOR SUPPORT LEVEL AND MAY BE SIGNALING IMPENDING WEAKNESS IN GOLD.

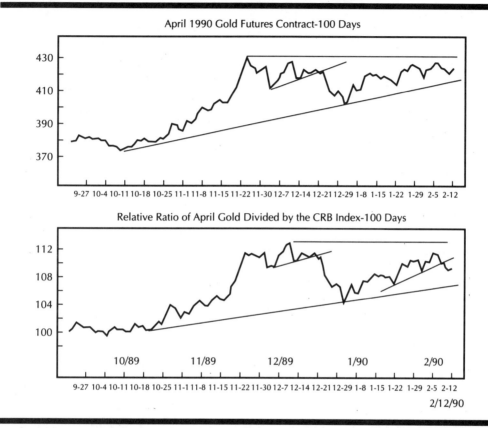

April 1990 Gold Futures Contract-100 Days

Relative Ratio of April Gold Divided by the CRB Index-100 Days

2/12/90

put on the long side of gold and platinum, if the trader is bullish on the group. If the trader is bearish on precious metals, silver would be the best short sale.

Ratio analysis within a group can also be helpful in finding the one or two commodities that are most likely to outperform the others. Ratio analysis will be applied to the precious metals markets to see what conclusions might be found. Figure 11.10 is a platinum/gold ratio during the 100 days from October 1989 to mid-February 1990. This is the same time horizon being used for all the examples. The chart on the top and the relative ratio along the bottom both show that gold has outperformed platinum over the past few months. Although both have been moving upward, gold has been the better relative performer. However, as the ratio chart on the bottom of Figure 11.10 shows, this may be changing. On a relative strength basis, the platinum/gold ratio has broken a down trendline and is breaking out to the upside. This relative action would suggest that traders in the precious metals should begin switching some capital out of gold into platinum on the assumption that platinum will now be the stronger of the two.

FIGURE 11.8
**PLATINUM FUTURES (UPPER CHART) COMPARED TO A PLATINUM/CRB INDEX RATIO (BOT-
TOM CHART). ALTHOUGH BOTH CHARTS ARE SIMILAR, THE RATIO LINE IS LAGGING BEHIND
PLATINUM FUTURES. THIS MINOR BEARISH DIVERGENCE MAY BE HINTING THAT THE PLAT-
INUM RALLY WILL BEGIN TO WEAKEN.**

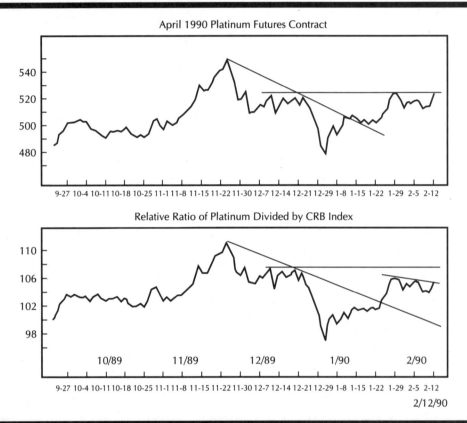

2/12/90

FIGURE 11.9
**SILVER FUTURES (UPPER CHART) COMPARED TO A SILVER/CRB INDEX RATIO (BOTTOM CHART).
SILVER HAS BEEN THE WEAKEST OF THE PRECIOUS METALS AND UNDERPERFORMED THE CRB
INDEX BY 4 PERCENT IN THE PRIOR 100 TRADING DAYS. UPSIDE BREAKOUTS IN SILVER FU-
TURES AND THE SILVER/CRB RATIO ARE NEEDED TO TURN THE CHART PICTURE BULLISH.**

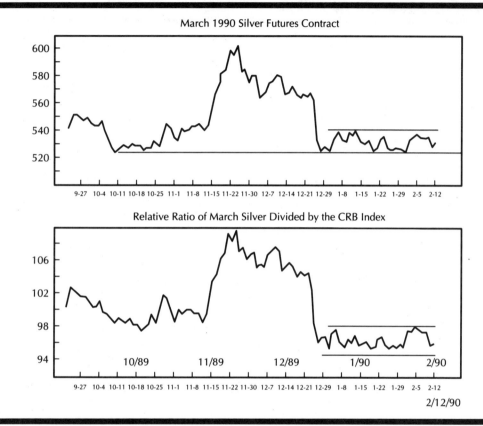

2/12/90

FIGURE 11.10
GOLD AND PLATINUM FUTURES (UPPER CHART) ARE COMPARED TO A PLATINUM/GOLD RATIO (BOTTOM CHART). ALTHOUGH GOLD WAS STRONGER DURING THE FOURTH QUARTER OF 1989, THE BREAKING OF THE DOWN TRENDLINE BY THE RATIO IN JANUARY 1990 SUGGESTS THAT PLATINUM IS NOW THE STRONGER. BULLISH TRADERS WOULD BUY PLATINUM. BEARISH TRADERS WOULD SHORT GOLD.

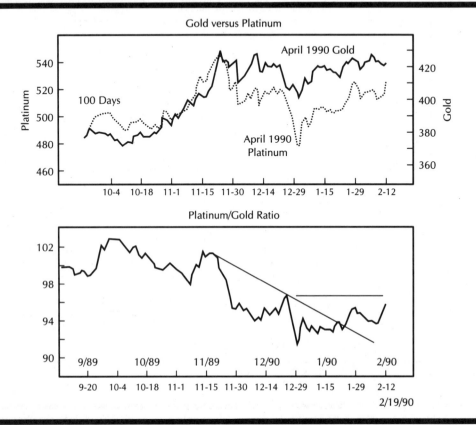

GOLD/SILVER RATIO

Figure 11.11 shows the gold/silver ratio over the same 100 days. Since the ratio line has been rising, we can see that gold has outperformed silver by a wide margin. However, the up trendline drawn from the November lows has been broken. If the ratio starts to weaken further, this would suggest that silver is undervalued relative to gold and implies that silver merits consideration as a buying candidate. The upper chart compares the actual performance of gold versus silver. While gold is stalled at overhead resistance, silver has yet to rise above its potential basing area. An upside breakout by silver, if accompanied by a falling gold/silver ratio, would suggest that silver is the better candidate for a long position of the two precious metals.

FIGURE 11.11
GOLD AND SILVER FUTURES (UPPER CHART) COMPARED TO A GOLD/SILVER RATIO (BOTTOM CHART). GOLD HAS OUTPERFORMED SILVER BY 14 PERCENT OVER THE PREVIOUS 100 DAYS. THE BREAKING OF THE RATIO UP TRENDLINE IS SUGGESTING THAT SILVER MAY NOW BE THE STRONGER. HOWEVER, SILVER STILL NEEDS AN UPSIDE BREAKOUT ON ITS CHART TO JUSTIFY TURNING BULLISH.

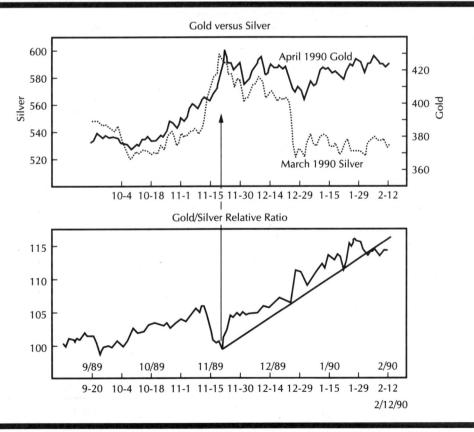

GOLD VERSUS OIL

It's also useful to compare performance between two different groups of commodities such as metals and energy. The top chart in Figure 11.12 compares gold and crude oil futures. The bottom chart plots a gold/oil ratio. When the ratio is rising (as happened during October and November 1989), gold is the better performer. Since the beginning of December, however, oil has been the better performer (since the gold/oil ratio is dropping). Considering that both gold and oil turned in strong performances during the fourth quarter of 1989, money could have been made on the long side of both markets. Relative-strength comparisons between those two strong markets, however, would have given the technical trader an added edge—the ability to direct more money into the stronger performing commodity.

RANKING INDIVIDUAL COMMODITIES

Another way to rank relative commodity performance is simply to bypass the groups and list the individual markets by their *relative ratios*. During this discussion, this

FIGURE 11.12
GOLD AND CRUDE OIL FUTURES (UPPER CHART) COMPARED TO A GOLD/CRUDE OIL RATIO (BOTTOM CHART). THROUGH NOVEMBER OF 1989, GOLD OUTPERFORMED OIL AND WAS THE BETTER PURCHASE. SINCE THE BEGINNING OF DECEMBER, OIL DID BETTER. TRADERS CAN USE RATIOS TO CHOOSE BETWEEN BULLISH ALTERNATIVES.

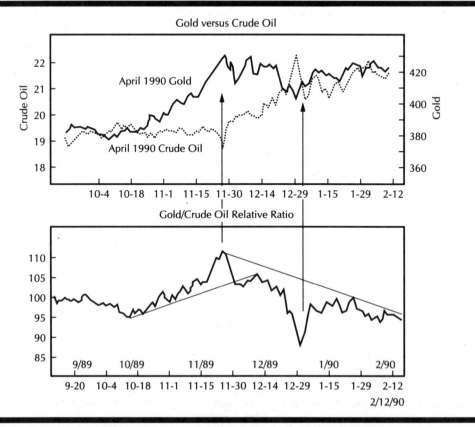

will be done for two separate time periods—100 days and 25 days. By using two different time periods, it can be determined if the relative rankings of the commodities are changing.

Commodity	Ranking (last 25 days)	Commodity	Ranking (last 100 days)
Lumber	105.70*	Orange juice	144.34
Orange juice	105.62	Crude oil	112.24
Platinum	105.59*	Gasoline	111.39
Crude oil	105.36	Hogs	109.41
Sugar	104.52*	Gold	109.20
Coffee	104.40*	Platinum	105.40
Gold	103.27	Lumber	104.40
Cattle	103.04*	Sugar	104.34
Cocoa	102.03*	Heating oil	103.11
Corn	101.61*	Cattle	102.79
Cotton	101.23*	Porkbellies	99.59
Gasoline	100.59	Corn	99.13
Soy. oil	100.40*	Coffee	97.71
Silver	100.28*	Wheat	96.81
Heating oil	98.29	Silver	95.92
Hogs	98.12	Soy. oil	93.91
Soybeans	97.24	Soybeans	91.16
Wheat	96.12	Oats	90.07
Oats	93.54	Soy. meal	89.04
Meal	93.04	Cotton	88.81
Copper	90.88*	Cocoa	87.28
Bellies	89.76	Copper	82.77

   In the preceding table, two columns of relative-strength rankings are shown. The second column from the left shows the relative ratio (individual commodity divided by the CRB Index) over the past 25 trading days. Column 4 uses a longer span of 100 days. While the longer time span might be more useful for studying longer-range trends, the shorter time interval can alert the trader to shorter-term shifts in relative strength. Column 4 shows that the six best performing markets during the previous five months were orange juice, crude oil, gasoline, hogs, gold, and platinum. Trend followers might want to concentrate on those markets that have been the strongest. Contrarians might focus on those near the bottom of the list such as copper, cocoa, cotton, the soybean complex, and silver on the theory that their downtrends are overdone.

   The asterisks alongside some commodities in column 2 mark those that improved their ranking over the previous five months. Those markets with asterisks that have gained ground in the previous 25 days include, in order of strength: lumber, platinum, sugar, coffee, cattle, cocoa, corn, cotton, soybean oil, silver, and copper. Since those markets are showing improved rankings, a trader looking for new long trades might want to use this list as a starting point in his search. Special emphasis would be placed on those candidates higher up on the list.

* Those commodities that moved up in the rankings

By using two different time spans (such as 100 and 25 days) the trader is able to study not only the rankings, but any shifts taking place in those rankings. Relative-strength numbers alone can be misleading. A market may have a relatively high ranking, but that ranking may be weakening. A market with a lower ranking may be strengthening. While the relative rankings are important, the *trend* of the rankings is more important. The final decision depends on the chart pattern of the ratio line. As in standard chart analysis, the trader wants to be a buyer in an early uptrend in the ratio line. Signs of a topping pattern in the ratio line (such as the breaking of an up trendline) would suggest a possible short sale. Figures 11.13 through 11.15 show relative ratios of six selected commodities in the 100 days from September 1989 to mid-February 1990.

SELECTED COMMODITIES

Figure 11.13 shows the lumber/CRB ratio in the upper box; the orange juice/CRB ratio is shown in the lower chart. These markets rank one and two over the past 25 days.

FIGURE 11.13
TWO STRONG PERFORMERS IN LATE 1989–EARLY 1990. THE TOP CHART SHOWS A LUM-BER/CRB INDEX RATIO. THE BOTTOM CHART USES A 40-DAY MOVING AVERAGE ON THE OR-ANGE JUICE/CRB RATIO. BOTH MARKETS HAVE BEEN STRONG BUT LOOK OVEREXTENDED. MARKETS WITH HIGH RELATIVE-STRENGTH RANKINGS ARE SOMETIMES TOO OVERBOUGHT TO BUY.

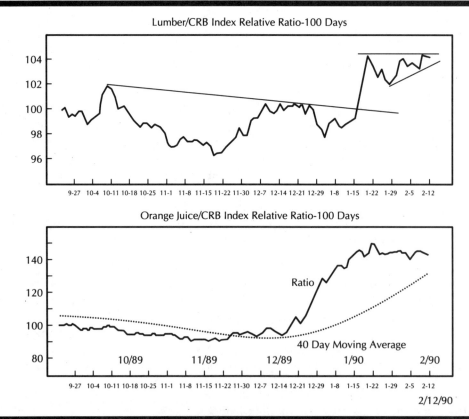

2/12/90

FIGURE 11.14
THE SUGAR/CRB RATIO (UPPER CHART) LOOKS BULLISH BUT NEEDS AN UPSIDE BREAKOUT TO RESUME ITS UPTREND. THE COFFEE/CRB RATIO (BOTTOM CHART) HAS JUST COMPLETED A BULLISH BREAKOUT. ALTHOUGH SUGAR HAS A HIGHER RATIO VALUE (104 FOR SUGAR VERSUS 97 FOR COFFEE), COFFEE HAS A BETTER TECHNICAL PATTERN. BOTH MARKETS ARE INCLUDED IN THE CRB IMPORTED GROUP INDEX AND ARE RALLYING TOGETHER.

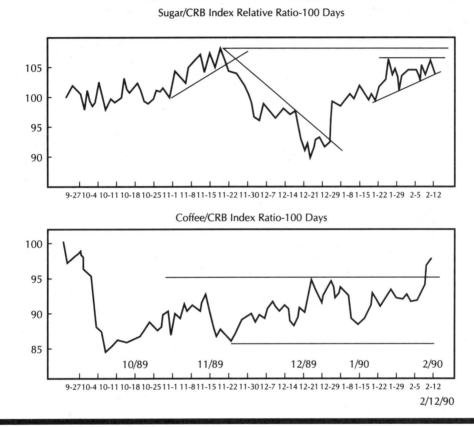

Sugar/CRB Index Relative Ratio-100 Days

Coffee/CRB Index Ratio-100 Days

(Orange juice ranked first over the previous 100 days, and lumber ranked seventh). Figure 11.14 shows the ratios for sugar (upper box) and coffee (lower). Although sugar has the higher ranking over the previous month, coffee has the better-looking chart. Figure 11.15 shows a couple of weaker performers that are showing some signs of bottoming action. The cotton ratio (upper box) and the soybean oil (lower chart) have just broken down trendlines and may be just starting a move to the upside. Figure 11.16 uses copper as an example of a market near the bottom of the relative strength ranking that is just beginning to turn up.

SUMMARY

This chapter applied *relative-strength* analysis to the commodity markets by using *ratios* of the individual commodities and commodity groups divided by the CRB Index. By using *relative ratios*, it is also possible to compare relative-strength numbers for purposes of *ranking* commodity groups and markets. The purpose of relative-strength analysis is to concentrate long positions in the strongest commodity markets

FIGURE 11.15
EXAMPLES OF TWO RATIOS THAT ARE JUST BEGINNING TO TURN UP IN THE FIRST QUARTER OF 1990. THE COTTON/CRB INDEX RATIO (UPPER CHART) AND THE SOYBEAN OIL/CRB INDEX (BOTTOM CHART) HAVE BROKEN DOWN TRENDLINES. SOYBEAN OIL HAS THE BETTER PATTERN AND HIGHER RELATIVE RATIO THAN COTTON.

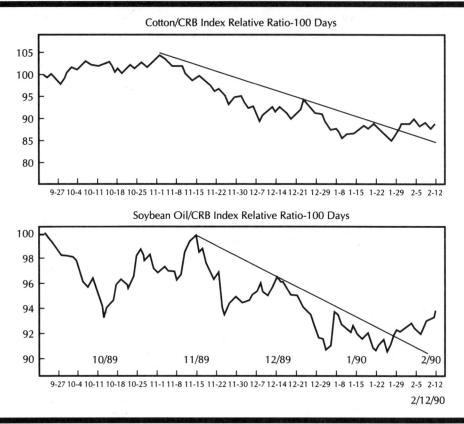

within the strongest commodity groups. One way to accomplish this is to isolate the strongest groups and then to concentrate on the strongest commodities within those groups. A second way is to rank the commodities individually. Short-selling candidates would be concentrated in the weakest commodities in the weakest groups.

The trend of the relative ratio is crucial. The best way to determine this trend is to apply standard chart analysis to the ratio itself. The ratio line should also be compared to the group or commodity for signs of *confirmation* or *divergence*. A second way is to compare the rankings over different time spans to see if those rankings are improving or weakening. The *trend* of the ratio is more important than its *ranking*. One caveat to the use of rankings is that those markets near the top of the list may be overbought and those near the bottom, oversold.

Ratio analysis enables traders to choose between markets that are giving simultaneous buy signals or simultaneous sell signals. Traders could buy the strongest of the bullish markets and sell the weakest of the bearish markets. Used in this fashion, ratio analysis becomes a useful supplement to traditional chart analysis. Ratio analysis can be used within commodity groups (such as the platinum/gold and gold/silver ratios) or between related markets (such as the gold/crude oil ratio).

FIGURE 11.16
AN EXAMPLE OF A DEEPLY OVERSOLD MARKET. COPPER HAD THE LOWEST RELATIVE-STRENGTH RANKING DURING THE PREVIOUS 100 TRADING DAYS. A LOW RANKING, COMBINED WITH AN UPTURN IN THE RATIO, USUALLY SIGNALS AN OVERSOLD MARKET THAT IS READY TO RALLY. CONTRARIANS CAN FIND BUYING CANDIDATES NEAR THE BOTTOM OF THE RELATIVE-STRENGTH RANKINGS AND SELLING CANDIDATES NEAR THE TOP OF THE RANKINGS.

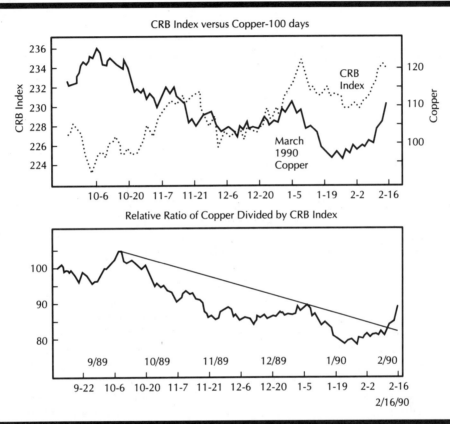

By applying relative-strength analysis to the commodity markets, technical traders are using intermarket principles as an adjunct to standard technical analysis. In addition to analyzing the chart action of individual markets, commodity traders are using data from related commodity markets to aid them in their trade selection. Another dimension has been added to the trading process. As in all intermarket work, traders are turning their focus outward instead of inward. They are learning that nothing happens in isolation and that all commodity markets are related in some fashion to other commodity markets. They are now using those interrelationships as part of their technical trading strategy.

While this chapter dealt with relative action within the commodity world, *relative-strength* analysis has important implications for all financial sectors, including bonds and stocks. Ratio analysis can be used to compare the various financial sectors for purposes of analysis and can be a useful tool in tactical asset allocation. Chapter 12 will focus on ratio analysis between the financial sectors—commodities, bonds, and stocks—and will also address the role of commodities as an asset class in the asset allocation process.

12

Commodities and Asset Allocation

In the preceding chapter, the concept of *relative-strength*, or *ratio*, analysis was applied within the commodity markets. This chapter will expand on that application in order to include the relative action between the commodity markets (represented by the CRB Index) and bonds and stocks. There are two purposes in doing so. One is simply to introduce another technical tool to demonstrate how closely these three financial sectors (commodities, bonds, and stocks) are interrelated and *to show how intermarket ratios can yield important clues to market direction*. Ratio charts can help warn of impending trend changes and can become an important supplement to traditional chart analysis. A rising CRB Index to bond ratio, for example, is usually a warning that inflation pressures are intensifying. In such an environment, commodities will outperform bonds. A rising CRB/bond ratio also carries bearish implications for stocks.

The secondary purpose is to address the feasibility of utilizing commodity markets as a separate asset class along with bonds and stocks. Up to this point, intermarket relationships have been used primarily as technical indicators to help trade the individual sectors. However, there are much more profound implications having to do with *the potential role of commodities in the asset allocation process*. If it can be shown, for example, that commodity markets usually do well when bonds and stocks are doing badly, why wouldn't a portfolio manager consider holding positions in commodity futures, both as a diversification tool and as a hedge against inflation? If bonds and stocks are dropping together, especially during a period of rising inflation, how is diversification achieved by placing most of one's assets in those two financial areas? Why not have a portion of one's assets in a group of markets that usually does well at such times and that actually benefit from rising inflation—namely, the commodity markets?

One of the themes that runs throughout this book has to do with the fact that the important role played by commodity markets in the intermarket picture has been largely ignored by financial traders. By linking commodity markets to bonds and stocks (through the impact of commodities on inflation and interest rates), a breakthrough has been achieved. The full implication of that breakthrough, however, goes beyond utilizing the commodity markets just as a technical indicator for bonds and stocks. It may very well be that *some utilization of commodity markets (such as*

*those represented in the CRB Index) in the asset allocation process, along with bonds,
stocks, and cash, is the most complete and logical application of intermarket analysis.*
While addressing this issue, the question of utilizing managed commodity funds as
another means for bond and stock portfolio managers to achieve diversification and
improve their overall results will also be briefly discussed.

RATIO ANALYSIS OF THE CRB INDEX VERSUS BONDS

This section will begin with a comparison of the CRB Index and Treasury bonds.
As stated many times before, *the inverse relationship of commodity prices to bond
prices is the most consistent and the most important link in intermarket analysis.* The
use of ratio analysis is another useful way to monitor this relationship. Ratio charts
provide chartists with another indicator to analyze and are a valuable supplement to
overlay charts. Traditional technical analysis, including support and resistance levels,
trendlines, moving averages, and the like, can be applied directly to the ratio lines.
These ratio lines will often provide early warnings that the relationship between the
two markets in question is changing.

Figures 12.1 to 12.3 compare the CRB Index to Treasury bonds during the five-
year period from the end of 1985 to the beginning of 1990. All of the figures are
divided into two charts. The upper charts provide an overlay comparison of the CRB
Index to Treasury bonds. The bottom chart in each figure is a relative ratio chart of
the CRB Index divided by Treasury bond futures prices. As explained in Chapter
11, the *relative ratio* indicator is a ratio of any two entities over a selected period of
time with a starting value of 100. By utilizing a starting value of 100, it is possible to
measure relative percentage performance on a more objective basis.

Figure 12.1 shows the entire five-year period. The ratio chart on the bottom was
dropping sharply as 1986 began. A disinflationary period such as that of the early
1980s will be characterized by falling commodity prices and rising bond prices.
Hence, the result will be a falling CRB/bond ratio. When the ratio is falling, as was
the case until 1986 and again from the middle of 1988 to the middle of 1989, inflation
is moderating and bond prices will outperform commodities. When the ratio is rising
(from the 1986 low to the 1988 peak and again at the end of 1989), inflation pressures
are building, and commodities will outperform bonds. As a rule, *a rising CRB/bond
ratio also means higher interest rates.*

The trendlines applied to the ratio chart in Figure 12.1 show how well this type of
chart lends itself to traditional chart analysis. Trendlines can be used for longer-range
trend analysis (see the down trendline break at the 1986 bottom and the breaking of
the two-year up trendline at the start of 1989). Trendline analysis can also be utilized
over shorter time periods, such as the up trendline break in the fall of 1987 and the
breaking of the down trendline in the spring of 1988.

The real message of this chart, however, lies in the simple recognition that there
are periods of time when bonds are the better place to be, and there are times when
commodities are the preferred choice. During the entire five-year period shown in
Figure 12.1, bonds outperformed the CRB Index by almost 30 percent. However, *from
1986 until the middle of 1988, commodities outperformed bonds (solely on a relative
price basis) by about 30 percent.*

Figure 12.2 shows the relative action from the mid-1988 peak in the ratio to
March of 1990. During that year and a half period, bonds outperformed the CRB
Index by about 20 percent. However, in the final six months, from August of 1989
into March of 1990, *the CRB Index outperformed bonds by approximately 12 percent.*

FIGURE 12.1

A COMPARISON OF THE CRB INDEX AND TREASURY BONDS FROM THE END OF 1985 TO EARLY 1990. THE UPPER CHART IS AN OVERLAY COMPARISON. THE BOTTOM CHART IS A RELATIVE RATIO CHART OF THE CRB INDEX DIVIDED BY BOND FUTURES. A RISING RATIO FAVORS COMMODITIES, WHEREAS A FALLING RATIO FAVORS BONDS. FROM 1986 TO MID-1988, COMMODITY PRICES OUTPERFORMED BONDS BY ABOUT 30 PERCENT. TRENDLINES HELP PINPOINT TURNS IN THE RATIO.

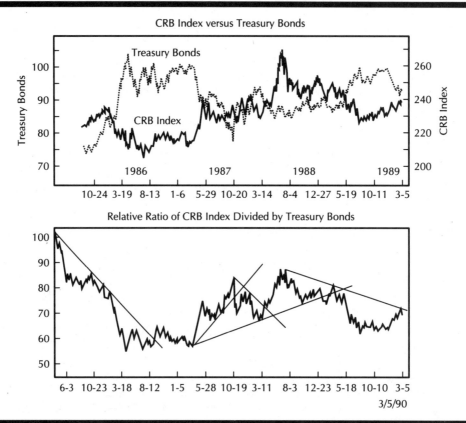

This chart also shows that the breakdown in the ratio in the spring of 1989 reflected a spectacular rally in the bond market and a collapse in commodities.

Figure 12.3 shows a closer picture of the rally in the CRB/bond ratio that began in the summer of 1989. This figure shows that the bottom in the ratio in August 1989 (bottom chart) coincided with a peak in the bond market and a bottom in the CRB Index (upper chart). Inflation pressures that began to build during the fourth quarter of 1989 began from precisely that point. And very few people noticed. The upside breakout in the ratio in Figure 12.3 near the end of December 1989 indicated that inflation pressures were getting more serious. This put upward pressure on interest rates and increased bearish pressure on bonds.

There are two lessons to be learned from these charts. The first is that turning points in the ratio line can be pinpointed with reasonable accuracy with trendlines and some basic chart analysis. The second is that traders now have a more useful

FIGURE 12.2
AN OVERLAY CHART OF THE CRB INDEX AND TREASURY BONDS (UPPER CHART) AND A RATIO CHART OF THE CRB INDEX DIVIDED BY BONDS (LOWER CHART) FROM EARLY 1988 TO EARLY 1990. THE FALLING RATIO FROM MID-1988 TO MID-1989 WAS BULLISH FOR BONDS. IN THE SEVEN MONTHS SINCE AUGUST OF 1989, THE CRB INDEX OUTPERFORMED BOND FUTURES BY ABOUT 12 PERCENT.

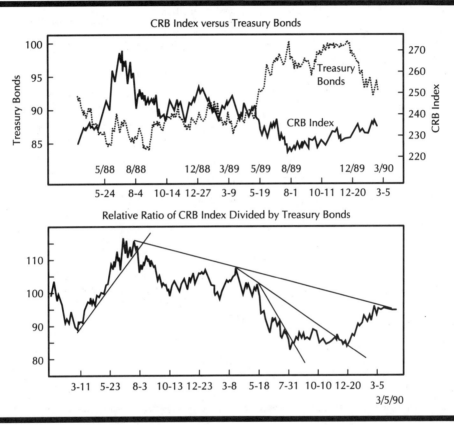

FIGURE 12.3
**THE CRB INDEX VERSUS TREASURY BOND FUTURES FROM FEBRUARY 1989 TO MARCH 1990.
IN AUGUST OF 1989, THE CRB/BOND RATIO HIT BOTTOM. IN DECEMBER, THE RATIO BROKE
OUT TO THE UPSIDE, SIGNALING HIGHER COMMODITIES AND WEAKER BONDS. A RISING
RATIO MEANS HIGHER INTEREST RATES.**

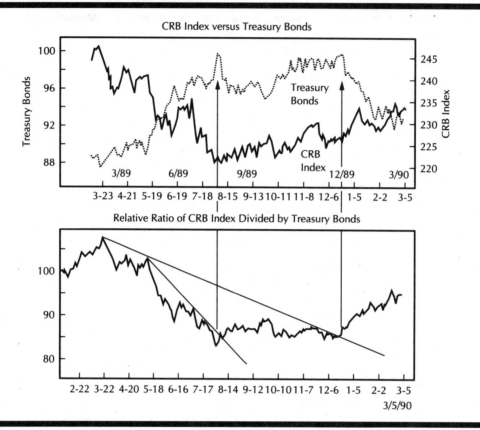

tool to enable them to shift funds between the two sectors. *When the ratio line is rising, buy commodities; when the ratio is falling, buy bonds.* The direction of the CRB Index/bond ratio also says something about the health of the stock market.

THE CRB INDEX VERSUS STOCKS

Figures 12.4 through 12.6 use the same relative-strength format that was employed in the previous figures, except this time the CRB index is divided by the S&P 500 stock index. The time period is the same five years, from the end of 1985 to the first quarter of 1990. The bottom chart in Figure 12.4 shows that the S&P 500 outperformed the CRB Index by almost 50 percent (on a relative price basis) over the entire five years. There were only two periods when commodities outperformed stocks. The first was in the period from the summer of 1987 to the summer of 1988. Not surprisingly, this period encompassed the stock market crash in the second half of 1987 and the

FIGURE 12.4
THE CRB INDEX VERSUS THE S&P 500 STOCK INDEX FROM LATE 1985 TO EARLY 1990. THE CRB/S&P RATIO (BOTTOM CHART) SHOWS THAT ALTHOUGH STOCKS HAVE OUTPERFORMED COMMODITIES DURING THOSE FIVE YEARS, COMMODITIES OUTPERFORMED STOCKS FROM MID-1987 TO MID-1988 AND AGAIN AS 1989 ENDED. COMMODITIES TEND TO DO BETTER WHEN STOCKS FALTER.

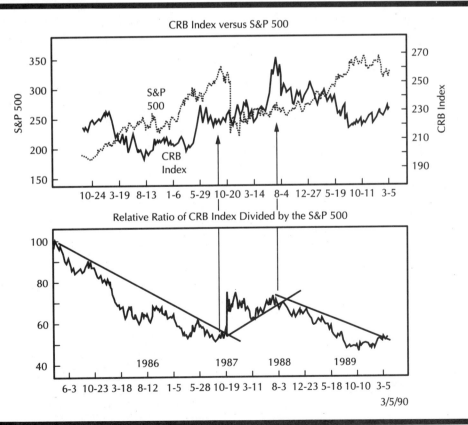

surge in commodity prices during the first half of 1988 owing to the midwest drought. *During these 12 months, the CRB Index outperformed the S&P 500 stock index by about 25 percent.* The second period began in the fourth quarter of 1989 and carried into early 1990.

Figure 12.5 shows a significant up trendline break in the CRB/stock ratio during the summer of 1988 and the completion of a "double top" in the ratio as 1989 began. This breakdown in the ratio confirmed that the pendulum had swung away from commodities and back to equities. In October of 1989, however, the pendulum began to swing back to commodities.

In mid-October of 1989, the U.S. stock market suffered a severe selloff as shown in the upper portion of Figure 12.6. A second peak was formed during the first week of January 1990. Stocks then dropped sharply again. The upper portion of Figure 12.6 also shows that commodity prices were rising while stocks were dropping. The lower portion of this chart shows two prominent troughs in the CRB/S&P ratio in October and January and a gradual uptrend in the ratio. From October 1989 to the end of February 1990, *the CRB Index outperformed the S&P 500 by about 14 percent.*

FIGURE 12.5
THE CRB INDEX VERSUS THE S&P 500 FROM 1987 TO EARLY 1990. THE *DOUBLE TOP* IN THE CRB/S&P RATIO (BOTTOM CHART) DURING THE SECOND HALF OF 1988 SIGNALED A SHIFT AWAY FROM COMMODITIES TO EQUITIES. IN THE FOURTH QUARTER OF 1989, COMMODITIES GAINED RELATIVE TO STOCKS.

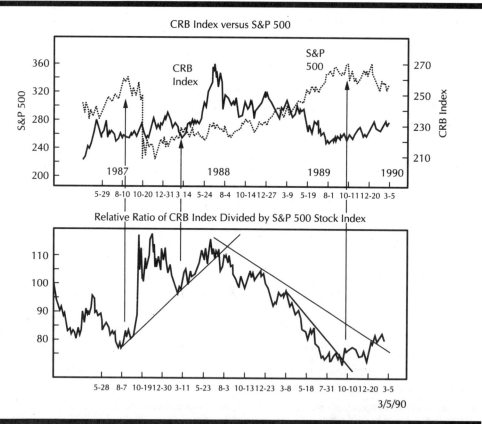

Reproduced with permission by Knight Ridder's Tradecenter. Tradecenter is a registered trademark of Knight Ridder's Financial Information.

FIGURE 12.6
**THE CRB INDEX VERSUS THE S&P 500 FROM MID-1989 TO MARCH OF 1990. THE CRB/S&P RA-
TIO (BOTTOM CHART) TROUGHED IN OCTOBER OF 1989 AND JANUARY OF 1990 AS STOCKS
WEAKENED. IN THE FIVE MONTHS SINCE THAT OCTOBER, THE CRB INDEX OUTPERFORMED
THE S&P 500 BY ABOUT 14 PERCENT. DURING STOCK MARKET WEAKNESS, COMMODITIES
USUALLY DO RELATIVELY BETTER.**

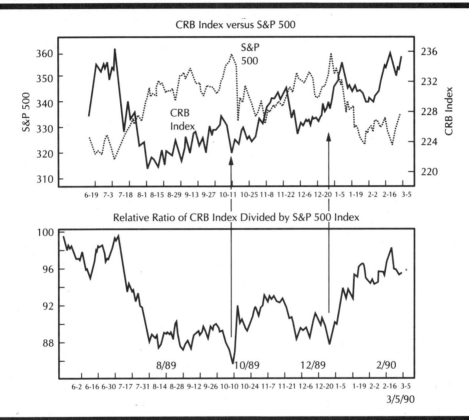

One clear message that emerges from a study of these charts is this. While stocks
have been the better overall performer during the most recent five years, *commodities
tend to do better when the stock market begins to falter.* There's no question that
during a roaring bull market in stocks, commodities appear to add little advantage.
However, it is precisely when stocks begin to tumble that commodities often rally.
This being the case, having some funds in commodities would seem to lessen the
impact of stock market falls and would provide some protection from inflation.

Another way of saying the same thing is that *stocks and commodities usually
do best at different times.* Commodities usually do best in a high inflation environment (such as during the 1970s), which is usually bearish for stocks. A low inflation
environment (when commodities don't do as well) is bullish for stocks. Relative-
strength analysis between commodities and stocks can warn commodity and stock
market traders that existing trends may be changing. A falling ratio would be supportive to stocks and suggests less emphasis on commodity markets. A rising com-
modity/stock ratio would suggest less stock market exposure and more emphasis on
inflation hedges, which would include some commodities.

Bonds and stocks are closely linked. One of the major factors impacting on the price of bonds is inflation. It follows, therefore, that a period of accelerating inflation (rising commodity prices) is usually bearish for bonds and will, in time, be bearish for stocks. Declining inflation (falling commodity prices) is usually beneficial for bonds and stocks. It should come as no surprise then, that *there is a positive correlation between the CRB Index/bond ratio and the CRB Index/S&P 500 ratio*. Figure 12.7 compares the CRB/bond ratio (upper chart) and the CRB/S&P 500 ratio (lower chart) from 1985 into early 1990.

Figure 12.7 shows a general similarity between the two ratios. Four separate trends can be seen in the two ratios. First, both declined during the early 1980s into the 1986–1987 period. Second, both rose into the middle of 1988. Third, both fell from mid-1988 to the third quarter of 1989. Fourth, both rallied as the 1980s ended. The charts suggest that *periods of strong commodity price action (rising inflation) usually have an adverse effect on both bonds and stocks.*

During periods of high inflation (characterized by rising CRB Index/bond-stock ratios), commodities usually outperform both bonds and stocks. This would suggest

FIGURE 12.7
A COMPARISON OF THE CRB/BOND RATIO (UPPER CHART) AND THE CRB/S&P 500 RATIO (LOWER CHART) IN THE FIVE YEARS SINCE 1985. THERE IS A SIMILARITY BETWEEN THE TWO RATIOS. RISING COMMODITY PRICES USUALLY HAVE A BEARISH IMPACT ON BOTH BONDS AND STOCKS, ALTHOUGH THE IMPACT ON BONDS IS MORE IMMEDIATE.

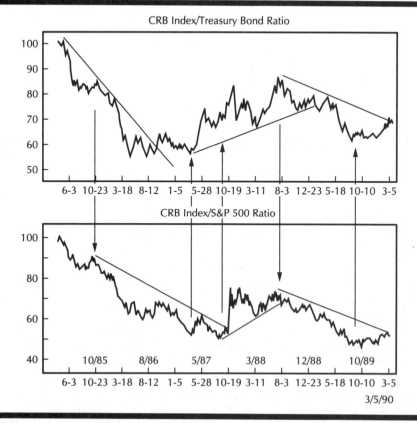

that limiting one's assets to bonds and stocks at such times does not really provide adequate protection against inflation and also falls short of achieving proper diversification. Diversification is achieved by holding assets in areas that are either poorly correlated or negatively correlated. In a high inflation environment, commodities fill both roles.

Figure 12.8 compares the commodity/bond ratio (upper chart) and the commodity/stock ratio (lower chart) from 1988 to early 1990. To the upper left, it can be seen that both ratios turned down at about the same time during the summer of 1988. These downtrends accelerated during the spring of 1989. However, both ratios bottomed out together during the summer of 1989 and rose together into March of 1990. Once again, the similar performance of the two ratios demonstrates the relatively close linkage between bonds and stocks and the negative correlation of commodities to both financial sectors. Traders who attempt to diversify their funds and, at the same time protect against inflation by switching between stocks and bonds,

FIGURE 12.8
A COMPARISON OF THE CRB/BOND RATIO (UPPER CHART) AND THE CRB/S&P RATIO (BOTTOM CHART) FROM EARLY 1988 TO EARLY 1990. BOTH RATIOS PEAKED AT ABOUT THE SAME TIME IN MID-1988 AND BOTTOMED DURING THE SECOND HALF OF 1989. SINCE BOTH RATIOS OFTEN DECLINE AT THE SAME TIME, NEITHER BONDS NOR STOCKS APPEAR TO PROVIDE AN ADEQUATE HEDGE AGAINST INFLATION.

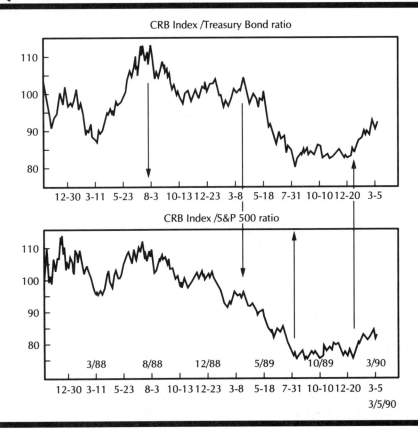

are actually achieving little of each. At times when both bonds and stocks are beginning to weaken, the only area that seems to offer not only protection, but real profit potential, lies in the commodity markets represented by the CRB Index.

THE CRB/BOND RATIO LEADS THE CRB/STOCK RATIO

Another conclusion that can be drawn from studying these two ratios shown in Figure 12.7 and 12.8 is that *the CRB Index/bond ratio usually leads the CRB Index/S&P 500 ratio*. This is easily explained. The bond market is more sensitive to inflation pressures and is more closely tied to the CRB Index. The negative impact of rising inflation on stocks is more delayed and not as strong. Therefore, it would seem logical to expect the commodity/bond ratio to turn first. Used in this fashion, *the CRB/bond ratio can be used as a leading indicator for stocks*. The CRB/bond ratio started to rally strongly in the spring of 1987 while the CRB/stock ratio was still falling (Figure 12.7). The result was the October 1987 stock market crash. The CRB/bond ratio bottomed out in August of 1989 and preceded the final bottom in the CRB/stock ratio two months later in October. In both instances, turning points in the CRB/stock ratio were anticipated by turns in the CRB Index/bond ratio. Figure 12.9 provides another way to study the effect of the commodity/bond ratio on stocks.

Figure 12.9 compares the commodity/bond ratio (bottom chart) with the action in the S&P 500 Index over the five years since 1986. By studying the areas marked off by the arrows, it can be seen that *a rising CRB Index/bond ratio has usually been followed by or accompanied by weak stock prices*. The two most striking examples occurred during 1987 and late 1989. The rising ratio during the first half of 1988 didn't actually push stock prices lower but prevented equities from advancing. The major advance in stock prices during 1988 didn't really begin until the CRB/bond ratio peaked out that summer and started to drop.

A falling ratio has usually been accompanied by firm or rising stock prices. The most notable examples of the bullish impact of a falling ratio on stocks in Figure 12.9 can be seen from the fourth quarter of 1986 to the first quarter of 1987 and the period from the summer of 1988 to the summer of 1989. A falling ratio during the early 1980s also provided a bullish environment for stocks (not shown here). The study of the CRB Index/bond ratio tells a lot about which way the inflation winds are blowing, which of these two markets is in the ascendancy at the moment, and sheds light on prospects for the stock market. *A falling CRB/bond ratio is bullish for stocks. A sharply rising ratio is a bearish warning.*

CAN FUTURES PLAY A ROLE IN ASSET ALLOCATION?

With the development of financial futures over the past twenty years, futures traders can now participate in all financial sectors. Individual commodities, representing the oldest sector of the futures world, can be traded on various exchanges. Metals and energy markets are traded in New York, whereas most agricultural commodities are traded in Chicago. CRB Index futures provide a way to use a basket approach to the commodity markets.

Interest-rate futures provide exposure to Treasury bills, notes, and bonds as well as the short-term Eurodollar market. Stock index futures offer a basket approach to trading general trends in the stock market. Foreign currency futures and the U.S. Dollar Index provide vehicles for participation in foreign exchange trends. All four sectors

FIGURE 12.9
A COMPARISON OF THE S&P 500 STOCK INDEX (UPPER CHART) AND A CRB/TREASURY BOND RATIO (LOWER CHART) SINCE 1986. A RISING CRB/BOND RATIO IS USUALLY BEARISH FOR STOCKS. A FALLING RATIO IS BULLISH FOR EQUITIES. A RISING RATIO DURING 1987 WARNED OF THE IMPENDING MARKET CRASH IN THE FALL OF THAT YEAR. A FALLING RATIO FROM MID-1988 TO MID-1989 HELPED SUPPORT A STRONG UPMOVE IN THE STOCK MARKET.

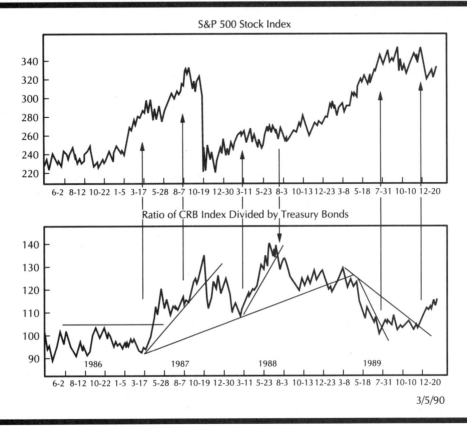

3/5/90

are represented in the futures markets—commodities, currencies, interest rates, and equities. Futures contracts exist on the Japanese and British bond and stock markets as well as on several other overseas financial markets.

Futures traders, therefore, have a lot to choose from. In many ways, *the futures markets provide an excellent asset allocation forum.* Futures traders can easily swing money among the four sectors to take advantage of both short- and long-term market trends. They can emphasize long positions in bond and stock index futures when these financial markets are outperforming the commodity markets, and reverse the process just as easily when the financial markets start to slip and commodities begin to outperform. During periods of rising inflation, they can supplement long positions in commodity markets with long positions in foreign currencies (such as the Deutsche mark), which usually rise along with American commodities (during periods of dollar weakness).

A GLIMPSE OF THE FOUR FUTURES SECTORS

Figure 12.10 provides a glimpse at the four sectors of the futures markets during the 100 days from November of 1989 to the first week of March 1990. The two charts on the left (the Deutsche mark on the upper left and the CRB Index on the bottom left) have been rising for several months. Both areas benefited from a sharp drop in the U.S. dollar (not shown) during that time, which boosted inflation pressures in the states. At such times, traders can buy individual commodity markets (such as gold and oil) or the CRB Index as a hedge against inflation. Or they can buy foreign currency futures, which also rise as the U.S. dollar falls. If they prefer the short side of the market, they can sell the U.S. Dollar Index short and benefit directly from a declining American currency.

FIGURE 12.10
A COMPARISON OF THE FOUR FINANCIAL SECTORS REPRESENTED BY THE FUTURES MARKETS AS 1989 ENDED AND 1990 BEGAN: CURRENCIES (UPPER LEFT), COMMODITIES (LOWER LEFT), BONDS (LOWER RIGHT), AND STOCKS (UPPER RIGHT). BY INCLUDING ALL FOUR SECTORS, FUTURES MARKETS PROVIDE A BUILT-IN ASSET ALLOCATION FORUM. FOREIGN CURRENCIES AND COMMODITIES WILL USUALLY RISE DURING DOWNTURNS IN THE BOND AND STOCK MARKETS.

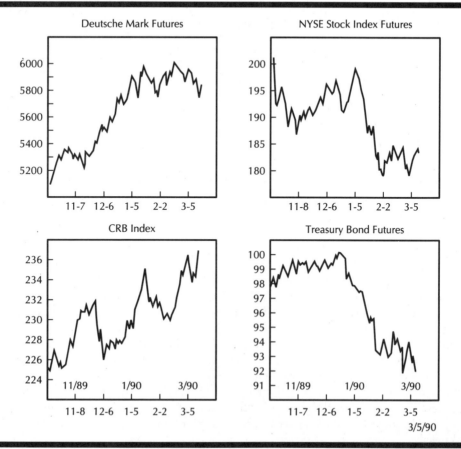

The two charts to the right of Figure 12.10 (NYSE stock index futures on the upper right and Treasury bond futures on the lower right) have been dropping for essentially the same reasons that commodities and foreign currencies have been rising—namely, a falling U.S. dollar and renewed inflation pressures. Futures traders could have chosen to liquidate long positions in bonds and stock index futures during that period and concentrate long positions in commodities and currencies. Or they could have benefited from declining financial markets by initiating short positions in interest rate and stock index futures.

By selling short, a trader actually makes money in falling markets. The nature of futures trading makes short selling as easy as buying. As a result, futures professionals have no bullish or bearish preference. They can buy a rising market or sell a falling market short. The upshot of all of this is an amazing number of choices available to futures traders. They can participate in all market sectors, and trade from both the long and the short side. They can benefit from periods of inflation and periods of disinflation. The futures markets provide an excellent environment for the application of tactical asset allocation, which refers to the switching of funds among various asset classes to achieve superior performance. The fact that futures contracts trade on only 10 percent margin also makes that process quicker and cheaper. Given these facts, professionally managed futures funds would seem to be an ideal place for portfolio managers to seek diversification and protection from inflation.

THE VALUE OF MANAGED FUTURES ACCOUNTS

Over the past few years, money managers have begun to consider the potential benefits of allocating a portion of their assets to managed futures accounts to achieve diversification and some protection against inflation. Attention started to focus on this area with the work of Professor John Lintner of Harvard University. In the spring of 1983, Lintner presented a paper at the annual conference of the Financial Analysts Federation in Toronto, Canada.

The paper entitled "The Proposed Role of Managed Commodity-Financial Futures Accounts (and/or Funds) In Portfolios of Stocks and Bonds" drew attention to the idea of including managed futures accounts as a portion of the traditional portfolio of bonds and stocks. Since then, other researchers have updated Lintner's results with similar conclusions. Those conclusions show that futures portfolios have higher returns and higher risks. However, since returns on futures portfolios tend to be poorly correlated with returns on bonds and stocks, *significant improvements in reward/risk ratios can be achieved by some inclusion of managed futures.* Lintner's paper contained the following statement:

> Indeed, the improvements from holding efficiently selected portfolios of managed accounts or funds are so large—*and* the correlations between the returns on the futures-portfolios and those on the stock and bond portfolios are so surprisingly low (sometimes even negative)—that the return/risk tradeoffs provided by *augmented portfolios,* consisting partly of funds invested with appropriate groups of futures managers (or funds) combined with funds invested in portfolios of stocks alone (or in mixed portfolios of stocks and bonds), clearly dominate the tradeoffs available from portfolios of stocks alone (or from portfolios of stocks and bonds). . . . The combined portfolios of stocks (or stocks and bonds) *after* including judicious investments in appropriately selected . . . managed futures accounts (or funds) show substantially less risk at every possible level of expected return than portfolios of stocks (or stocks and bonds) alone.

WHY ARE FUTURES PORTFOLIOS POORLY CORRELATED WITH STOCKS AND BONDS?

There are two major reasons why futures funds are poorly correlated with bonds and stocks. The first lies in the diversity of the futures markets. Futures fund managers deal in all sectors of the futures markets. *Their trading results are not dependent on just bonds and stocks.* Most futures fund managers are trend-followers. During financial bull markets, they buy interest rate and stock index futures and benefit accordingly. During downturns in bonds and stocks, however, their losses in the financial area will be largely offset by profits in commodities and foreign currencies, which tend to rise at such times. *They have built in diversification by participating in four different sectors which are usually negatively correlated.*

The second reason has to do with short selling. Futures managers are not tied to the long side of any markets. They can benefit from bear markets in bonds and stocks by shorting futures in these two areas. In such an environment, they can hold short positions in the financial markets and long positions in commodities. In this way, they can do very well during periods when financial markets are experiencing downturns, especially if inflation is the major culprit. And this is precisely when traditional bond and stock market portfolio managers need the most help.

The late Dr. Lintner's research and that of other researchers is based on the track records of Commodity Trading Advisors and publicly-traded futures mutual funds, which are monitored and published by *Managed Account Reports* (5513 Twin Knolls Road, Columbia, MD 21045). The purpose in mentioning it here is simply to alert the reader to work being done in this area and to suggest that the benefits of intermarket trading, which is more commonly practised in the futures markets, may someday become more widely recognized and utilized in the investment community.

Let's narrow the focus and concentrate on one portion of the futures portfolio— *the traditional commodity markets.* This book has focused on this group's importance as a hedge against inflation and its interrelationships with the other three sectors— currencies, bonds, and stocks. The availability of the widely-watched Commodity Research Bureau Futures Price Index and the existence of a futures contract on that index have allowed the use of one commodity index for intermarket comparisons. Utilizing an index to represent all commodity markets has made it possible to look at the commodity markets as a whole instead of several small and unrelated parts. Serious work in intermarket analysis (linking commodity markets to the financial markets) began with the introduction of CRB Index futures in 1986 as traders began to study that index more closely on a day-to-day basis.

Why not carry the use of the CRB Index a step further and examine whether or not its components qualify as a separate asset class and, if so, whether any benefits can be achieved by incorporating a *basket* approach to commodity trading into the more traditional investment philosophy? To explore this avenue further, I'm going to rely on statistics compiled by Powers Research Associates, L.P. (30 Montgomery Street, Jersey City, NJ 07306) and published by the New York Futures Exchange in a work entitled "Commodity Futures as an Asset Class" (January 1990).

COMMODITY FUTURES AS AN ASSET CLASS

The study first compares the returns of the four categories (government bonds, corporate bonds, U.S. stocks, and the CRB Index) from 1961 through 1988. U.S. stocks are represented by the S&P 500 Index and U.S. corporate bonds by the Salomon Brothers

Long-Term High-Grade Corporate Bond Index. Government bonds use an approximate maturity of 20 years. The commodity portion is represented by a return on the CRB Index plus 90 percent of the return on Treasury Bills (since a CRB Index futures position only requires a 10 percent margin deposit). Table 12.1 summarizes some of the results.

Over the entire 30-year period, U.S. stocks were the best overall performer (1428.41) whereas the CRB Index came in second (1175.26). In the two periods beginning in 1965 and 1970 to 1988, the CRB Index was the best performer (974.70 and 787.97, respectively), while U.S. stocks took second place (766.78 and 650.69, respectively). Those two periods include the inflationary 1970s when commodities experienced enormous bull markets. In the fifteen years since 1975, stocks regained first place (555.69) while corporate bonds took second place (338.23). The CRB Index slipped to third place (336.47). Since 1980, corporate bonds turned in the best returns (300.58), with stocks and government bonds just about even in second place. The CRB Index, reflecting the low inflation environment of the 1980s, slipped to last. During the final period, from 1985 to 1988, stocks were again the best place to be, with bonds second. Commodities turned in the worst performance in the final four years.

Although financial assets (bonds and stocks) were clearly the favored investments during the 1980s, commodities outperformed bonds by a wide margin over the entire 30-year span and were the best performers of the three classes during the most recent 20- and 25-year spans. The rotating leadership suggests that each asset class has "its day in the sun," and argues against taking too short a view of the relative performance between the three sectors.

WHAT ABOUT RISK?

Total returns are only part of the story. Risk must also be considered. Higher returns are usually associated with higher risk, which is just what the study shows. During the 30 years under study, stock market returns showed an average standard deviation of 3.93, the largest of all the asset classes. (Standard deviation measures portfolio variance and is a measure of risk. The higher the number, the greater the risk.) The CRB Index had the second highest with 2.83. Government and corporate bonds showed

TABLE 12.1
YEARLY RETURNS: BONDS, EQUITIES, AND COMMODI-
TIES (ASSUMING A $100 INVESTMENT IN EACH CLASS
DURING EACH TIME PERIOD)

	Govt. Bonds	Corp. Bonds	U.S. Stocks	CRB Index
1960–1988	442.52	580.21	1428.41	1175.26
1965–1988	423.21	481.04	766.78	974.70
1970–1988	423.58	452.70	650.69	787.97
1975–1988	314.16	338.23	555.69	336.47
1980–1988	288.87	300.58	289.27	153.68
1985–1988	132.79	132.32	145.62	128.13

the lowest relative risk, with standard deviations of 2.44 and 2.42, respectively. It may come as a surprise to some that a portfolio of stocks included in the S&P 500 Index carries greater risk that an *unleveraged* portfolio of commodities included in the CRB Index.

Other statistics provided in the study have an important bearing on the potential role of commodities as an appropriate diversification tool and as a hedge against inflation. Over the entire 30 years, the CRB index showed negative correlations of −0.1237 and −0.1206 with government and corporate bonds, respectively, and a small positive correlation of 0.0156 with the S&P 500. *The fact that commodities show a slight negative correlation to bonds and a positive correlation to stocks that is close to zero would seem to support the argument that commodities would qualify as an excellent way to diversify portfolio risk.*

A comparison of the CRB Index to three popular inflation gauges—the Consumer Price Index (CPI), the Producer Price Index (PPI), and the implicit GNP deflator—over the 30-year period shows that commodity prices were highly correlated to all three inflation measures, with correlations above 90 percent in all cases. *That strong positive correlation between the CRB Index and those three popular inflation measures supports the value of utilizing commodity markets as a hedge against inflation.*

PUSHING THE EFFICIENT FRONTIER

The *efficient frontier* is a curve on a graph that plots portfolio risk (standard deviation) on the horizontal axis and expected return on the vertical axis. The efficient frontier slopes upward and to the right, reflecting the higher risk associated with higher returns. Powers Research first developed a set of optimized portfolios utilizing only stocks and bonds. By solving for the highest expected return for each level of risk, an efficient frontier was created. After determining optimal portfolios using only bonds and stocks, commodity futures were added at three different levels of commitment. The result was four portfolios—one with no commodities, and three other portfolios with commodity commitments of 10 percent, 20 percent, and 30 percent. Figure 12.11 shows the effects of introducing the CRB Index at those three levels of involvement.

Four lines are shown in Figure 12.11. The one to the far right is the *efficient frontier* for a portfolio of just stocks and bonds. Moving to the left, the second line has a CRB exposure of 10 percent. The third line to the left commits 20 percent to commodities, whereas the line to the far left places 30 percent of its portfolio in the CRB Index. The chart demonstrates that increasing the level of funds committed to the CRB Index has the beneficial effect of moving the efficient frontier upward and to the left, meaning that *the portfolio manager faces less risk for a given level of return when a basket of commodities is added to the asset mix.* Statistics are also presented that measure the change in the reward to risk ratios that take place as the result of including commodities along with bonds and stocks. To quote directly from page 8 of the report:

> Note in all cases, the addition of commodity futures to the portfolio increased the ratio, i.e., lowered risk and increased return. The increase grows as more commodity futures replace other domestic assets...the more of your portfolio allocated to commodity futures (up to 30 percent) the better off you are.

FIGURE 12.11
THE *EFFICIENT FRONTIERS* OF FOUR DIFFERENT PORTFOLIOS. THE LINE TO THE FAR RIGHT INCLUDES JUST BONDS AND STOCKS. THE LINES SHIFT UPWARD AND TO THE LEFT AS COMMODITIES ARE ADDED IN INCREMENTS OF 10 PERCENT, 20 PERCENT, AND 30 PERCENT. THE EFFICIENT FRONTIER PLOTS PORTFOLIO RISK (STANDARD DEVIATION) ON THE HORIZONTAL AXIS AND EXPECTED RETURN ON THE VERTICAL AXIS. (SOURCE: "COMMODITY FUTURES AS AN ASSET CLASS," PREPARED BY POWERS RESEARCH ASSOCIATES, L.P., PUBLISHED BY THE NEW YORK FUTURES EXCHANGE, JANUARY 1990.)

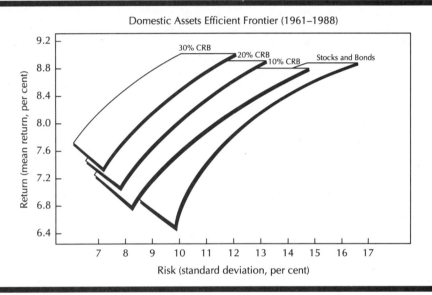

Domestic Assets Efficient Frontier (1961–1988)

SUMMARY

This chapter has utilized ratio analysis to better monitor the relationship between commodities (the CRB Index) and bonds and stocks. Ratio analysis provides a useful technical tool for spotting trend changes in these intermarket relationships. Trendline analysis can be applied directly to the ratio lines themselves. A rising CRB/bond ratio suggests that commodities should be bought instead of bonds. A falling CRB/bond ratio favors long commitments in bonds. A rising CRB/bond ratio is also bearish for equities. Rising commodities have an adverse impact on both bonds and stocks. The CRB/bond ratio usually leads turns in the CRB/S&P 500 ratio and can be used as a leading indicator for stocks.

The commodities included in the CRB Index should qualify as an asset class along with bonds and stocks. Because commodity markets are negatively correlated to bonds and show little correlation to stocks, an *unleveraged* commodity portfolio (with 10 percent committed to a commodity position and 90 percent in Treasury bills) could be used to diversify a portfolio of stocks and bonds. The risks usually associated with commodity trading are the result of low margin requirements (around 10 percent) and the resulting high leverage. By using a conservative (unleveraged) approach of keeping the unused 90 percent of the futures funds in Treasury bills, much of the risk associated with commodity trading are reduced and its use by portfolio managers becomes more realistic. The high correlation of the CRB index to inflation gauges qualify commodities as a reliable inflation hedge.

Futures markets—including commodities, currencies, bonds, and stock index futures—provide a built-in forum for asset allocation. Because their returns are poorly correlated with bond and stock market returns, professionally managed futures funds may qualify as a legitimate diversification instrument for portfolio managers. There are two separate approaches involved in the potential use of futures markets by portfolio managers. One has to do with the use of *professionally managed futures accounts*, which invest in all four sectors of the futures markets—*commodities, currencies, bond, and stock index futures*. In this sense, the futures portfolio is treated as a separate entity. The term *futures* refers to all futures markets, of which *commodities* are only one portion. The second approach treats the *commodity* portion of the futures markets as a separate asset class and utilizes a basket approach to trading those 21 commodities included in the CRB Index.

13

Intermarket Analysis
and the Business Cycle

Over the past two centuries, the American economy has gone through repeated boom and bust cycles. Sometimes these cycles have been dramatic (such as the Great Depression of the 1930s and the runaway inflationary spiral of the 1970s). At other times, their impact has been so muted that their occurrence has gone virtually unnoticed. Most of these cycles fit somewhere in between those two extremes and have left a trail of fairly reliable business cycle patterns that have averaged about four years in length. Approximately every four years the economy experiences a period of expansion which is followed by an inevitable contraction or slowdown.

The contraction phase often turns into a *recession*, which is a period of negative growth in the economy. The recession, or slowdown, inevitably leads to the next period of expansion. During an unusually long economic expansion (such as the 8-year period beginning in 1982), when no recession takes place, the economy usually undergoes a slowdown, which allows the economy to 'catch its breath' before resuming its next growth phase. Since 1948, the American economy has experienced eight recessions, the most recent one lasting from July 1981 to November 1982. The economic expansions averaged 45 months and the contractions, 11 months.

The business cycle has an important bearing on the financial markets. These periods of expansion and contraction provide an economic framework that helps explain the linkages that exist between the bond, stock, and the commodity markets. In addition, the business cycle explains the chronological sequence that develops among these three financial sectors. A trader's interest in the business cycle lies not in economic forecasting but in obtaining a better understanding as to why these three financial sectors interact the way they do, when they do.

For example, during the early stages of a new expansion (while a recession or slowdown is still in progress), bonds will turn up ahead of stocks and commodities. At the end of an expansion, commodities are usually the last to turn down. A better understanding of the business cycle sheds light on the intermarket process, and reveals that what is seen on the price charts makes sense from an economic perspective. Although it's not the primary intention, intermarket analysis could be used to help determine where we are in the business cycle.

Some understanding of the business cycle (together with intermarket analysis of bonds, stocks, and commodities) impacts on the *asset allocation* process, which was discussed in chapter 12. Different phases of the business cycle favor different asset classes. The beginning of an economic expansion favors financial assets (bonds and stocks), while the latter part of an expansion favors commodities (or inflation hedges such as gold and oil stocks). Periods of economic expansion favor stocks, whereas periods of economic contraction favor bonds.

In this chapter, the business cycle will be used to help explain the chronological rotation that normally takes place between bonds, stocks and commodities. Although I'll continue to utilize the CRB Futures Price Index for the commodity portion, the relative merits of using a couple of more industrial-based commodity averages will be discussed such as the Spot Raw Industrials Index of the Journal of Commerce Index. Since copper is one of the most widely followed of the industrial commodities, its predictive role in the economy and some possible links between copper and the stock market will be considered. Since many asset allocators use gold as their commodity proxy, I'll show where the yellow metal fits into the picture. Because the bond market plays a key role in the business cycle and the the intermarket rotation process, the bond market's value as a leading indicator of the economy will be considered.

THE CHRONOLOGICAL SEQUENCES OF BONDS, STOCKS, AND COMMODITIES

Figure 13.1 (courtesy of the *Asset Allocation Review*, written by Martin J. Pring, published by the International Institute for Economic Research, P.O. Box 329, Washington Depot, CT 06794) shows an idealized diagram of how the three financial sectors interact with each other during a typical business cycle. The curving line shows the path of the economy during expansion and contraction. A rising line indicates ex-

---

FIGURE 13.1
AN IDEALIZED DIAGRAM OF HOW BONDS (B), STOCKS (S), AND COMMODITIES (C) INTERACT DURING A TYPICAL BUSINESS CYCLE. (SOURCE: *ASSET ALLOCATION REVIEW* BY MARTIN J. PRING, PUBLISHED BY THE INTERNATIONAL INSTITUTE FOR ECONOMIC RESEARCH, P.O. BOX 329, WASHINGTON DEPOT, CT 06794.)

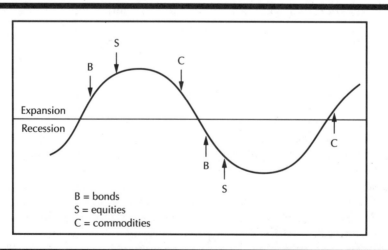

pansion and a falling line, contraction. The horizontal line is the equilibrium level that separates positive and negative economic growth. When the curving line is above the horizontal line but declining, the economy is slowing. When it dips below the horizontal line, the economy has slipped into recession. The arrows represent the direction of the three financial markets—*B* for bonds, *S* for stocks, and *C* for commodities.

The diagram shows that as the expansion matures, bonds are the first of the group to turn down. This is due to increased inflation pressures and resulting upward pressure on interest rates. In time, higher interest rates will put downward pressure on stocks, which turn down second. Since inflation pressures are strongest near the end of the expansion, commodities are the last to turn down. Usually by this time, the economy has started to slow and is on the verge of slipping into recession. A slowdown in the economy reduces demand for commodities and money. Inflation pressures begin to ease. Commodity prices start to drop (usually led by gold). At this point, all three markets are dropping.

As interest rates begin to soften as well (usually in the early stages of a recession), bonds begin to rally. Within a few months, stocks will begin to turn up (usually after the mid-point of a recession). Only after bonds and stocks have been rallying for awhile, and the economy has started to expand, will inflation pressures start to build contributing to an upturn in gold and other commodities. At this point, all three markets are rising. Of the three markets, bonds seem to be the focal point.

Bonds have a tendency to peak about midway through an expansion, and bottom about midway through a contraction. The peak in the bond market during an economic expansion is a signal that a period of healthy noninflationary growth has turned into an unhealthy period of inflationary growth. This is usually the point where commodity markets are starting to accelerate on the upside and the bull market in stocks is living on borrowed time.

GOLD LEADS OTHER COMMODITIES

Although gold is often used as a proxy for the commodity markets, it should be remembered that *gold usually leads other commodity markets at tops and bottoms.* Chapter 7 discussed gold's history as a leading indicator of the CRB Index. It's possible during the early stages of an expansion to have bonds, stocks, and gold in bull markets at the same time. This is exactly what happened in 1982 and again in 1985. During 1984, the bull markets in bonds and stocks were stalled. Gold had resumed its major downtrend from an early 1983 peak. Bonds turned up in July of 1984 followed by stocks a month later. Gold hit bottom in February of 1985, about half a year later. For the next 12 months (into the first quarter of 1986), *all three markets rallied together.* However, the CRB Index didn't actually hit bottom until the summer of 1986.

This distinction between gold and the general commodity price level may help clear up some confusion about the interaction of the commodity markets with bonds. In previous chapters, we've concentrated on the inverse relationship between the CRB Index and the bond market. The peak in bonds in mid-1986 coincided with a bottom in the CRB Index. In the spring of 1987, an upside breakout in the CRB Index helped cause a collapse in the bond market. A rising gold market can coexist with a rising bond market, but it is an early warning that inflation pressures are starting to build. *A rising CRB Index usually marks the end of the bull market in bonds.* Conversely, a falling CRB Index during the early stages of a recession (or economic slowdown) usually coincides with the bottom in bonds. It's unlikely that all three groups will be rising or falling together for long if the CRB index is used in place of the gold market.

ARE COMMODITIES FIRST OR LAST TO TURN?

The diagram in Figure 13.1 shows that bonds turn down first, stocks second, and commodities last. As the economy bottoms, bonds turn up first, followed by stocks, and then commodities. In reality, it's difficult to determine which is first and which is last since all three markets are part of a never-ending cycle. Bonds turn up *after commodities have turned down*. Conversely, *the upturn in commodities precedes the top in bonds*. Viewed in this way, commodities are the *first* market to turn instead of the *last*. Stocks hit an important peak in 1987. Bonds peaked in 1986. Gold started to rally in 1985 and the CRB Index in 1986. It could be argued that the rally in gold (and the CRB Index) signaled a renewal of inflation, which contributed to the top in bonds which contributed to the top in stocks. It's just a matter of where the observer chooses to start counting.

THE SIX STAGES OF THE BUSINESS CYCLE

In his *Asset Allocation Review*, Martin Pring divides the business cycle into six stages (Figure 13.2). Stage one begins as the economy is slipping into a recession and ends with stage six, where the economic expansion has just about run its course. Each stage is characterized by a turn in one of the three asset classes—bonds, stocks, or commodities. The following table summarizes Pring's conclusions:

Stage 1 ... *Bonds turn up*   (stocks and commodities falling)
Stage 2 ... *Stocks turn up*   (bonds rising, commodities falling)
Stage 3 ... *Commodities turn up*   (all three markets rising)
Stage 4 ... *Bonds turn down*   (stocks and commodities rising)
Stage 5 ... *Stocks turn down*   (bonds dropping, commodities rising)
Stage 6 ... *Commodities turn down*   (all three markets dropping)

FIGURE 13.2
THE SIX STAGES OF A TYPICAL BUSINESS CYCLE THROUGH RECESSION AND RECOVERY. EACH STAGE IS CHARACTERIZED BY A TURN IN ONE OF THE THREE SECTORS—BONDS, STOCKS, AND COMMODITIES. (SOURCE: *ASSET ALLOCATION REVIEW* BY MARTIN J. PRING.)

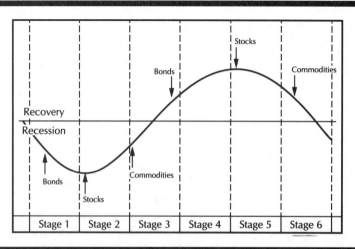

The implications of the above sequence for asset allocators should be fairly obvious. As inflation and interest rates begin to drop during a slowdown (Stage 1), bonds are the place to be (or interest-sensitive stocks). After bonds have bottomed, and as the recession begins to take hold on the economy (Stage 2), stocks become attractive. As the economy begins to expand again (Stage 3), gold and gold-related assets should be considered as an early inflation hedge. As inflation pressures begin to pull other commodity prices higher, and interest rates begin to rise (Stage 4), commodities or other inflation hedges should be emphasized. Bonds and interest-sensitive stocks should be de-emphasized. As stocks begin a topping process (Stage 5), more assets should be funneled into commodities or other inflation-hedges such as gold and oil shares. When all three asset groups are falling (Stage 6), *cash is king.*

The chronological sequence described in the preceding paragraphs does not imply that bonds, stocks, and commodities *always* follow that sequence exactly. Life isn't that simple. There have been times when the markets have peaked or troughed out of sequence. The diagram describes the *ideal* rotational sequence that *usually* takes place between the three markets, and gives us a useful roadmap to follow. When the markets are following the ideal pattern, the analyst knows what to expect next. When the markets are diverging from their normal rotation, the analyst is alerted to the fact that something is amiss and is warned to be more careful. While the analyst may not always understand exactly what the markets are doing, it can be helpful to know what they're *supposed* to be doing. Figure 13.3 shows how commodity prices behaved in the four recessions between 1970 and 1982.

THE ROLE OF BONDS IN ECONOMIC FORECASTING

The bond market plays a key role in intermarket analysis. It is the fulcrum that connects the commodity and stock markets. The direction of interest rates tells a lot about inflation and the health of the stock market. Interest rate direction also tells a lot about the current state of the business cycle and the strength of the economy. Toward the end of an economic expansion, the demand for money increases, resulting in higher interest rates. Central bankers use the lever of higher interest rates to rein in inflation, which is usually accelerating.

At some point, the jump in interest rates stifles the economic expansion and is a major cause of an economic contraction. *The event that signals that the end is in sight is usually a significant peak in the bond market.* At that point, an early warning is being given that the economy has entered a dangerous inflationary environment. This signal is usually given around the midway point in the expansion. After the bond market peaks, stocks and commodities can continue to rally for sometime, but stock investors should start becoming more cautious. Economists also should take heed.

During an economic contraction, demand for money decreases along with inflation pressures. Interest rates start to drop along with commodities. The combined effect of falling interest rates and falling commodity prices causes the bond market to bottom. This usually occurs in the early stages of the slowdown (or recession). Stocks and commodities can continue to decline for awhile, but stock market investors are given an early warning that the time to begin accumulating stocks is fast approaching. Economists have an early indication that the end may be in sight for the economic contraction. The bond market fulfills two important roles which are sometimes hard to separate. One is its role as a leading indicator of stocks (and commodities). The other is its role as a leading indicator of the economy.

Bond prices have turned in an impressive record as a leading indicator of the economy, although the lead time at peaks and troughs can be quite long. In his book,

FIGURE 13.3
A MONTHLY CHART OF THE CRB FUTURES PRICE INDEX THROUGH THE LAST FOUR BUSINESS CYCLE RECESSIONS (MARKED BY SHADED AREAS). COMMODITY PRICES USUALLY WEAKEN DURING A RECESSION AND BEGIN TO RECOVER AFTER THE RECESSION HAS ENDED. THE 1980 PEAK IN THE CRB INDEX OCCURRED AFTER THE 1980 RECESSION ENDED BUT BEFORE THE 1981-1982 RECESSION BEGAN. (SOURCE: *1984 COMMODITY YEAR BOOK*, COMMODITY RESEARCH BUREAU, INC.)

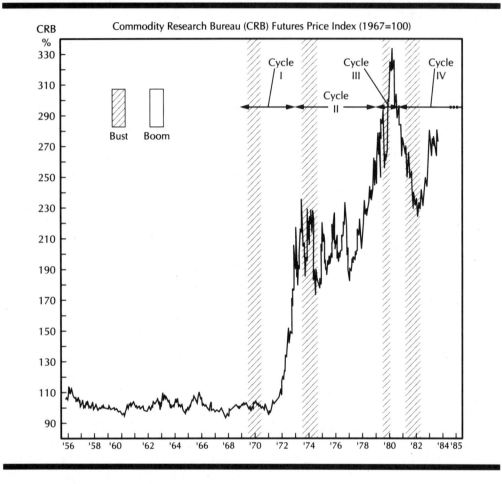

Leading Indicators for the 1990s (Dow Jones-Irwin, 1990), Geoffrey Moore, one the nation's most highly regarded authorities on the business cycle, details the history of bonds as a long-leading indicator of business cycle peaks and troughs. *Since 1948, the U.S. economy has experienced eight business cycles.* The Dow Jones 20 Bond Average led each of the 8 business cycle peaks by an average of 27 months. At the 8 business cycle troughs, the bond lead was a shorter 7 months on average. *Bond prices led all business cycle turns combined since 1948 by an average of seventeen months.*

LONG- AND SHORT-LEADING INDEXES

Dr. Moore, head of the Center for International Business Cycle Research at Columbia University in New York City, suggests utilizing bond prices as part of a "long-leading index," which would provide earlier warnings of business cycle peaks and troughs than the current list of eleven leading indicators published monthly by the U.S. Department of Commerce in the *Business Conditions Digest*. The long-leading index, comprised of four indicators (the Dow Jones 20 Bond Average, the ratio of price to unit labor cost in manufacturing, new housing permits, and M2 money supply), has led business cycle turns by 11 months on average.

Moore also recommends adoption of a new "short-leading index" of 11 indicators. The short-leading index has led business cycle turns by an average of five months, slightly shorter than the six-month lead of the current leading indicator index. (Figure 13.4 shows the CIBCR long- and short-leading indexes in the eight recessions since 1948.) Moore suggests changing the number of leading indicators from 11 to 15 and using his long- and short-leading indexes in place of the current leading index of 11 indicators. Both the current leading index and Moore's short-leading index include two components of particular interest to analysts—stock and commodity prices.

FIGURE 13.4
THE LONG- AND SHORT-LEADING INDEXES DEVELOPED BY GEOFFREY H. MOORE AND COL-UMBIA UNIVERSITY'S CENTER FOR INTERNATIONAL BUSINESS CYCLE RESEARCH (CIBCR). BOND PRICES (DOW JONES BOND AVERAGE) ARE PART OF THE LONG-LEADING INDEX, WHEREAS STOCKS (S&P 500) AND COMMODITIES (JOURNAL OF COMMERCE INDEX) ARE PART OF THE SHORT-LEADING INDEX. (SOURCE: *BUSINESS CONDITIONS DIGEST*, U.S. DE-PARTMENT OF COMMERCE, BUREAU OF ECONOMIC ANALYSIS, FEBRUARY 1990.) SHADED AREAS MARK RECESSIONS.

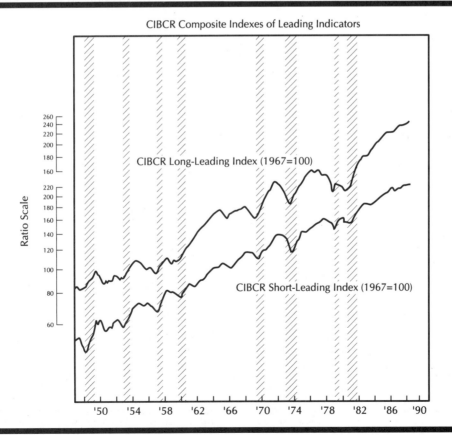

CIBCR Composite Indexes of Leading Indicators

STOCKS AND COMMODITIES AS LEADING INDICATORS

Stocks and commodities also qualify as leading indicators of the business cycle, although their warnings are much shorter than those of bonds. Research provided by Dr. Moore (in collaboration with Victor Zarnowitz and John P. Cullity) in the previously-cited work on "Leading Indicators for the 1990s" provides us with lead and lag times for all three sectors—bonds, stocks, and commodities—relative to turns in the business cycle, supporting the rotational process described in Figure 13.1.

In the eight business cycles since 1948, *the S&P 500 stock index led turns by an average of seven months*, with a nine-month lead at peaks and five months at troughs. *Commodity prices (represented by the Journal of Commerce Index) led business cycle turns by an average of six months*, with an eight-month lead at peaks and two months at troughs. Several conclusions can be drawn from these numbers.

FIGURE 13.5

A COMPARISON OF THE DOW JONES BOND AVERAGE, THE DOW JONES INDUSTRIAL AVER-AGE, AND GOLD DURING 1987. THE THREE MARKETS PEAKED DURING 1987 IN THE CORRECT ROTATION—BONDS FIRST (DURING THE SPRING), STOCKS SECOND (DURING THE SUMMER), AND GOLD LAST (IN DECEMBER). GOLD CAN RALLY FOR A TIME ALONG WITH BONDS AND STOCKS BUT PROVIDES AN EARLY WARNING OF RENEWED INFLATION PRESSURES.

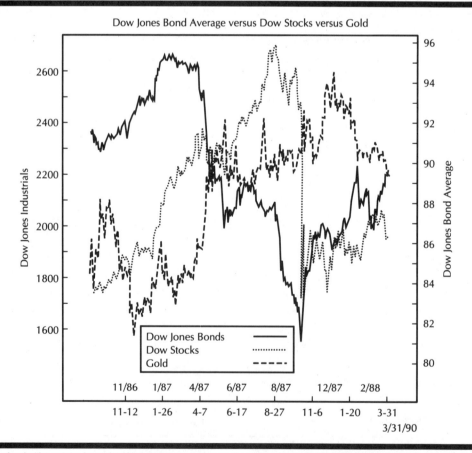

One is that technical analysis of bonds, stocks, and commodities can play a role in economic analysis. Another is that the rotational nature of the three markets, as pictured in Figure 13.1, is confirmed. Bonds turn first (17 months in advance), stocks second (seven months in advance), and commodities third (six months in advance). That rotational sequence of bonds, stocks, and commodities turning in order is maintained at both peaks and troughs. In all three markets, the lead at peaks is much longer than at troughs. The lead time given at peaks by bonds can be extremely long (27 months on average) while commodities provide a very short warning at troughs (two months on average). The lead time for commodities may vary depending on the commodity or commodity index used. Moore favors the Journal of Commerce Index which he helped create. (Figures 13.5 through 13.8 demonstrate the rotational nature of bonds, stocks, and commodities from 1986 to early 1990.)

FIGURE 13.6

A COMPARISON OF THE DOW JONES BOND AVERAGE, THE DOW JONES INDUSTRIAL AVER-AGE, AND THE CRB FUTURES PRICE INDEX DURING 1987 AND 1988. THREE MAJOR PEAKS CAN BE SEEN IN THE NORMAL ROTATIONAL SEQUENCE—BONDS FIRST, STOCKS SECOND, AND COMMODITIES LAST. ALTHOUGH THE CRB INDEX DIDN'T PEAK UNTIL MID-1988, GOLD TOPPED OUT SIX MONTHS EARLIER AND PLAYED ITS USUAL ROLE AS A LEADING INDICATOR OF COMMODITIES.

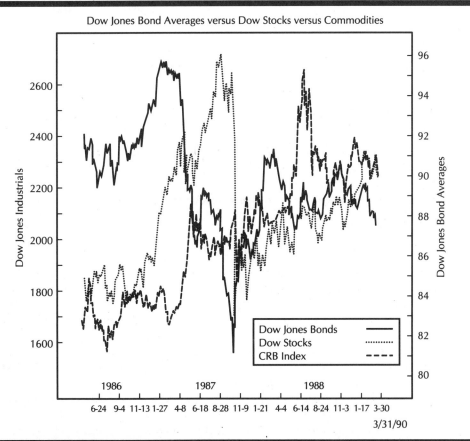

Dow Jones Bond Averages versus Dow Stocks versus Commodities

3/31/90

FIGURE 13.7
THE UPPER CHART COMPARES TREASURY BOND FUTURES PRICES WITH THE DOW JONES INDUSTRIAL AVERAGE FROM 1986 THROUGH THE FIRST QUARTER OF 1990. THE BOTTOM CHART SHOWS THE CRB INDEX DURING THE SAME PERIOD. THE CRB INDEX RALLY IN EARLY 1987 COINCIDED WITH THE PEAK IN BONDS, WHICH PRECEDED THE STOCK MARKET PEAK. THE COMMODITY PEAK IN MID-1988 LAUNCHED A NEW UPCYCLE FOR THE FINANCIAL MARKETS. IN LATE 1989, THE COMMODITY RALLY PRECEDED DOWNTURNS IN BONDS AND STOCKS. NOTICE THE ORDER OF TOPS IN 1986 (BONDS), 1987 (STOCKS), AND 1988 (COMMODITIES).

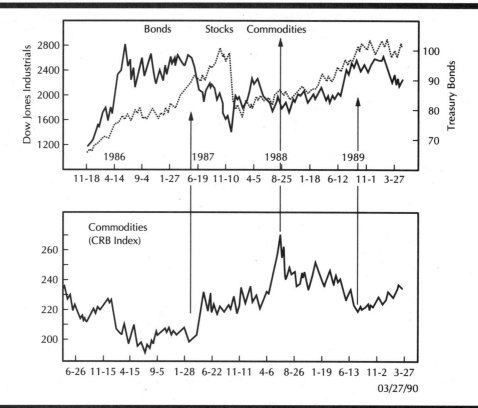

Chapter 7 includes a discussion of the various commodity indexes, including the CRB Futures Price Index, the CRB Spot Index, the CRB Spot Raw Industrials Index, the CRB Spot Foodstuffs Index, and the Journal of Commerce Index of 18 key raw industrials. Readers unfamiliar with the composition of the indexes might want to refer back to Chapter 7, which also includes a discussion of the relative merits of commodity indexes. Moore and some economists prefer commodity indexes that utilize only *industrial* prices on the premise that they are better predictors of inflation and are more sensitive to movements in the economy.

Martin Pring in the previously-cited work, the *Asset Allocation Review*, prefers the CRB Spot Raw Industrials Index. Pring and many economists believe that the CRB Futures Price Index, which includes *food* along with *industrial* prices, is often influenced more by weather than by economic activity. I've expressed a preference for

FIGURE 13.8
THE UPPER CHART COMPARES TREASURY BOND FUTURES PRICES WITH THE DOW JONES INDUSTRIALS DURING THE SECOND HALF OF 1989 AND THE FIRST QUARTER OF 1990. THE BOTTOM CHART SHOWS THE CRB FUTURES INDEX DURING THE SAME PERIOD. THE NORMAL ROTATIONAL SEQUENCE BETWEEN THE THREE MARKETS CAN BE SEEN. THE COMMODITY TROUGH DURING THE SUMMER OF 1989 CONTRIBUTED TO THE DOWNTURN IN BONDS, WHICH EVENTUALLY PULLED STOCKS LOWER.

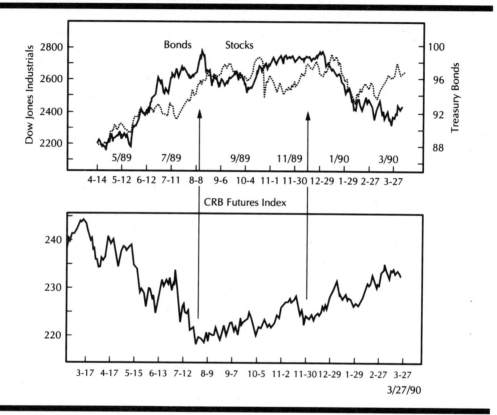

Reproduced with permission by Knight Ridder's Tradecenter. Tradecenter is a registered trademark of Knight Ridder's Financial Information.

the CRB Futures index because of my belief that food is a part of the inflation picture and can't be ignored. It's up to the reader to decide which of the many commodity indexes to employ. Since none of the commodity indexes are perfect, *it's probably a good idea to keep an eye on all of them.*

COPPER AS AN ECONOMIC INDICATOR

Copper is a key industrial commodity. It's importance is underlined by the fact that it is included in every major commodity index. This is not true of some other important commodities. No precious metals are included in the Journal of Commerce Index or the Spot Raw Industrials Index. Crude oil is included in the Journal of Commerce Index but not in the Raw Industrials Index. The only other industrial commodity that is included in every major commodity index is the cotton market. (All of the previously-mentioned commodities are included in the CRB Futures Index.)

Because copper is used in the automotive, housing and electronics industries, a lot can be learned about the strength of the economy by studying the strength of the copper market. During periods of economic strength, demand from the three industries just cited will keep copper prices firm. When the economy is beginning to show signs of weakness, demand for copper from these industries will drop off, resulting in a declining trend in the price of copper. In the four recessions since 1970, the economic peaks and troughs have coincided fairly closely with the peaks and troughs in the copper market.

Copper hit a major top at the end of 1988 and dropped sharply throughout most of 1989 (Figure 13.9). Weakness in copper futures suggested that the economy was slowing and raised fears of an impending recession. At the beginning of 1990, however, copper prices stabilized and started to rally sharply. Many observers breathed a sigh of relief at the copper rally (and that of other industrial commodities) and interpreted the price recovery as a sign that the economy had avoided recession (Figure 13.10).

FIGURE 13.9
A COMPARISON OF COPPER FUTURES PRICES (UPPER CHART) WITH THE DOW INDUSTRIALS (LOWER CHART) FROM 1987 TO THE FOURTH QUARTER OF 1989. COPPER PEAKED AFTER STOCKS IN LATE 1987, BEFORE BOTH RESUMED THEIR UPTRENDS. THE COLLAPSE IN COPPER DURING 1989 RAISED FEARS OF RECESSION, WHICH BEGAN TO HAVE A BEARISH INFLUENCE ON STOCK PRICES. COPPER HAS A PRETTY GOOD TRACK RECORD AS A BAROMETER OF ECONOMIC STRENGTH.

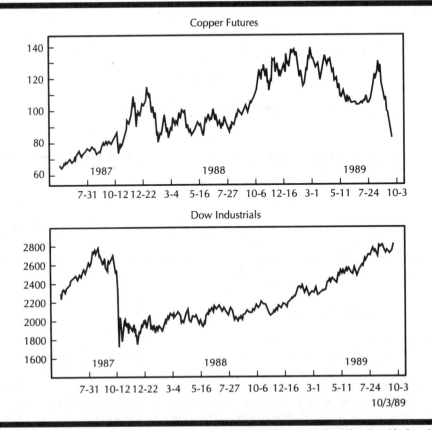

FIGURE 13.10

COPPER FUTURES COMPARED TO THE DOW INDUSTRIALS FROM MID-1989 THROUGH THE FIRST QUARTER OF 1990. BOTH MARKETS SHOWED A STRONG POSITIVE CORRELATION DURING THOSE NINE MONTHS BECAUSE BOTH WERE REACTING TO SIGNS OF ECONOMIC STRENGTH AND WEAKNESS. BOTH PEAKED TOGETHER IN OCTOBER OF 1989 AND THEN TROUGHED TOGETHER DURING THE FIRST QUARTER OF 1990.

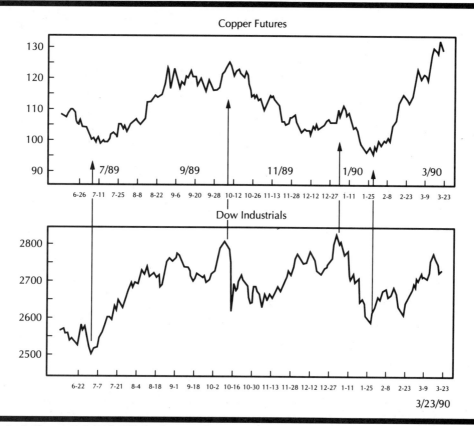

COPPER AND THE STOCK MARKET

Recession fears played on the minds of equity investors as 1989 ended. During the nine months from July 1989 to March of 1990, the correlation between the copper market and the stock market was unusually strong (Figure 13.10). It almost seemed that both markets were feeding off one another. The stock market selloff that started in October of 1989 coincided with a peak in the copper market. The strong rally that began in American equities during the first week of February 1990 began a week after the copper market hit a bottom and also started to rally sharply. Although the link between the stock market and copper is not usually that strong on a day-to-day basis, there are times (such as the period just cited) when their destinies are closely tied together. Stocks are considered to be a leading indicator of the economy. Copper is probably better classified as a coincident indicator. Turns in the stock market usually lead turns in copper. However, both are responding to (or anticipating) the health of the economy. As a result, their fortunes are tied together. (Figure 13.11 compares copper prices to automobile stocks.)

FIGURE 13.11
**COPPER FUTURES (UPPER CHART) ALSO SHOWED A STRONG CORRELATION WITH AUTO-
MOBILE STOCKS (BOTTOM CHART) IN THE NINE MONTHS FROM MID-1989 THROUGH THE
FIRST QUARTER OF 1990. THE AUTOMOBILE INDUSTRY IS ONE OF THE HEAVIEST USERS OF
COPPER, AND THEIR FORTUNES ARE OFTEN TIED TOGETHER.**

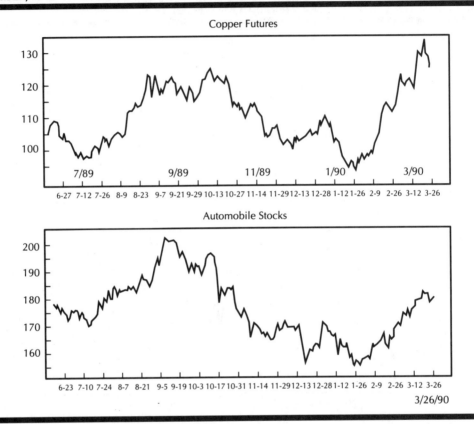

A strong copper market implies that the economic recovery is still on sound footing and is a positive influence on the stock market. A falling copper market implies that an economic slowdown (or recession) may be in progress and is a negative influence on the stock market. One of the advantages of using the copper market as a barometer of the economy (and the stock market) is that copper prices are available on a daily basis at the Commodity Exchange in New York (as well as the London Metal Exchange). Copper also lends itself very well to technical analysis. (Figure 13.12 shows copper and other industrial prices rallying in early 1990 after falling in late 1989.)

SUMMARY

The 4-year business cycle provides an economic framework for intermarket analysis and explains the chronological sequence that is usually seen between the bond, stock, and commodity markets. Although not a rigid formula, the peaks and troughs that take place in these three asset classes usually follow a repetitive pattern where bonds

FIGURE 13.12

WEAKNESS IN COPPER PRICES (UPPER CHART) AND THE JOURNAL OF COMMERCE INDEX OF 18 INDUSTRIAL MATERIALS (BOTTOM CHART) DURING 1989 RAISED FEARS OF RECESSION. HOWEVER, AS INDUSTRIAL COMMODITIES RECOVERED IN EARLY 1990, MANY TOOK THIS AS A SIGN THAT A RECESSION HAD BEEN POSTPONED. ECONOMISTS PAY CLOSE ATTENTION TO INDUSTRIAL COMMODITIES.

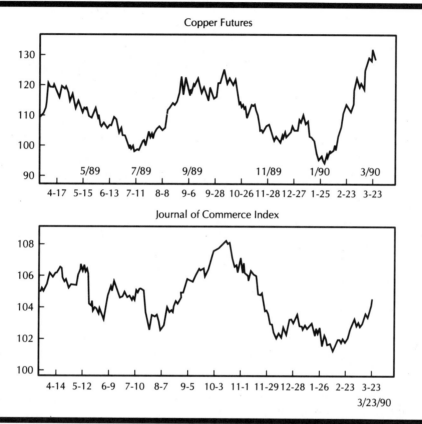

turn first at peaks and troughs, stocks second, and commodities third. The turn in the bond market is usually activated by a turn in the commodity markets in the opposite direction. Gold usually leads the general commodity price level and can be used as an early warning of inflation pressures.

The chronological rotation of the three sectors has important implications for the asset allocation process. The early stages of recovery favor financial assets, whereas the latter part of the expansion favors commodity prices or other inflation hedges. Bonds play a dual role as a leader of stocks and commodities and also as a long-leading economic indicator. Copper also provides clues to the strength of the economy and, at times, will track the stock market very closely.

14

The Myth of Program Trading

One recent Friday morning, one of New York's leading newspapers used the following combination of headlines and lead-ins to describe the previous day's events in the financial markets:

Cocoa futures surged to seven-month highs...
The dollar dropped sharply...
Prices of Treasury securities plummeted...
Tokyo stocks off sharply
Program sales hurt stocks; Dow off 15.99
    (*New York Times*, 3/30/90)

Despite the fact that all of the first four stories were bearish for stocks, "program sales" were used to explain the weakness in the Dow. The next day, the same paper carried these two headlines:

Prices of Treasury Issues Still Falling
Dow Off 20.49 After "Buy" Programs End
    (*New York Times*, 3/31/90)

This time, the culprit wasn't "sell" programs, but the absence of "buy" programs. The real explanation (the drop in Treasury issues) was mentioned briefly in paragraph five of the stock market story. Earlier that same week, two other financial papers explained a stock market rally with these headlines:

Dow Up 29 as Programs Spark Advance
    (*Investor's Daily*, 3/28/90)

Industrials Advance 29.28 Points on Arbitrage Buying
    (*Wall Street Journal*, 3/28/90)

The international markets are not immune to this type of reporting. A couple of weeks earlier, one of the papers carried the following headline in a story on the international stock markets:

Tokyo Stocks Drop Sharply on Arbitrage Selling by Foreign Brokers...
    (*Wall Street Journal*, 3/8/90)

The same story, which used arbitrage selling to explain the drop in Tokyo, began its explanation of a rally in the London stock market with the following sentence:

> London stocks notched gains amid sketchy trading as futures-related buying and a bullish buy recommendation... pulled prices higher.
>
> (*Wall Street Journal*, 3/8/90)

A reader of the financial press can't help but notice how often "program trading" is used to explain moves in the stock market. Even on an intra-day basis, a morning's selloff will be attributed to rounds of "program selling" only to be followed by an afternoon rally attributed to rounds of "program buying." After a while, "program trading" takes on a life of its own and is treated as an independent, market-moving force. A reader could be forgiven for wondering what moved the stock market on a day-to-day basis before "program trading" captured the imagination of the financial media. A reader could also be forgiven for starting to believe the printed reports that "program trading" really is the dominant force behind stock market moves. In this chapter, the *myth* of "program trading" as a market-moving force will be explored. An attempt will be made to demonstrate that market forces that are usually blamed on "program trading" are nothing more than intermarket linkages at work.

PROGRAM TRADING—AN EFFECT, NOT A CAUSE

It's easy to see why most observers mistakenly treat program trading as a *cause* of stock market trends. It provides an easy explanation and eliminates the need to dig deeper for more adequate reasons. Consider how program trading looks to the casual observer. As stock index futures rise sharply, arbitrage activity leads traders to buy a basket of stocks and sell stock index futures in order to bring the futures and cash prices of a stock index back into line. A strong upsurge in stock index futures *causes* "buy programs" to kick in and is considered bullish for stocks. A sharp drop in stock index futures has the opposite effect. When the drop in stock index futures goes too far, traders sell a basket of stocks and buy the stock index futures. The resulting "sell programs" pull stock prices lower and are considered to be bearish for stocks.

It appears on the surface (and is usually reported) that the stock market rose (or fell) *because* of the program buying (or selling). As is so often the case, however, the quick and easy answer is seldom the right answer. Unfortunately, market observers see "program trading" impacting on the stock market and treat it as an isolated, market-moving force. What they fail to realize is that the moves in stock index futures, which activate the program trading in the first place, are themselves usually caused by moves in related markets—the bond market, the dollar, and commodities. And this is where the real story lies.

WHAT CAUSES PROGRAM TRADING?

Instead of treating program trading as the *cause* of a stock market move and ending the story there, the more pertinent question to be asked is "what caused the program trading in the first place?" Suppose S&P 500 stock index futures surge higher at 10:00 A.M. on a trading day. The rally in stock index futures is enough to push the futures price too far above the S&P 500 cash value, and "program buying" is activated. How would that story be treated? Most often, the resulting rally in the stock market would be attributed to "program buying." *But what caused the program buying?* What caused the stock index futures to rally in the first place?

The program buying didn't get activated until the S&P stock index futures rallied far enough above the S&P 500 cash index to place them temporarily "out of line." The program trading didn't *cause* the rally in the stock index futures—*the program buying reacted to the rally in stock index futures*. It was the rally in stock index futures that started the ball rolling. What caused the rally to begin in stock index futures, which led to the program buying? If observers are willing to ask that question, they will begin to see how often the sharp rally or drop in stock index futures is the direct result of a corresponding sharp rise or drop in the bond market, the dollar, or maybe the oil market.

Viewed in this fashion, it can be seen that the *real* cause of a sudden stock market move is often a sharp move in the bond market or crude oil. However, the ripple effect that starts in a related financial market (such as the bond market) doesn't hit the stock market directly. The intermarket effect flows through stock index futures first, which then impact on the stock market. In other words, the program trading phenomenon (which is nothing more than an adjustment between stock index futures and an underlying cash index) is the last link in an intermarket chain that usually begins in the other financial markets. *Program trading, then, can be seen as an effect, not a cause.*

PROGRAM TRADING AS SCAPEGOAT

The problem with using program trading as the main culprit, particularly during stock market drops, is that it masks the real causes and provides an easy scapegoat. Outcries against index arbitrage really began after the stock market crash of 1987 and again during the mini-crash two years later in October of 1989. Critics argued that index arbitrage was a destabilizing influence on the stock market and should be banned. These critics ignored some pertinent facts, however. The introduction of stock index futures in 1982 coincided with the beginning of the greatest bull market in U.S. history. If stock index futures were destabilizing, how does one explain the enormous stock market gains of the 1980s?

A second, often-overlooked factor pertaining to the 1987 crash was the fact that *the stock market collapse was global in scope*. No world stock market escaped un-scathed. Some world markets dropped much more than ours. Yet, *index arbitrage didn't exist in these other markets.* How then do we explain their collapse? If index arbitrage caused the collapse in New York, what caused the collapse in the other markets around the globe?

A dramatic example of the dangers of using program trading to mask the real events behind a stock market drop was seen during the first quarter of 1990 in Japan. During the early stages of the plunge in the Japanese stock market, index arbitrage was frequently cited as the main culprit. At first, the stock market plunge wasn't taken too seriously. However, a deeper analysis revealed a very dangerous intermarket situation (as described in Chapter 8). The Japanese yen had started to drop dramatically, and Japanese inflation had turned sharply higher. Japanese bonds were in a freefall. These bearish factors were ignored, at least initially, in deference to cries for the banning of index arbitrage.

By the end of the first quarter of 1990, the Japanese stock market had lost about 32 percent. Two major contributing factors to that debacle were a nine percent loss in the Japanese yen versus the U.S. dollar and a 13 percent loss in the Japanese bond market. The intermarket picture in Japan as 1990 began looked very ominous for the Japanese market (and was not unlike the situation in the United States during 1987 with a falling dollar, rising commodity prices, and a falling bond market). However, it wasn't until the stock market plunge in Japan took on more serious proportions that market observers began to look beyond the "program trading" mirage for the more serious problems facing that country.

Chapter 2 described the events leading up to the stock market crash in the American stock market in 1987. Preceding the stock market crash, the dollar had been dropping sharply, commodity prices had broken out of a basing pattern and were rallying sharply higher, and the bond market had collapsed. Textbook intermarket analysis would categorize this intermarket picture as bearish for stocks. Yet, stocks continued to rally into the summer and fall of 1987, and no one seemed concerned. When the bubble finally burst in October of 1987, "program trading" was most often cited as the reason for the collapse. Many observers at the time claimed that no other reasons could explain the sudden stock market plunge. They said the same thing in Japan in 1990.

The events in the United States in 1987 and Japan in 1990 illustrate how the preoccupation with program trading often masks more serious issues. Program trading is the conduit through which the bearish (or bullish) influence of intermarket forces is carried to the stock market. The stock market is usually the last sector to react. As awareness of these intermarket linkages described in the preceding chapters grows, market observers should become more aware of the ripple effect that flows through all the markets, even on an intra-day basis.

Program trading has no bullish or bearish bias. In itself, it is inherently neutral. It simply reacts to outside forces. Unfortunately, it also speeds up and usually exaggerates the impact of these forces. Program trading is more often the "messenger" bearing bad (or good) news than the cause of that news. Up to now, too much focus has been placed on the messenger and not enough on the message being brought.

AN EXAMPLE FROM ONE DAY'S TRADING

One way to demonstrate the lightning-quick impact of these intermarket linkages and their role in program trading is to study the events of one trading day. The day under discussion is Friday, April 6, 1990. We're going to study the intra-day activity that took place that morning in the financial markets following the release of an unemployment report, and how those events were reported by a leading news service.

At 8:30 A.M. (New York time), the March unemployment report was released and looked to be much weaker than expected. U.S. non-farm payroll jobs in March were up 26,000—a much smaller figure than economists expected. Since the report signaled economic weakness, the bond market rallied sharply while the dollar slumped. The weak dollar boosted gold. Stocks benefitted from the strong opening in bonds. Some of the morning's headlines produced by Knight-Ridder Financial News read as follows:

—8:57 A.M.... Dollar softens on unexpectedly weak jobs data
—9:08 A.M.... Bonds surge 16/32 on weak March jobs data
—10:26 A.M.... Jun gold up 3.2 dollars...
—10:27 A.M.... US Stock Index Opening: Move higher, follow bonds...

—11:07 A.M.... CBT Jun T-bonds break to 92 18/32...

—11:07 A.M.... US stock index futures slide as T-bonds drop...

—11:10 A.M.... Dow down 19 at 2701 amid sell programs, extends loss

—11:32 A.M.... W. German Credit Review: Bonds plunge...

—11:33 A.M.... CBT/IMM Rates: Bonds plunge; Bundesbank report cited

—11:44 A.M.... NY Stocks: Dow off 15; extends loss on sell-programs

The intermarket linkages among the four market sectors can be seen in the morning's trading. The dollar weakened and gold rallied. Bonds rallied initially and pulled stocks higher. Bonds then tumbled, pulling stock index futures down with them. The resulting selloff in stock index futures activated sell programs, which helped pull the Dow lower. As the headlines at 11:32 and 11:33 state, one of the reasons for the plunge in bonds at mid-morning was a plunge in the German bond market. The stock market plunge was the result of a plunge in the U.S. bond market, which in turn was partially caused by a sharp selloff in the German bond market. A selloff in the dollar around mid-morning was also a bearish factor.

The two headlines at 11:10 and 11:44 cite "sell programs" as the Dow was falling. These two headlines are misleading if they are read out of context. They seem to indicate that the sell-programs were *causing* the stock market selloff when the sharp slide in the bond market was the main reason why the stock rally faltered. Fortunately, the Knight-Ridder Financial News service provided plenty of other information to allow the reader to understand what was really happening and the reasons why it was happening. Not all financial reports are as thorough.

Sometimes the financial media, under pressure to give quick answers, picks up the "sell-program" headlines and ignores the rest. It's easy to see how someone scanning the headlines can focus on the sell-programs and not understand everything else that is happening. There is also a disturbing tendency in some sectors of the financial media to focus on sell programs when the Dow is falling, while forgetting to mention buy programs when the Dow is rising.

A VISUAL LOOK AT THE MORNING'S TRADING

Figures 14.1 and 14.2 show the price activity in the dollar, bonds, and stocks during the same morning and provide a picture of the events that have just been described. Figure 14.1 compares the June Dollar Index (bottom chart) to the June S&P 500 futures index from 8:30 A.M. (New York time) to noon. Notice how closely they track each other during the morning. After selling off initially, the dollar rallied until about 10:00 before rolling over to the downside again. The June S&P contract weakened at about the same time. Both markets bottomed together after 11:00.

Figure 14.2 compares the June bond contract (upper chart) to the June S&P 500 futures contract (bottom chart). The bond market had already peaked before the stock index futures started trading (9:30 A.M., New York time). Bonds started to bounce again around 9:30 and rallied to just after 10:00. Bond and stock index futures started to weaken around 10:15. Both markets also bottomed together just after 11:00 (along with the dollar). The plunge in the bond market around 11:00 was partially caused by the collapse in the German bond market (not shown).

The moral of the preceding exercise was to demonstrate how closely the financial markets are linked on a minute-by-minute basis. The stock market is heavily influenced by events in surrounding markets, most notably the dollar and bonds. To fully

FIGURE 14.1

AN INTRA-DAY COMPARISON OF STANDARD & POOR'S 500 STOCK INDEX FUTURES (TOP CHART) AND U.S. DOLLAR INDEX FUTURES (BOTTOM CHART) ON THE MORNING OF APRIL 6, 1990. BOTH MARKETS FELL TOGETHER JUST AFTER 10:00 IN THE MORNING AND BOTTOMED TOGETHER ABOUT AN HOUR LATER. STOCK MARKET MOVES ON A MINUTE-BY-MINUTE BASIS CAN OFTEN BE EXPLAINED BY WATCHING MOVEMENTS IN THE DOLLAR.

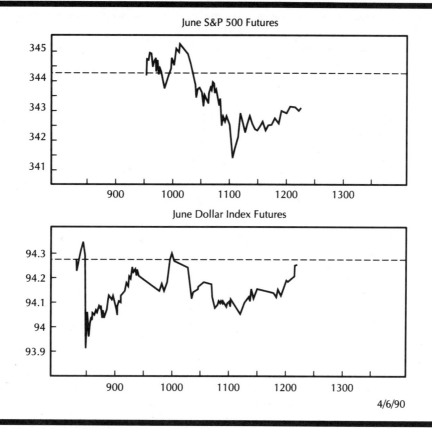

understand why the stock market suddenly dropped at 10:00 on the morning of April 6 and then bottomed at 11:00, the trader had to be aware of what was happening in the bond market and the dollar (not to mention gold and the other commodities). Those who didn't bother to monitor the bond and dollar futures that morning couldn't have possibly understood what was happening. (Figures 14.3 and 14.4 show stock index trading during the entire day of April 6. Figure 14.5 shows the entire week's trading.)

Those who choose not to educate themselves in these lightning-fast intermarket linkages are doomed to fall back on artificial reasons such as sell-programs and program trading, instead of the real reasons having to do with activity in the surrounding markets. Those whose job it is to report on the activity in the financial markets on a daily basis owe it to their clients to dig for the real reasons why the stock market moves up and down and to stop going for the quick and easy answers (see Figures 14.6 through 14.8).

FIGURE 14.2
AN INTRA-DAY COMPARISON OF S&P 500 STOCK INDEX FUTURES (BOTTOM CHART) AND TREASURY BOND FUTURES (TOP CHART) DURING THE SAME MORNING (APRIL 6). MOMENTARY SHIFTS IN STOCK INDEX FUTURES (WHICH AFFECT THE STOCK MARKET) ARE HEAVILY INFLUENCED BY ACTIVITY IN THE BOND MARKET. NOTICE THE PLUNGE IN BOTH MARKETS AROUND 11:00 A.M. SUDDEN STOCK MARKET MOVES THAT ARE BLAMED ON PROGRAM TRADING CAN USUALLY BE EXPLAINED BY INTERMARKET LINKAGES.

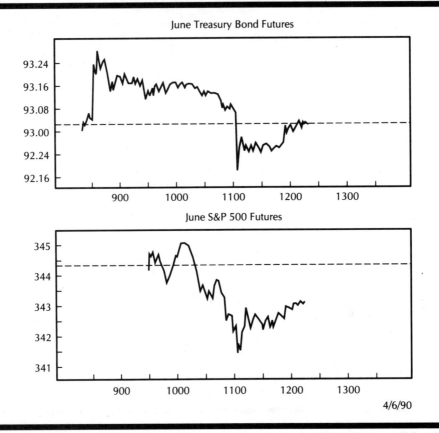

FIGURE 14.3
A COMPARISON OF S&P 500 FUTURES (TOP CHART) AND THE DOW INDUSTRIALS ON APRIL 6, 1990. BOTH INDEXES BOTTOMED AROUND 11:00 (ALONG WITH THE BOND MARKET) AND RALLIED THROUGH THE BALANCE OF THE DAY. ALTHOUGH BOTH INDEXES TREND TOGETHER, STOCK INDEX FUTURES USUALLY LEAD THE DOW BY A FEW SECONDS AND ARE QUICKER TO REACT TO INTERMARKET FORCES.

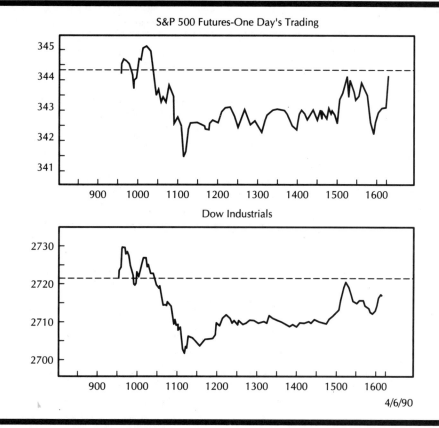

4/6/90

FIGURE 14.4

A COMPARISON OF S&P 500 FUTURES (TOP CHART) AND THE S&P 500 CASH INDEX (BOTTOM CHART) ON APRIL 6. ALTHOUGH THE FUTURES CONTRACT SHOWS MORE VOLATILITY, THE PEAKS AND TROUGHS ARE SIMILAR. PROGRAM TRADING IS ACTIVATED WHEN THE FUTURES AND CASH INDEX MOVE TOO FAR OUT OF LINE.(STOCK INDEX FUTURES TRADE 15 MINUTES LONGER THAN THE CASH INDEX.)

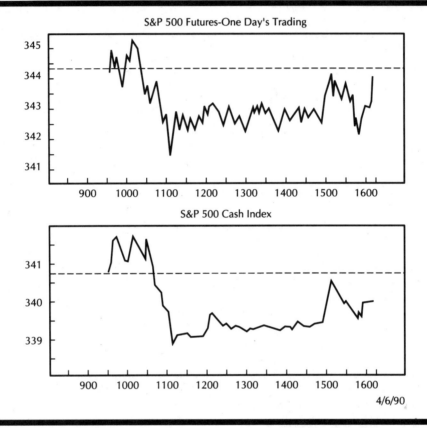

Reproduced with permission by Knight Ridder's Tradecenter. Tradecenter is a registered trademark of Knight Ridder's Financial Information.

FIGURE 14.5

A COMPARISON OF S&P 500 FUTURES (UPPER LINE) AND THE S&P 500 CASH INDEX (BOTTOM LINE) DURING THE FIRST WEEK OF APRIL 1990. NOTICE HOW SIMILAR THE TWO LINES LOOK. ARBITRAGE ACTIVITY (PROGRAM TRADING) KEEPS THE TWO LINES FROM MOVING TOO FAR AWAY FROM EACH OTHER. PROGRAM TRADING DOESN'T ALTER THE EXISTING TREND BUT MAY EXAGGERATE IT.

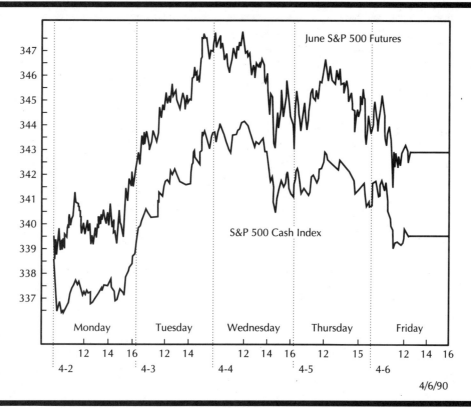

FIGURE 14.6

A COMPARISON OF THE FOUR MARKET SECTORS—THE CRB INDEX (BOTTOM LEFT), TREA-SURY BONDS (UPPER LEFT), THE U.S. DOLLAR (UPPER RIGHT), AND THE DOW INDUSTRIALS (LOWER RIGHT) DURING ONE TRADING DAY (MARCH 29, 1990). ONE LEADING NEWSPAPER ATTRIBUTED THE SELLOFF IN THE STOCK MARKET TO PROGRAM TRADING. THE MORE LIKELY REASONS WERE THE SHARP SELLOFF IN THE DOLLAR AND BONDS AND THE SHARP RALLY IN COMMODITIES. INTERMARKET LINKAGES CAN BE SEEN EVEN ON INTRA-DAY CHARTS.

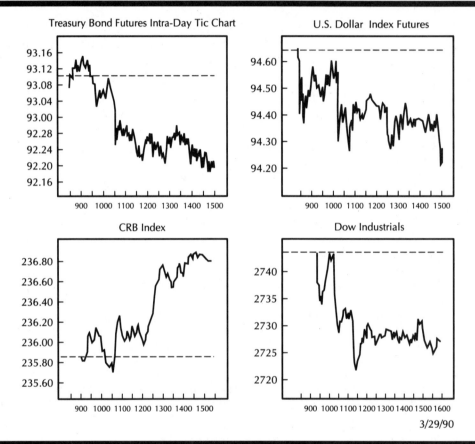

3/29/90

FIGURE 14.7
**THE COLLAPSE IN THE JAPANESE STOCK MARKET DURING THE FIRST QUARTER OF 1990
WAS INITIALLY BLAMED ON PROGRAM SELLING. MORE CONVINCING REASONS WERE THE
COLLAPSE IN THE JAPANESE YEN AND THE JAPANESE BOND MARKET. BLAMING PROGRAM
TRADING FOR STOCK MARKET DECLINES USUALLY MASKS THE REAL REASONS.**

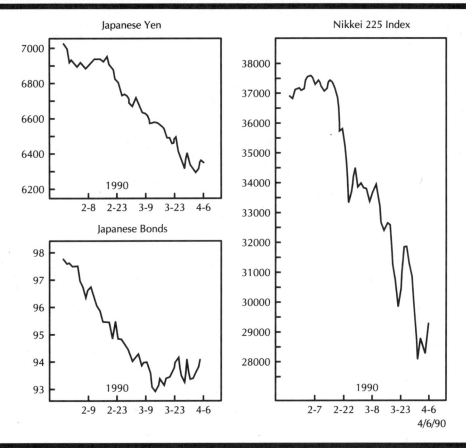

SUMMARY

This chapter discusses the *myth* of program trading as the *primary* cause of stock
market trends on a day-to-day and minute-by-minute basis, and shows that what is
often attributed to program trading is usually a manifestation of intermarket linkages
at work. This discussion is not meant as a defense of program trading. Nor is it meant
to ignore the role program trading can play in exaggerating stock market declines
once they start. There are many legitimate concerns surrounding the practice of program trading which need to be addressed and corrected if necessary. However, a lot
of misunderstanding exists concerning the role of program trading on a day-to-day
basis. Whenever the stock market rallies, it is almost a certainty that program buying
is present. It is equally certain that program selling usually takes place during a stock
market selloff. Telling us that program trading is present at such times is similar to
telling us that there is more buying than selling during rallies or more selling than

FIGURE 14.8
THE FOUR SECTORS OF THE AMERICAN MARKETS DURING 1987. THE INTERMARKET PICTURE GOING INTO THE SECOND HALF OF 1987 WAS BEARISH FOR EQUITIES—A FALLING DOLLAR, RISING COMMODITIES, AND A COLLAPSING BOND MARKET. MANY OBSERVERS MISTAKENLY BLAMED THE STOCK MARKET CRASH ON PROGRAM TRADING.

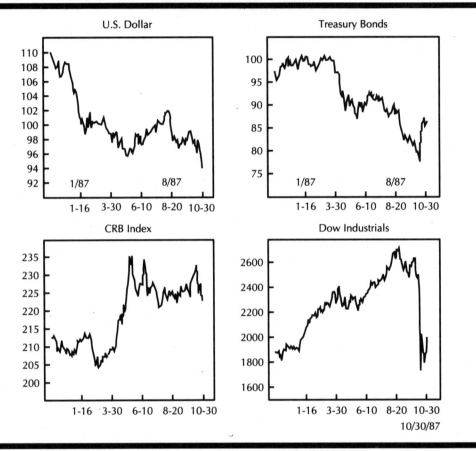

buying during declines. In other words, telling us that program trading is present tells us nothing. It states the obvious.

What's worse, reporting on program trading as a primary market moving force masks the real reasons behind a stock market trend. It also gives the false impression that program trading actually *causes* the move when, in reality, program trading is usually a *reaction* to intermarket pressures. A better understanding of how the financial markets are constantly interacting may help dispel some of the paranoia concerning program trading. It may also prove helpful in regulatory attempts to correct any abuses in the practice.

15

A New Direction

Having examined the various intermarket relationships in isolation, let's put them all back together again. This chapter will also review some of the general principles and guidelines of intermarket analysis. Although the scope of intermarket comparisons can seem intimidating at times, a firm grasp of a few basic principles can go a long way in helping to comprehend so many market forces continually interacting with each other. The main purpose in this chapter will be to summarize what intermarket analysis is and to show why this type of analysis represents a new and necessary direction in technical work.

INTERMARKET TECHNICAL ANALYSIS—
A MORE OUTWARD FOCUS

As stated at the outset of the book, technical analysis has always had an inward focus. Primary emphasis has always been placed on the market being traded, whether that market was equities, Treasury bonds, or gold. Technicians tried not to be influenced By outside events so as not to cloud their chart interpretation. Hopefully, the previous pages have shown why that attitude is no longer sufficient.

No market trades in isolation. The stock market, for example, is heavily influenced by the bond market. In a very real sense, activity in the bond market acts as a leading indicator for stocks. It's hard to imagine stock traders not taking bond market activity into consideration in their technical analysis of the stock market. Intermarket analysis utilizes price activity in one market, such as Treasury bonds, as a technical indication of the likely direction prices will trend in another market such as the stock market. This approach redefines the meaning of a technical indicator. Instead of just looking at *internal* technical indicators for a given market, the intermarket analyst looks to the price action of related markets for directional clues. Intermarket work expands the scope and the definition of technical analysis and gives it a more outward focus.

The bond market is heavily influenced by commodities. It has been shown why it's dangerous to analyze the bond market without keeping an eye on commodities.

During the latter part of 1989 and early 1990, many traders were looking for lower interest rates. They failed to consider the rising CRB Index which was signaling higher interest rates and lower bond prices. The collapse in bond prices during the first half of 1990 was a surprise only to those who weren't watching the commodity markets. The tumble in bond prices in the spring of that year also put downward pressure on stock prices. Since commodities and bonds are so closely linked, *analysis of the commodity markets is almost a requirement for a thorough analysis of the bond market.*

Finally, there is the U.S. dollar. The inflation problem that surfaced in early 1990 as commodity prices rose was the direction result of a collapse in the U.S. dollar during the fourth quarter of 1989. Weakness in the U.S. currency reawakened inflation pressures as 1989 ended, pushing commodity prices higher. Interest rates rose along with commodities, putting downward pressure on the bond market. Falling bond prices put downward pressure on U.S. stocks. *Technical analysis of the U.S. dollar (currencies), the CRB Index (commodities), Treasury bonds (interest rates), and stocks must always be combined.*

THE EFFECT OF GLOBAL TRENDS

Global forces were also at work as the new decade began. Global interest rates were trending higher, putting overseas bond markets under pressure. Falling bond markets began to take their toll on the Japanese and British equities markets. During the first quarter of 1990, the Japanese stock market lost almost a third of its value, owing to a collapsing yen and falling Japanese bond prices—an example of classic intermarket analysis. Falling bond prices (owing to rising inflation fears) also pushed British stock prices lower. Bearish global forces in bonds and stocks were just beginning to impact on the American stock market in the spring of 1990. Surging oil prices during the second half of 1990 pushed global bond and stock markets into more serious bear market declines.

TECHNICAL ANALYSTS AND INTERMARKET FORCES

What it all means is that technical analysts have to understand how these intermarket linkages work. What does a falling dollar mean for commodities? What does a rising dollar mean for U.S. bonds and stocks? What are the implications of the dollar for the gold market? What does a rising or a falling gold market mean for the CRB Index and the inflation outlook? What do rising or falling commodities mean for bonds and stocks? And what is the impact of rising or falling Japanese and British bond and stock markets on their American counterparts? These are the types of questions technical analysts must begin to ask themselves.

To ignore these interrelationships is to cheat oneself of enormously valuable price information. What's worse, it leaves technical analysts in the position of not understanding the *external* technical forces that are moving the market they are trading. *The days of following only one market are long gone.* Technical analysts have to know what's happening in all market sectors, and must understand the impact of trends in related markets all over the globe. For this purpose, technical analysis is uniquely suited because of its reliance on price action. For the same reason, it seems only logical that technical analysts should be at the forefront of intermarket analysis.

KEY INTERMARKET PRINCIPLES AND RELATIONSHIPS

Some of the key intermarket principles and relationships that we've covered in the preceding chapters are:

- All markets are interrelated.
- No market moves in isolation.
- Chart action in related markets should be taken into consideration.
- Technical analysis is the preferred vehicle for intermarket work.
- Intermarket analysis adds a new dimension to technical analysis.
- The four key sectors are currencies, commodities, bonds, and stocks.
- The U.S. dollar usually trends in the *opposite* direction of the gold market.
- The U.S. dollar usually trends in the *opposite* direction of the CRB Index.
- Gold *leads* turns in the CRB Index in the *same* direction.
- The CRB Index normally trends in the *opposite* direction of the bond market.
- Bonds normally trend in the *same* direction as the stock market.
- Bonds *lead* turns in the stock market.
- The Dow Utilities *follow* the bond market and *lead* stocks.
- The U.S. bond and stock markets are *linked* to global markets.
- Some stock groups (such as oil, gold mining, copper, and interest-sensitive stocks) are influenced by related futures markets.

INTERMARKET ANALYSIS AND THE FUTURES MARKETS

Heavy emphasis has been placed on the futures markets throughout the book. This is mainly due to the fact that the evolution of the futures markets during the 1970s and 1980s has played a major role in intermarket awareness. Whereas the stock market world has remained relatively static during the past two decades, the futures markets have expanded to include virtually every financial sector—currencies, commodities, interest rate, and stock index futures. Global futures markets have grown dramatically. The price discovery mechanism provided by instant quotations in the futures markets all over the world and the quickness with which they interact with each other have provided a fertile proving ground for intermarket work.

Those readers unfamiliar with the specific workings of the futures markets need not be concerned. Cash markets exist in every sector studied in this book. As an illustration, bond futures and stock index futures trend in the same direction as their respective cash markets (sometimes with a slight lead time). The futures markets used in this book can be viewed simply as proxies for their respective cash markets. *The use of futures markets in the various examples doesn't in any way diminish the usefulness and relevance of intermarket analysis in the respective cash markets.*

COMMODITIES AS THE MISSING LINK

Another theme running throughout the book has been the important role played by the commodity markets in the intermarket picture. This is due to the belief that commodities have been the least understood and the least appreciated of the four sectors. *The biggest breakthrough in intermarket analysis lies in the recognition of the close linkage between commodity markets, measured by the Commodity Research Bureau (CRB) Index, interest rates, and bond prices.*

By establishing this link, commodity prices also becomes linked with activity in the currency and stock markets. It's not possible to analyze the other three sectors from an intermarket perspective without considering the key role play by commodities because of the link between commodity price action and inflation. Greater appreciation of the role played by commodities and their generally negative correlation to the three other financial sectors may encourage the view of commodities as an asset class and as a potential vehicle for tactical asset allocation.

Admittedly, most of the emphasis in these pages has centered on the past twenty years. This raises the inevitable question as to whether or not these studies have reached back far enough in time. It also raises the question of whether these linkages are a new phenomenon and whether they are likely to continue. How far back in history can or should the markets be researched for intermarket comparisons? This book's focus on the past two decades is due largely to reliance on the futures markets, most of which were introduced during that period, and the belief that a lot has changed during the past twenty years in the way we view the world markets. Let's consider some of those changes.

Prior to 1970, the world had fixed exchange rates. Trends in the U.S. dollar and foreign currencies simply didn't exist. Given the important role played by the currency markets today, it's impossible to measure their possible impact prior to 1970. Gold was set at a fixed price and couldn't be owned by Americans until the mid-1970s. Gold's relationship with the dollar and its role as a leading indicator of inflation was impossible to measure prior to that time since its price didn't fluctuate. The price of oil was regulated until the early 1970s. All of these parts of the intermarket puzzle weren't available before 1970.

Gold futures were introduced in 1974 and oil futures in 1983. Currency futures were started in 1972. Their impact on each other could only be measured from those points in time. Futures contracts in Treasury bonds, Treasury Bills, and Eurodollars were developed later in the 1970s. Futures markets in stock index futures, the U.S. dollar, and the CRB Index weren't introduced until the 1980s. When one considers how important each of these markets is to the intermarket picture, it can be seen why it's so hard to study intermarket analysis prior to 1970. In most cases, the data simply isn't available. Where the data is available, it's only in bits and pieces.

COMPUTERIZATION AND GLOBALIZATION

The trends toward computerization and globalization in the past two decades have also made a major contribution to expanding our global perspective. Thanks to these two trends, the world seems much smaller and much more interdependent. Most people didn't watch the overseas markets ten years ago and didn't care what they were doing. Now many begin the day with quotes from Tokyo and London. The entrance of computers enabled traders to view these markets on terminal screens and watch them trade off each other on a minute-by-minute basis. Financial futures contracts now exist all over the globe, and their price action is reported instantaneously on quote machines and video screens to every other part of the globe. To put it mildly, much has changed in the financial markets in the past two decades and in the observer's ability to monitor them.

There is probably a self-fulfilling prophecy at work in intermarket analysis. Years ago, traders weren't as aware of the linkages between the various markets. Now, as these markets are freely traded, with quotes and pictures so readily available on terminal screens all over the globe, traders react much more quickly to changing market events. A selloff in Tokyo can cause a selloff in London, which will influence the opening on Wall Street. A sudden selloff in the German bond market can cause a similar selloff in Chicago Treasury bond futures within seconds (which may impact on the stock market in New York a few seconds later). Trading activity in the United States sets the tone for overnight trading overseas. It seems incredible to think that the British stock market started dropping almost a year before the American stock market in 1929, and either no one in the States noticed, or hardly anyone seemed to care. Today, such a selloff in London would have more immediate repercussions.

There will be those who will want to go back further in time to study intermarket linkages. My belief, however, is that the growing evidence of intermarket linkages parallels the evolution of the futures markets since the 1970s and our enhanced ability to track them. It seems safe to say that with newer markets and instant communications, the world's markets have truly changed and so has our ability to react to those changes. For these reasons, comparisons before that time may not be very helpful. The more pertinent question isn't whether intermarket linkages were as obvious forty years ago, but whether they will still be obvious forty years from now. My guess is that they will.

INTERMARKET ANALYSIS—A NEW DIRECTION

Technical analysis appears to be going through an evolutionary phase. As its popularity grows, so has the recognition that technical analysis has many applications beyond the traditional study of *isolated* charts and *internal* technical indicators. *Intermarket analysis represents another step in the evolution of technical theory.* With the growing recognition that all markets are linked—financial and non-financial, domestic and international—traders will be taking these linkages into consideration more and more in their analysis. Because of its flexibility and its universal application to all markets, *technical analysis is uniquely suited to perform this type of analysis.*

Intermarket analysis simply adds another step to the process and provides a more useful framework for understanding analysis of the individual sectors. For the past century, technical analysis has had an inward focus. My guess is the next century will witness a broader application of technical principles in the areas of financial and economic forecasting. Even the Federal Reserve Board has been known to peek at charts of the financial markets on occasion. The principles presented in this text are admittedly only the first steps in a new direction for technical analysis. However, I believe that as technical analysis continues to grow in popularity and respectability, intermarket analysis will play an increasingly important role in its future.

APPENDIX

As the reader has probably detected from the computer-generated charts in the preceding chapters, this book was written over a span of several months. In each chapter, the most recent market data was utilized. Naturally, each succeeding chapter included more recent price data. Instead of going back to update the earlier charts and edit market observations with the benefit of hindsight, the decision was made to leave the earlier chapters alone and to include the more recent data as the book progressed. As a result, the material has a dynamic quality to it as I assimilated new market data into the intermarket equation.

The purpose of this Appendix is to update the most important intermarket relationships through the third quarter of 1990 as we go to press. Some relationships have performed better than others in the past year, but, as I hope you'll agree, most have held up quite well. It's gratifying, for example, to see how well the markets followed the intermarket script even during the hectic days of the Mideast crisis that gripped the global financial markets during the summer of 1990. Chart examples utilized in any book quickly become outdated. The important point to remember is that even though the chart data is constantly changing, the basic principles of intermarket technical analysis stay the same.

FIGURE A.1

CHARTS OF THE FOUR SECTORS—THE DOLLAR, CRB INDEX, STOCKS, AND BONDS— THROUGH THE THIRD QUARTER OF 1990. A WEAK DOLLAR DURING MOST OF 1990 HELPED SUPPORT COMMODITY PRICES AND PUT DOWNWARD PRESSURE ON BONDS AND STOCKS.

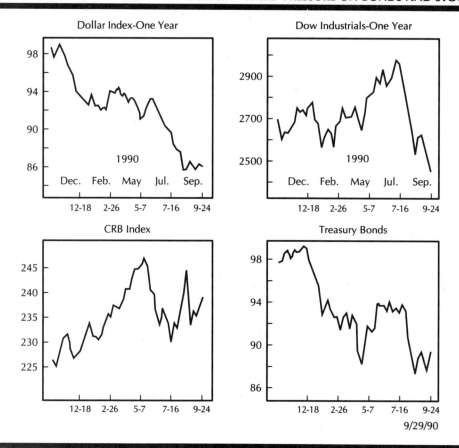

FIGURE A.2
A COMPARISON OF THE CRB INDEX AND TREASURY BONDS FROM LATE 1989 THROUGH THE THIRD QUARTER OF 1990. DURING THE FIRST HALF OF 1990, COMMODITIES RALLIED WHILE BONDS WEAKENED. THE BOND BOTTOMS IN EARLY MAY AND LATE AUGUST (SEE ARROWS) WERE ACCOMPANIED BY PEAKS IN COMMODITY PRICES.

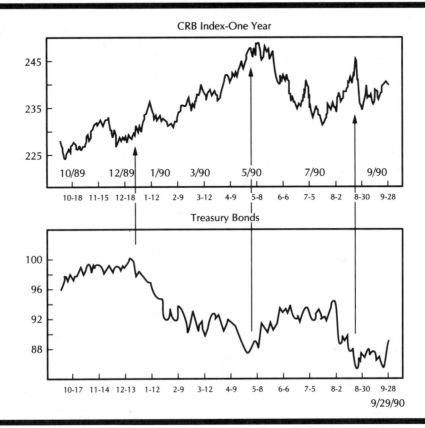

FIGURE A.3
STOCKS VERSUS BONDS FROM LATE 1989 THROUGH SEPTEMBER 1990. AFTER FALLING THROUGH THE EARLY PORTION OF 1990, THE BOND TROUGH IN EARLY MAY HELPED SUPPORT THE STOCK RALLY. BONDS FAILED TO CONFIRM THE DOW'S MOVE TO NEW HIGHS DURING THE SUMMER. BOTH MARKETS THEN TUMBLED TOGETHER.

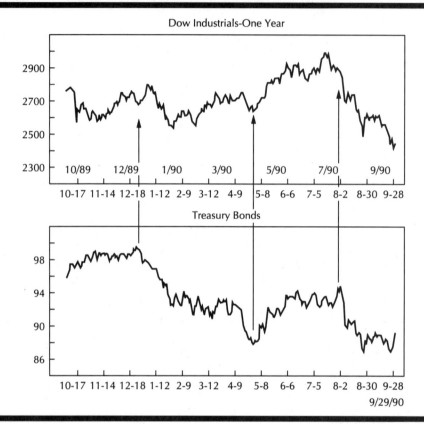

Dow Industrials-One Year

Treasury Bonds

9/29/90

FIGURE A.4
A COMPARISON OF THE DOW INDUSTRIALS, DOW UTILITIES, AND TREASURY BONDS FROM AUTUMN OF 1989 THROUGH THE THIRD QUARTER OF 1990. RELATIVE WEAKNESS IN THE DOW UTILITIES FROM THE BEGINNING OF 1990 PROVIDED AN EARLY BEARISH WARNING FOR THE DOW INDUSTRIALS. NOTICE THE CLOSE CORRELATION BETWEEN THE DOW UTILITIES AND TREASURY BONDS.

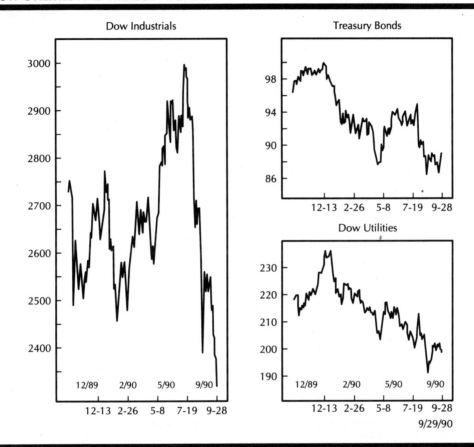

FIGURE A.5
A COMPARISON OF THE CRB INDEX TO THE U.S. DOLLAR FROM LATE 1989 TO SEPTEMBER 1990. THE FALLING DOLLAR, WHICH IS INFLATIONARY, HELPED COMMODITY PRICES ADVANCE DURING 1990. A BOUNCE IN THE DOLLAR DURING MAY CONTRIBUTED TO THE CRB PEAK THAT MONTH. COMMODITIES FIRMED AGAIN DURING THE SUMMER AS THE DOLLAR DROPPED TO NEW LOWS.

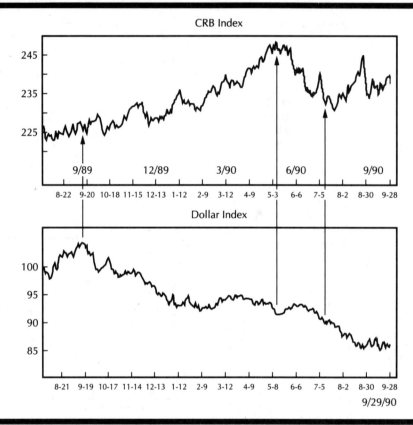

FIGURE A.6
THE U.S. DOLLAR VERSUS GOLD FROM LATE 1989 THROUGH SEPTEMBER 1990. THE DECLINING DOLLAR DURING MOST OF 1990 WASN'T ENOUGH TO TURN THE GOLD TREND HIGHER. HOWEVER, THE INVERSE RELATIONSHIP CAN STILL BE SEEN, ESPECIALLY DURING THE DOLLAR SELLOFFS IN LATE 1989 AND JUNE 1990, WHEN GOLD RALLIED. THE INTERIM BOTTOM IN THE DOLLAR IN FEBRUARY 1990 WAS ENOUGH TO PUSH GOLD PRICES LOWER.

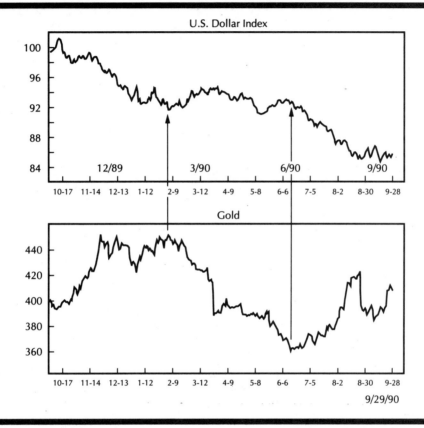

FIGURE A.7
GOLD VERSUS THE DOW INDUSTRIALS FROM THE SUMMER OF 1989 TO THE AUTUMN OF 1990. THE GOLD RALLY IN THE FALL OF 1989 COINCIDED WITH STOCK MARKET WEAKNESS. THE FEBRUARY 1990 PEAK IN GOLD COINCIDED WITH A RALLY IN STOCKS. GOLD ROSE DURING THE SUMMER OF 1990 AS STOCKS WEAKENED. THROUGHOUT THE PERIOD SHOWN, GOLD DID BEST WHEN THE STOCK MARKET FALTERED.

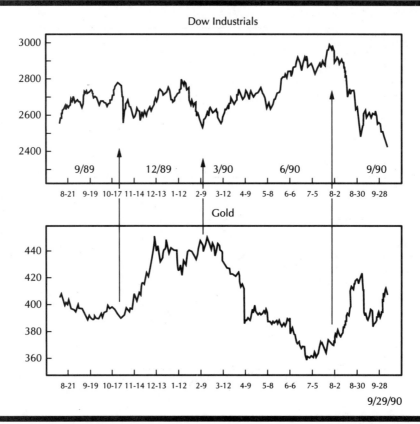

FIGURE A.8
**A COMPARISON OF AMERICAN, BRITISH, AND JAPANESE STOCK MARKETS IN THE 18-MONTH
PERIOD ENDING IN THE THIRD QUARTER OF 1990. ALL THREE MARKETS DROPPED SHARPLY
AT THE BEGINNING OF 1990 AND THEN RALLIED IN THE SPRING. NEITHER OF THE FOREIGN
MARKETS CONFIRMED THE AMERICAN RALLY TO NEW HIGHS DURING THE SUMMER OF 1990.
THE "TRIPLE TOP" IN BRITAIN AND THE COLLAPSE IN JAPAN HELD BEARISH IMPLICATIONS
FOR AMERICAN EQUITIES. GLOBAL MARKETS THEN COLLAPSED TOGETHER.**

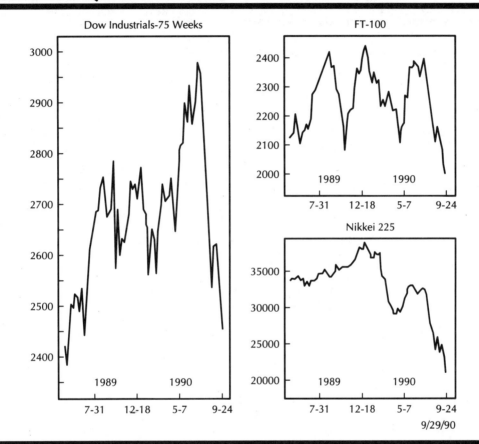

FIGURE A.9
AMERICAN VERSUS JAPANESE STOCK MARKETS FROM SEPTEMBER 1989 TO SEPTEMBER 1990. BOTH MARKETS TURNED DOWN IN JANUARY. ALTHOUGH THE AMERICAN MARKET APPEARED TO SHRUG OFF THE JAPANESE COLLAPSE DURING THE FIRST QUARTER OF 1990, THE SECOND FALL IN JAPAN DURING THE SUMMER TOOK ITS TOLL ON ALL GLOBAL MARKETS. THE JAPANESE RALLY FROM MAY INTO JULY HELPED STABILIZE THE AMERICAN MARKET. HOWEVER, THE AMERICAN RALLY TO NEW HIGHS WASN'T CONFIRMED BY THE JAPANESE MARKET, WHICH BARELY RETRACED HALF OF ITS PREVIOUS LOSSES.

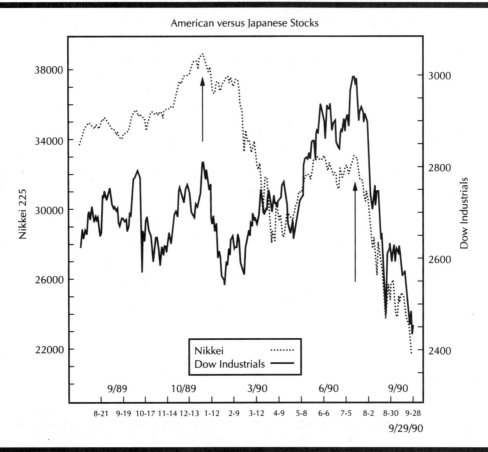

American versus Japanese Stocks

FIGURE A.10

A COMPARISON OF THE AMERICAN, BRITISH, GERMAN, AND JAPANESE BOND MARKETS DURING THE SUMMER OF 1990. GLOBAL BOND MARKETS TUMBLED AS OIL PRICES SURGED FOLLOWING IRAQ'S INVASION OF KUWAIT ON AUGUST 2, 1990. JAPANESE BONDS TURNED IN THE WORST PERFORMANCE (OWING TO JAPAN'S GREATER DEPENDENCE ON OIL), NOT ONLY LEADING GLOBAL BOND PRICES LOWER BUT ALSO ACCOUNTING FOR THE COLLAPSE OF JAPANESE EQUITIES.

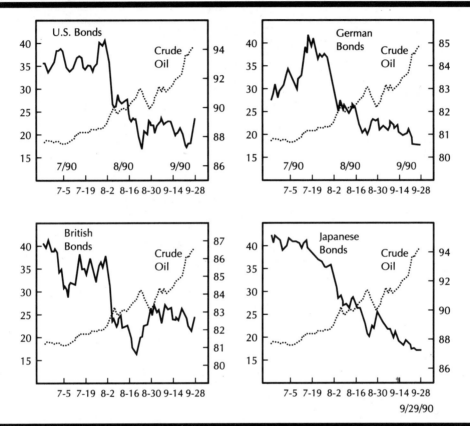

Reproduced with permission by Knight Ridder's Tradecenter. Tradecenter is a registered trademark of Knight Ridder's Financial Information.

FIGURE A.11
DOW INDUSTRIALS VERSUS CRUDE OIL DURING THE SUMMER OF 1990. THE INFLATIONARY IMPACT OF SURGING OIL PRICES DURING THE SUMMER OF 1990 TOOK A BEARISH TOLL ON EQUITY PRICES EVERYWHERE ON THE GLOBE. OIL BECAME THE DOMINANT COMMODITY DURING 1990 AND DEMONSTRATED HOW SENSITIVE BOND AND STOCK MARKETS ARE TO ACTION IN THE COMMODITY SECTOR.

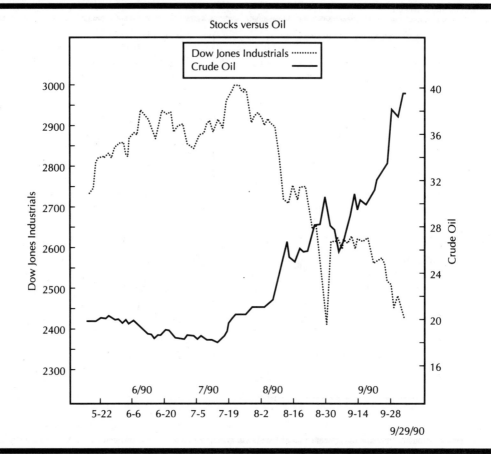

FIGURE A.12
CRUDE OIL VERSUS OIL STOCKS DURING 1990. OIL STOCKS HAD SPENT THE FIRST HALF OF 1990 IN A HOLDING PATTERN WHILE OIL PRICES WEAKENED. OIL STOCKS EXPLODED TO NEW HIGHS IN EARLY JULY WHEN OIL BOTTOMED. AS THE THIRD QUARTER OF 1990 ENDED, HOWEVER, FALLING OIL SHARES HAVE SET UP A "NEGATIVE DIVERGENCE" WITH THE PRICE OF OIL, WHICH IS TESTING ITS ALL-TIME HIGH AT $40.

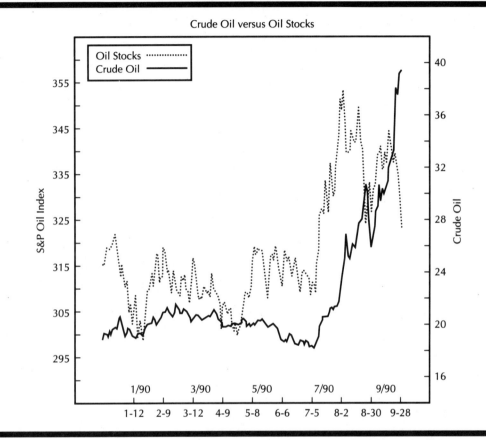

Crude Oil versus Oil Stocks

GLOSSARY

Advance/Decline Line: One of the most widely-used indicators to measure the *breadth* of a stock market advance or decline. Each day (or week) the number of advancing issues is compared to the number of declining issues. If advances outnumber declines, the net total is added to the previous cumulative total. If declines outnumber advances, the net difference is subtracted from the previous cumulative total. The advance/decline line is usually compared to a popular stock average such as the Dow Jones Industrial Average. They should trend in the same direction. When the advance/decline line begins to diverge from the stock average, an early indication is given of a possible trend reversal.

Arms Index: Also called *Trin*, this contrary indicator is the average volume of declining stocks divided by the average volume of advancing stocks. A reading below 1.0 indicates more volume in rising stocks. A reading above 1.0 reflects more volume in declining issues. However, an extreme high reading suggests an oversold market and an extreme low reading, an overbought market.

Ascending Triangle: A sideways price pattern between two converging trendlines, in which the lower line is rising while the upper line is flat. This is generally a bullish pattern.

Bar Chart: The most common type of price chart used by market technicians. On a daily bar chart, each bar represents one day's activity. The vertical bar is drawn from the day's highest price to the day's lowest price (the range). A tic to the left of the bar marks the opening price, whereas a tic to the right of the bar marks the closing price. Bar charts can be constructed for any time period, including monthly, weekly, hourly, and selected minute periods.

Breakaway Gap: A price gap that forms on the completion of an important price pattern. A *breakaway gap* usually signals the beginning of an important price move.

Bullish Consensus: Weekly numbers based on a poll of newsletter writers published by Hadady Publications in Pasadena, California. When 80 percent of newsletter writers are bullish on a market, that market is considered to be overbought and vulnerable to a price decline. Readings below 30 percent are indicative of an oversold market and are considered bullish.

Channel Line: Straight lines drawn parallel to the basic trendline. In an uptrend, the channel line slants up to the right and is drawn above rally peaks; in a downtrend, the channel line is drawn down to the right below price troughs. Prices will often meet resistance at rising channel lines and support at falling channel lines.

Confirmation: Having as many technical factors as possible agreeing with one another. For example, if prices and volume are rising together, volume is *confirming* the price action. The opposite of confirmation is *divergence*.

Continuation Patterns: Price formations that imply a pause or consolidation in the prevailing trend, after which the prior trend is resumed. The most common types are *triangles, flags,* and *pennants*.

Descending Triangle: A sideways price pattern between two converging trendlines, in which the upper line is declining while the lower line is flat. This is generally a bearish pattern.

Divergence: A situation where two indicators are not confirming each other. For example, in *oscillator* analysis, prices trend higher while an oscillator starts to drop. *Divergence* usually warns of a trend reversal.

Double Top: This price pattern displays two prominent peaks. The reversal is complete when the middle trough is broken. The *double bottom* is a mirror image of the top.

Down Trendline: A straight line drawn down and to the right above successive rally peaks in a downtrend. A violation of the down trendline usually signals a change in the trend.

Dow Theory: One of the oldest and most highly regarded of technical theories. A Dow Theory buy signal is given when the Dow Industrial and Dow Transportation Averages close above a prior rally peak. A sell signal is given when both averages close below a prior reaction low.

Elliott Wave Analysis: An approach to market analysis that is based on repetitive wave patterns and the Fibonacci number sequence. An ideal Elliott Wave pattern shows a five-wave advance followed by a three-wave decline. The Fibonacci number sequence (1, 2, 3, 5, 8, 13, 21, 34, 55, 89, 144 ...) is constructed by adding the first two numbers to arrive at the third. The ratio of any number to the next larger number is 62 percent, which is a popular Fibonacci retracement number. The inverse of 62 percent, which is 38 percent, is also used as a Fibonacci retracement number. The ratio of any number to the next smaller number is 1.62 percent, which is used to arrive at Fibonacci price targets. Elliott Wave Analysis incorporates the three elements of pattern (wave identification), ratio (Fibonacci ratios and projections), and time. Fibonacci time targets are arrived at by counting Fibonacci days, weeks, months, or years from prominent peaks and troughs.

Exhaustion Gap: A price gap that occurs at the end of an important trend and signals that the trend is ending.

Exponential Smoothing: A moving average that uses all data points, but gives greater weight to more recent price data.

Flag: A continuation price pattern, generally lasting less than three weeks, which resembles a parallelogram that slopes against the prevailing trend. The *flag* represents a minor pause in a dynamic price trend.

Fundamental Analysis: The opposite of technical analysis. Fundamental analysis relies on economic supply/demand information as opposed to market activity.

Gaps: Gaps are spaces left on the bar chart where no trading has taken place. An *up gap* is formed when the lowest price on a trading day is higher than the highest high of the previous day. A *down gap* is formed when the highest price on a day is lower than the lowest price of the prior day. An up gap is usually a sign of market strength, whereas a down gap is a sign of market weakness. Three types of gaps are *breakaway*, *runaway* (also called *measuring*), and *exhaustion* gaps.

Head and Shoulders: The best known of the reversal price patterns. At a market top, three prominent peaks are formed with the middle peak (or head) slightly higher than the two other peaks (shoulders). When the trendline (neckline) connecting the two intervening troughs is broken, the pattern is complete. A bottom pattern is a mirror image of a top and is called an *inverse head and shoulders*.

Intermarket Analysis: An additional aspect of technical analysis that takes into consideration the price action of related market sectors. The four sectors are currencies, commodities, bonds, and stocks. International markets are also included. This approach is based on the premise that all markets are interrelated and impact on one another.

Island Reversal: A combination of an *exhaustion* gap in one direction and a *breakaway* gap in the other direction within a few days. Toward the end of an uptrend, for example, prices gap upward and then downward within a few days. The result is usually two or three trading days standing alone with gaps on either side. The *island reversal* usually signals a trend reversal.

Key Reversal Day: In an uptrend, this one-day pattern occurs when prices open in new highs and then close below the previous day's closing price. In a downtrend, prices open lower and then close higher. The wider the price range on the *key reversal day* and the heavier the volume, the greater the odds that a reversal is taking place.

Line Charts: Price charts that connect the *closing* prices of a given market over a span of time. The result is a curving line on the chart. This type of chart is most useful with overlay or comparison charts that are commonly employed in intermarket analysis.

Momentum: A technique used to construct an overbought/oversold oscillator. *Momentum* measures price *differences* over a selected span of time. To construct a 10-day momentum line, the closing price 10 days earlier is subtracted from the latest price. The resulting positive or negative value is plotted above or below a zero line.

Moving Average: A trend-following indicator that works best in a trending environment. Moving averages smooth out price action but operate with a time lag. A simple 10-day moving average of a stock, for example, adds up the last 10 days' closing prices and divides the total by 10. This procedure is repeated each day. Any number of moving averages can be employed, with different time spans, to generate buy and sell signals. When only one average is employed, a buy signal is given when the price closes above the average. When two averages are employed, a buy signal is given when the shorter average crosses above the longer average. Technicians use three types: simple, weighted, and exponentially smoothed averages.

Open Interest: The number of options or futures contracts that are still unliquidated at the end of a trading day. A rise or fall in open interest shows that money is flowing into or out of a futures contract or option, respectively. Open interest also measures liquidity.

Oscillators: Technical indicators that are utilized to determine when a market is in an *overbought* and *oversold* condition. Oscillators are plotted at the bottom of a price chart. When the oscillator reaches an upper extreme, the market is overbought. When the oscillator line reaches a lower extreme, the market is oversold. Two types of oscillators use *momentum* and *rates of change*.

Overbought: A term usually used in reference to an *oscillator*. When an oscillator reaches an upper extreme, it is believed that a market has risen too far and is vulnerable to a selloff.

Oversold: A term usually used in reference to an *oscillator*. When an oscillator reaches a lower extreme, it is believed that market has dropped too far and is due for a bounce.

Pennant: This continuation price pattern is similar to the *flag*, except that it is more horizontal and resembles a small *symmetrical triangle*. Like the *flag*, the *pennant* usually lasts from one to three weeks and is typically followed by a resumption of the prior trend.

% Investment Advisors Bullish: This measure of stock market bullish sentiment is published weekly by Investor's Intelligence in New Rochelle, New York. When only 35 percent of professionals are bullish, the market is considered oversold. A reading of 55 percent is considered to be overbought.

Price Patterns: Patterns that appear on price charts that have predictive value. Patterns are divided into *reversal* patterns and *continuation* patterns.

Put/Call Ratio: The ratio of volume in put options divided by the volume of call options is used as a contrary indicator. When put buying gets too high relative to call buying (a high put/call ratio), the market is oversold. A low put/call ratio represents an overbought market condition.

Rate of Change: A technique used to construct an overbought/oversold oscillator. *Rate of change* employs a price *ratio* over a selected span of time. To construct a ten-day Rate of Change oscillator, the last closing price is divided by the close price ten days earlier. The resulting value is plotted above or below a value of 100.

Ratio Analysis: The use of a *ratio* to compare the *relative strength* between two entities. An individual stock or industry group divided by the S&P 500 index can determine whether that stock or industry group is outperforming or underperforming the stock market as a whole. Ratio analysis can be used to compare any two entities. A rising ratio indicates that the numerator in the ratio is outperforming the denominator. Ratio analysis can also be used to compare market sectors such as the bond market to the stock market or commodities to bonds. Technical analysis can be applied to the ratio line itself to determine important turning points.

Relative-Strength Index (RSI): A popular oscillator developed by Welles Wilder, Jr., and described in his 1978 book, *New Concepts in Technical Trading Systems*. RSI is plotted on a vertical scale from 0 to 100. Values above 75 are considered to be overbought and values below 25, oversold. When prices are over 75 or below 25 and diverge from price action, a warning is given of a possible trend reversal. RSI usually employs time spans of 9 or 14 days.

Resistance: The opposite of *support*. *Resistance* is marked by a previous price peak and provides enough of a barrier above the market to halt a price advance.

Retracements: Prices normally retrace the prior trend by a percentage amount before resuming the original trend. The best known example is the 50 percent retracement. Minimum and maximum retracements are normally one-third and two-thirds, respectively. Elliott Wave Theory uses Fibonacci retracements of 38 percent and 62 percent.

Reversal Patterns: Price patterns on a price chart that usually indicate that a trend reversal is taking place. The best known of the reversal patterns are the *head and shoulders* and *double* and *triple* tops and bottoms.

Runaway Gap: A price gap that usually occurs around the midpoint of an important market trend. For this reason, it is also called a *measuring* gap.

Saucer: A price reversal pattern that represents a very slow and gradual shift in trend direction.

Sentiment Indicators: Psychological indicators that attempt to measure the degree of bullishness or bearishness in the stock market or in individual markets. These are contrary indicators and are used in much the same fashion as overbought or oversold oscillators. Their greatest value is when they reach upper or lower extremes.

Simple Average: A moving average that gives *equal* weight to each day's price data.

Stochastics: An overbought/oversold oscillator that is based on the principle that as prices advance, the closing price moves to the upper end of its range. In a downtrend, closing prices usually appear near the bottom of their recent range. Time periods of 9 and 14 days are usually employed in its construction. Stochastics uses two lines—%K and its 3-day moving average, %D. These two lines fluctuate in a vertical range between 0 and 100. Readings above 80 are overbought, while readings below 20 are oversold. When the faster %K line crosses above the slower %D line and the lines are below 20, a buy signal is given. When the %K crosses below the %D line and the lines are over 80, a sell signal is given. There are two stochastics versions: *fast* stochastics and *slow* stochastics. Most traders use the slower version because of its smoother look and more reliable signals. The formula for *fast* stochastics is:

$$\text{fast } \%K = \frac{\text{latest price } - \text{ lowest low for n periods}}{\text{n period highest high } - \text{ lowest low}}$$

fast %D = 3 day average of fast %K

In the formula, *n* usually refers to the number of days, but can also mean months, weeks, or hours. The formula for *slow* stochastics is:

slow %K = fast %D

slow %D = 3 day average of fast %D.

Support: A price, or price zone, *beneath* the current market price, where buying power is sufficient to halt a price decline. A previous reaction low usually forms a support level.

Symmetrical Triangle: A sideways price pattern between two converging trendlines in which the upper trendline is declining and lower trendline is rising. This pattern represents an even balance between buyers and sellers, although the prior trend is usually resumed. The breakout through either trendline signals the direction of the price trend.

Technical Analysis: The study of market action, usually with price charts, which also includes volume and open interest patterns.

Trend: Refers to the direction of prices. Rising peaks and troughs constitute an *uptrend*; falling peaks and troughs constitute a *downtrend*. A *trading range* is characterized by horizontal peaks and troughs. Trends are generally classified into major (longer than six months), intermediate (one to six months), or minor (less than a month).

Trendlines: Straight lines drawn on a chart below reaction lows in an uptrend, or above rally peaks in a downtrend, that determine the steepness of the current trend. The breaking of a trendline usually signals a trend change.

Triangles: Sideways price patterns in which prices fluctuate within converging trendlines. The three types of triangles are the *symmetrical*, the *ascending*, and the *descending*.

Triple Top: A price pattern with three prominent peaks, similar to the *head and shoulders* top, except that all three peaks occur at about the same level. The *triple bottom* is a mirror image of the top.

Up Trendline: A straight line drawn upward and to the right below reaction lows in an uptrend. The longer the up trendline has been in effect and the more times it has been tested, the more significant it becomes. Violation of the trendline usually signals that the uptrend may be changing direction.

Volume: The level of trading activity in a stock, option, or futures contract. Expanding volume in the direction of the current price trend confirms the price trend.

Weighted Average: A moving average that uses a selected time span but gives greater weight to more recent price data.

Index